UNREACHED PEOPLES '79

The Challenge of the Church's Unfinished Business

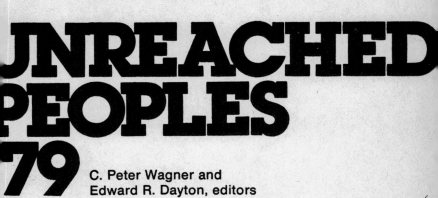

UNREACHED PEOPLES '79

C. Peter Wagner and
Edward R. Dayton, editors

David C. Cook Publishing Co.

ELGIN, ILLINOIS—WESTON, ONTARIO

First printing, January 1979
Second printing, June 1979

© 1978 David C. Cook Publishing Co.

The material contained in the Unreached People Register may be reproduced
or copied in any form provided appropriate credit is given. Portions of the rest
of this book may only be used with written permission from the publisher.

Edited by Marshall Shelley
Design by Kurt Dietsch
Cover illustration by Rod Burke
Printed in U.S.A.

ISBN 0-89191-146-4
LC 78-57642

Contents

Introduction

This book is being produced as a contribution toward fulfilling Jesus' command to "Go and make disciples of all nations" (Matthew 28:19). It is designed as a tool to be used by those who in one way or another are participating in contemporary world evangelization.

The rationale for this approach emerged from the Strategy Working Group of the Lausanne Committee for World Evangelization (LCWE). The two great world congresses on evangelization, held in Berlin in 1966 and in Lausanne, Switzerland, in 1974, drew the attention of Christian people everywhere to the immense unfinished task yet before us. While we rejoice in the fact that Christian churches are multiplying in virtually every part of the world at rates unprecedented in two thousand years of Christian history, we have no reason to relax our evangelistic efforts. Over 3 billion people have yet to hear about Jesus and respond to his love.

This challenge stimulated the 2,400 participants in the International Congress on World Evangelization to request the formation of an ongoing structure to stimulate the practical implementation of the Lausanne vision for reaching the unreached. In Mexico City, January 20-23, 1975, the Lausanne

Committee for World Evangelization was officially constituted. It was composed of forty-eight members from around the world.

The structure, as it has taken shape, consists of the international body, seven regional committees that deal with evangelistic challenges in their specific parts of the world, an executive committee of twelve, and four working groups: theology and education; intercession; communication; and strategy. The names of those who currently serve on those committees are given at the conclusion of this introduction.

The basic task of the Strategy Working Group is to (1) iden tify and describe the world's unreached peoples; (2) identify existing forces for evangelism which may be able to reach them and/or suggest the development of new forces for evan gelism; and (3) suggest methodologies that could help in crease the effectiveness of evangelistic efforts.

This book is a step toward accomplishing the first task. From its very inception the Strategy Working Group established a functional relationship with the MARC (Missions Advanced Research and Communication) Center of World Vision International. MARC pioneered research into unreached peoples and challenged the 1974 Lausanne meeting with the preliminary results. Its office facilities, computer capability, competent staff, and accumulated expertise in the field qualifies it as the central research agency worldwide for unreached peoples. MARC director Edward R. Dayton is a key member of the Strategy Working Group and coeditor of this book. Assisting him in preparing materials were David Fraser, James Griffith, Casey Klimasauskas, and Dan Brewster.

This book is intended to be the first of a series of annual publications on unreached people. The series will constitute a growing reference library for mission executives, missionaries, professors of mission, church mission committees, seminary libraries, and Christians with a higher than average interest in and commitment to world evangelization.

Each book in the series will contain indepth articles by recognized missiologists on reaching the unreached, detailed case studies of some specific unreached peoples, general descriptions of eighty to a hundred other unreached peoples with some indication of their receptivity to the gospel, and a cumulative index which will cover the entire series in each year's volume. This index will be a handy reference tool, saving the reader the time otherwise necessary to check back through the indices of each preceding volume.

What is it for? It is a planning guide for those responsible for making missions happen. Hopefully, those who want to participate more fully in world evangelization will be able to use this reference series as a starting point. Where are workers needed? Where has God ripened the harvest? Where should we concentrate our prayers, our funds, and our personnel at this particular moment of history? This book will help answer those questions.

Ed Dayton and I welcome feedback and suggestions. This is our first effort. The second will be an improvement if readers cooperate with their constructive criticisms and suggestions for revision.

The editors commend the David C. Cook Publishing Company for handling this series. It is not the kind of publishing project that many publishers could handle with the grace and patience and understanding that the staff at David C. Cook, particularly Mr. Ron Wilson, have shown. Their contribution represents an important part of the task of world evangelization.

C. Peter Wagner, Chairman
LCWE Strategy Working Group
and Associate Professor of
Church Growth, Fuller Seminary
School of World Mission

Pasadena, California
April, 1978

Lausanne Committee for World Evangelization as of 1978
Francisco Anabalon, Chile
Ramez Atallah, Canada
Saphir Athyal, India
Peter Beyerhaus, West Germany
Henri Blocher, France
Vonette Bright, U.S.A.
Michael Cassidy, South Africa
Wilson Hay Him Chan, Hong Kong
Chongnahm Cho, Korea
Chae Ok Chun, Korea
Robert Coleman, U.S.A.
Mariano DiGangi, Canada
Nilson Fanini, Brazil
Ajith Fernado, Sri Lanka
Leighton Ford, U.S.A.
Bruno Frigoli, Bolivia
Andrew Furuyama, Japan
Geziel Nunes Gomes, Brazil
Billy Graham (ex officio), U.S.A.
Edward Hill, U.S.A.
Fritz Hoffmann, East Germany
C. B. Hogue, U.S.A.
Donald Hoke, U.S.A.
Armin Hoppler, Switzerland
Abdul Istafanous, Egypt
Festo Kivengere, Uganda
A. T. Victor Koh, Singapore
Gordon Landreth, England
Samuel Libert, Argentina
Branco Lovrec, Yugoslavia
Emmy Matiti, Kenya
Billy Melvin, U.S.A.
Stanley Mooneyham, U.S.A.
Agne Norlander, Sweden
Petrus Octavianus, Indonesia
Samuel Odunaike, Nigeria

10

Gottfried Osei-Mensah, Kenya
Pablo Perez, Mexico
Ted Raedeke, U.S.A.
John Reid, Australia
John Richard, India
Subhas Sangma, Bangladesh
Peter Schneider, Germany
John Stott, England
C. Peter Wagner, U.S.A.
Ben Wati, India
Warren Webster, U.S.A.
James Wong, Singapore
Thomas Zimmerman, U.S.A.
Isaac Zokoue, Ivory Coast

Executive Committee
Leighton Ford, North America, chairman
Saphir Athyal, West Asia, deputy chairman
Donald Hoke, North America, treasurer
Gottfried Osei-Mensah, Africa, executive secretary
Armin Hoppler, Europe, Intercession Working Group chairman
John Stott, United Kingdom, Theology and Education Working Group chairman
C. Peter Wagner, North America, Strategy Working Group chairman
Thomas Zimmerman, North America, Communications Working Group chairman
Bruno Frigoli, Latin America
Andrew Furuyama, East Asia
Samuel Odunaike, Africa
John Reid, Oceania

Stretegy Working Group
C. Peter Wagner, U.S.A., chairman
Fourad Accad, Arabian Gulf
Edward Dayton, U.S.A.

11

David Gitari, Kenya
Tom Houston, England
Harmon Johnson, U.S.A.
John Masuda, Japan
George Samuel, India
James Wong, Singapore

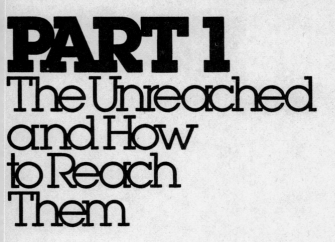

PART 1
The Unreached and How to Reach Them

To Reach the Unreached

by Edward R. Dayton

The Lord Jesus Christ has commanded his Church to make disciples of every nation. Every Christian in every local church, in every country of the world, is called upon to be a witness to the saving power of Jesus Christ. No matter who we are and where we are, if we claim Jesus as Lord, God's good intention for us is that we should proclaim our faith by what we say and how we live.

The Church *is* multiplying its witness around the world. On every continent men and women are gossiping the gospel to their friends, to their neighbors, to the village or city within which they live. However, in addition to these local witnesses, God has set apart certain men and women to go forth from where they live to reach those villages, towns, and cities where there is no witness. And if the world is to be evangelized, if every person in the world is to have an opportunity to know Jesus Christ as Lord and Savior, then these special ambassadors, these cross-cultural missionaries, need to understand the people to whom they are called. They need to uncover God's strategy, God's plans, for reaching these people, and they need to sense that God is setting them

15

aside to be about his business in a particular part of the world.

It is with this great need in mind that the Lausanne Committee for World Evangelization's Strategy Working Group, in conjunction with the Missions Advanced Research and Communication Center (MARC) of World Vision, has been attempting to think through *approaches* to reaching the world.

Let us begin with some definitions. What do we mean by world evangelization?

Nature: The nature of evangelization is the communication of the Good News.

Purpose: To give individuals and groups a valid opportunity to accept Jesus Christ.

Goal: The persuading of men and women to accept Jesus Christ as Lord and Saviour, and to serve him in the fellowship of his Church.

We divide this definition into *nature, purpose* and *goal* so as to build a bridge between God's intention and our response. Only the Lord really knows whether a man or a woman has given true allegiance to Jesus Christ. But it is the *nature* of evangelization that the Good News, the gospel, be communicated.

It is the *purpose* of evangelization that ultimately every individual and group of people in the world should have a valid opportunity to accept Jesus Christ as Lord and Savior.

But if this is to be carried out in any meaningful way, we need a measurable *goal.* Thus we state that the *goal* of world evangelization, and the only biblical goal that we can actually observe, is that men and women should not only come to accept Jesus Christ as Lord and Savior but that they should come to serve him in the fellowship of his Church.

Every man and woman in the world . . . How do we think about the entire world? The task seems so enormous. We find few people today talking about *world* evangelization. Somehow that seems like too big a dream in a world that every day grows more complex, a world torn by disasters, political upheaval, and starving people. Where do we begin? We might begin with population:

THE WORLD: 4.1 BILLION PEOPLE

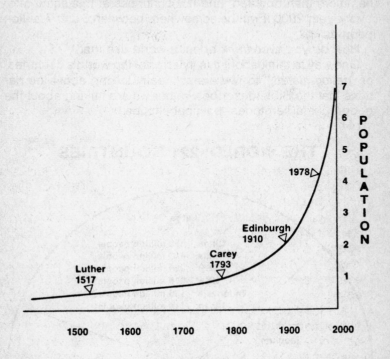

When we look at today's world population we are surprised at what has happened in such a few years. Between the time of Jesus' birth, when the population of the world was estimated at 250 million, and Martin Luther's dramatic challenge at Wittenberg, the population only doubled. In other words, it took fifteen hundred years for the population of the world to move from 250 million to 500 million. In 1793, William Carey, the "father of modern missions" set sail for India. In a little over 250 years the population had doubled again.

By the time of the Edinburgh Missionary Conference in 1910 the population had doubled again and now stood at over 2 billion.

THE UNREACHED AND HOW TO REACH THEM

In the brief sixty-eight years since that time the population has more than doubled, and if it continues at this same rate, by the year 2000 it will be somewhere between 6 and 7 billion people.

How do you even *think* about a world like that?

One way to think about it is in terms of the world's countries, or *"nation-states,"* for we are not really talking about the nations that the Bible describes, rather we are talking about the geographical territories, political entities.

THE WORLD: 221 COUNTRIES

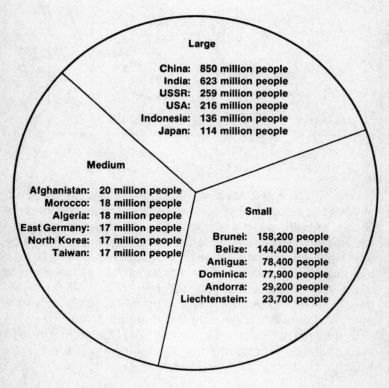

Large

China:	850 million people
India:	623 million people
USSR:	259 million people
USA:	216 million people
Indonesia:	136 million people
Japan:	114 million people

Medium

Afghanistan:	20 million people
Morocco:	18 million people
Algeria:	18 million people
East Germany:	17 million people
North Korea:	17 million people
Taiwan:	17 million people

Small

Brunei:	158,200 people
Belize:	144,400 people
Antigua:	78,400 people
Dominica:	77,900 people
Andorra:	29,200 people
Liechtenstein:	23,700 people

The 221 countries of the world come in all sizes. We have shown them here as large, medium and small. Nations range in size from the estimated 850 million people in China down to the mere 23,700 people in Liechtenstein. That tremendous variation shows how difficult it is to talk about world evangelization in terms of the countries. It is one thing to evangelize Liechtenstein. It is quite another to reach the 136 million people on the many islands of Indonesia.

Another way to think about the world is in terms of its religions.

THE WORLD: ITS RELIGIONS

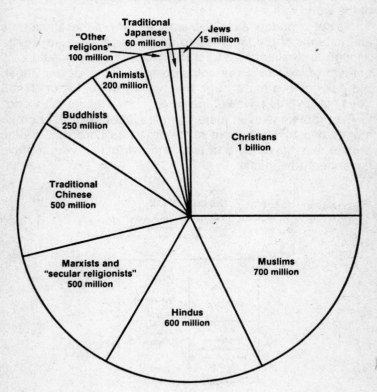

THE UNREACHED AND HOW TO REACH THEM

Christians, those who acknowledge Jesus Christ as Lord, number approximately one billion. The second largest religion in the world is Islam, with an estimated 700 million followers. The 600 million Hindus are found all over the world; the majority in India.

Marxism and what we might call "secular religons," things to which men and women have given their hearts, include approximately 500 million people.

There are estimated to be 500 million traditional Chinese. There are 250 million Buddhists in the world and 200 million animists, those who worship nature and the spirit world. Traditional Japanese, 15 million Jews, and all of the other religions of the world make up the balance.

It is not important as to how accurate any of these numbers are. In terms of proportions and magnitude they are accurate enough to challenge us with the fact that approximately 75 percent of the world's peoples do not worship Jesus Christ. But it is obvious that though this breakdown helps us, it still does not give us a workable strategy for reaching the world.

The problem is even more complex. In our world, approximately one billion people name Jesus as Lord, one billion people may have heard of him, and two billion people have never heard his name.

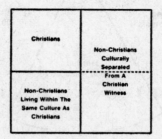

THE CHALLENGE

THE WORLD: 1 Billion people name Jesus as Lord
1 Billion people may have heard of Him
2 Billion people have never heard His Name

Christians

Non-Christians
Culturally
Separated
From A
Christian
Witness

Non-Christians
Living Within The
Same Culture As
Christians

What we have tried to show in this figure is that the approximate three billion people who are not Christians, only 1/3, or one billion, have neighbors who know Jesus and can share his love. To put that in reverse, no matter how earnest all of the local churches in the world were to reach out to their neighbors, only a third of the non-Christians in the world could be reached by Christians who speak their language and understand their culture. Dr. Ralph Winter, of the U. S. Center for World Mission, has tried to put this in perspective for us.

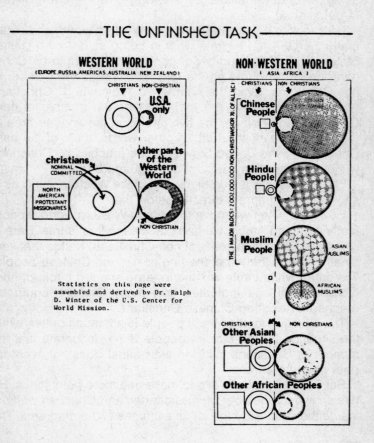

—————THE UNFINISHED TASK—————

WESTERN WORLD
(EUROPE,RUSSIA,AMERICAS,AUSTRALIA NEW ZEALAND)

CHRISTIANS NON-CHRISTIAN

U.S.A. only

christians
NOMINAL
COMMITTED

other parts of the Western World

NORTH AMERICAN PROTESTANT MISSIONARIES

NON CHRISTIAN

Statistics on this page were assembled and derived by Dr. Ralph D. Winter of the U.S. Center for World Mission.

NON-WESTERN WORLD
(ASIA AFRICA)

THE 3 MAJOR BLOCS: 2,002,000,000 NON CHRISTIANS(OR 70% OF ALL NC)

CHRISTIANS NON CHRISTIANS

Chinese People

Hindu People

Muslim People

ASIAN MUSLIMS

AFRICAN MUSLIMS

CHRISTIANS NON CHRISTIANS

Other Asian Peoples

Other African Peoples

THE UNREACHED AND HOW TO REACH THEM

In this diagram, the circles to the left of the vertical line represent the number of Christians, while the shaded circles to the right of the vertical line represent non-Christians.

But not all Christians are potential witnesses. Dr. Winter has estimated the number of "committed" Christians by placing a smaller circle inside the larger circle to the left of the vertical line.

Now to show us exactly what the unfinished task is, Dr. Winter has broken down the number of non-Christians who are living among Christians by showing a white circle in the larger shaded circle.

Let's look at the illustration on the Western world, and especially the USA to illustrate what is being said. In the United States, we find the number of people who claim to be Christian (the larger circle on the left) far exceeds the number of non-Christians. Even the number of "committed" Christians (the smaller circle to the left) exceeds the number of non-Christians. In addition, the two circles in the shaded area to the right are almost equal. In other words, most of the non-Christians in the United States can be reached by Christians without crossing any cultural or language barriers.

The same thing is true of the rest of the Western world as is shown in the diagram directly below that.

However, when we move to the non-Western world, specifically Asia and Africa, we find that the reverse is true. Here is where we find the majority of non-Christians. Notice that very small circle to the left of the line next to the Chinese people. The small white circle within the large shaded circle of non-Christian Chinese indicates how many Chinese could be reached by existing Chinese Christians.

The situation for the Hindu people is not much better, while the situation for the Muslim people is so desperate that the number of Christians living in their midst does not even appear on the diagram.

But Dr. Winter would like to make one more point for us. He has shown the number of missionaries and Christian workers inside the squares to the left of each one of the diagrams. The size of these squares indicates that the vast majority of North American Protestant missionaries are working in areas where there already are large numbers of Christians. We will give more thought to this as we move along.

How do you reach a world like that?

Not one country at a time, because countries vary so much. India, with its 623 million people, has 17 official languages, and 400 scheduled castes. Certainly the reaching of India is quite a different task than that of reaching Andorra with its 29,200 people.

Not one person at a time. As we have already tried to show, the ability of individuals who are already Christians to reach the rest of the world without some cross-cultural training and understanding is not adequate to do the job.

One people at a time is the way to do it.

What is a people? We define a people as "a significantly large sociological grouping of individuals who perceive themselves to have a common affinity for one aother because of their shared language, religion, ethnicity, residence, occupation, class or caste, situation, etc., or combinations of these."

For example:

● Urdu-speaking Muslim farmers of the Punjab

● Cantonese-speaking Chinese refugees from Viet Nam in France

● Welsh working-class miners

● Tamil-speaking Indian workers on Malaysian rubber plantations

● White, swinging singles in North American apartments

By a people we do not necessarily mean a tribal group. By a people we do not *necessarily* mean all the people living within a country. When we think of a people we try to think of them the way God sees them, to understand them *in terms of reaching them* with the gospel. We are attempting to define the world *in terms of world evangelization.*

Let's study the definition in chunks to see exactly what it means.

THE UNREACHED AND HOW TO REACH THEM

● By "significantly large" we mean a group usually large enough to believe it is a group.

● By "sociological grouping of individuals" we mean people who are relating to one another in a particular situation.

● "Who perceive themselves" needs some further defining. People who live in a high-rise apartment in New York City may know one another as a group of strangers, not as individuals. Yet in their individuality, and their statements about themselves, they see themselves as part of a group, which, from the view of world evangelization, has a commonness about it. There is "a common affinity for one another."

This sociological grouping, this perception, this common affinity, can be based on a lot of things. We have listed language, religion, ethnic background, where they live, their business or occupation, their class or caste, or anything about the situation which they are in, or any combination of these.

Perhaps our examples make the point. Notice the "boundaries" they place around a particular people. We speak not of just *Urdu-speaking* people. Not just Urdu-speaking *Muslims,* but Urdu-speaking Muslim *farmers* who happen to live in the *Punjab.*

There are lots of *Cantonese-speaking* Chinese. There are fewer of them who are *refugees.* The people we are describing here are Cantonese-speaking refugees from Viet Nam who right now are *living in France.*

To speak of evangelizing *Wales* is one thing. To speak of evangelizing the *working class* of Wales would narrow it down some. But to speak of evangelizing the Welsh working-class *miners* gets much more specific and defines a people.

There is not much point in trying to reach any one of these groups who are already reached. But how do we define *unreached?* The Strategy Working Group has adopted a working definition. *An unreached people is a group that is less than 20 percent practicing Christian.* What do we mean by *practicing?* Whatever *you mean!* How Christians will work out their religion in different places of the world will differ tremendously. The gospel has a marvelous ability to impregnate a culture and modify its Christian expression. Committed Christians within a particular group will know quite easily who are the practicing Christians and who are not.

We can turn back to the task that we had before: the 200,000 Turkana in northern Kenya; the 50,000 racetrack dwellers in the U.S.; the 1,000,000 high-rise residents in Singapore; the 300,000 Indians in South Africa; the 1,200,000 Turkish laborers in Germany; the 30,000,000 Ajlaf Muslim farmers in Bangladesh.

The world we are concerned with is the world of unreached people. Some of these groups are large. Some are small. The point is that we need to *discover God's strategies,* his best way for reaching these people. Certainly if the God of the universe is capable of being concerned with each individual in the world, he is just as concerned for the peoples of the world.

How do we reach them? Through their need.

● By trying to know them as God knows them.

● By attempting to meet their need as they see it.

● By communicating the saving power of Jesus Christ in their language and in their cultural understanding and in terms of where they are.

Too often some forms of evangelism have been carried out by people who had a solution and were looking for a problem. In other words, they assumed that there was one particular evangelistic method that would be appropriate in every setting. Evidently, God has not ordained it so. God's great love for humanity is expressed by his willingness to accept people wherever he finds them.

In order to communicate to people we have to begin where *they* perceive their need. We have to reach them *through* their need. We need *to know them as God knows them* and to begin by *attempting to meet their need as they see it.* When we have done this, we will have the potential for communicating the saving power of Jesus Christ in their language, and their cultural understanding, and in terms of where they find them-

THE UNREACHED AND HOW TO REACH THEM

selves. Understanding a people through their need is basic to the strategy that we are presenting here, a strategy that is useful anywhere in the world.

How do we discover their needs? What do we need to know about them?

● Where they are
● Why they should be considered a people group
● Where they are in their movement toward Christ
● Their potential receptivity to the gospel
● Their perceived spiritual needs

Where they are geographically is, of course, of first importance. But we need to go further and understand *why they should be considered a people group*. We need to put some boundaries around them.

A group of people is not static. Even in so-called traditional societies there is always movement. So we need to understand where this people is in terms of *their movement toward Christ*. Are they on the brink of receiving him, or are they completely unaware of his existence? The situations within which people find themselves will have a great deal to do with their receptivity to new things and thus their receptivity to the Gospel. We need to make some statements about that.

Finally, we need to understand their *perceived spiritual needs*. Jesus Christ is the answer to everyone's needs. But people have different needs at different times, and we must begin where they presently are.

In recent years some new tools have been developed to help us to better describe and thus better understand a people. One of these tools helps us to understand where people are in their movement toward Christ.

Notice that this scale shows a progression from no awareness of Christianity to being an active propagator. The scale is not special or peculiar to religion or Christianity. All of us, in making major decisions, go through some steps like this. And if we think back on our own conversion experience, we will discover that there were different people, different situations

WHERE IS THIS PEOPLE IN
THEIR MOVEMENT TOWARD CHRIST?
- The Engel Scale*

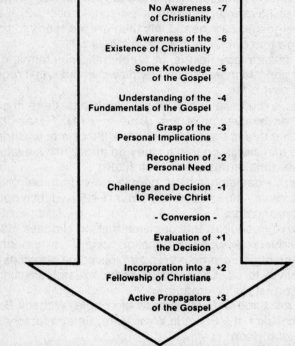

No Awareness of Christianity	-7
Awareness of the Existence of Christianity	-6
Some Knowledge of the Gospel	-5
Understanding of the Fundamentals of the Gospel	-4
Grasp of the Personal Implications	-3
Recognition of Personal Need	-2
Challenge and Decision to Receive Christ	-1
- Conversion -	
Evaluation of the Decision	+1
Incorporation into a Fellowship of Christians	+2
Active Propagators of the Gospel	+3

*This scale was originally proposed by Dr. James Engel of the Wheaton Graduate School.

that moved us toward Christ.

There was a day when, either because of ignorance or because of our extreme youth, we had absolutely *no awareness of Christianity* (-7 on this scale).

Most Westerners are aware or have some *awareness of Christianity* (-6 on our scale), and most Americans have *some knowledge of the gospel* (-5). The day came when some of us had an understanding of the *fundamentals of the gospel* (-4). What happened next and in what sequence is very difficult to

27

THE UNREACHED AND HOW TO REACH THEM

tell. It varies tremendously from individual to individual. But in addition to an intellectual understanding, each of us had to understand that this gospel was meant for us, we had to *grasp the personal implications* (-3). But even that is not enough. We must also have a *recognition of personal need* (-2) that we think the gospel can meet. Only then are we ready to have a *challenge and decision to receive Christ* (-1).

What takes place next is, in purely religious terms, called "conversion." In more biblical terms we would call it regeneration, a new birth.

But as is the case in most major decisions, there is almost always an *evaluation of the decision* (+1). Research has shown that this is the key time in the life of a new Christian. How we minister to people as they go through this evaluation will have a major impact on their future.

Once this decision is past, people move on to being *incorporated into a fellowship of Christians* (+2) and then *become active propagators* (+3).

We have described this decision-making process in terms of individuals. Actually, groups of people go through this same type of *group* process, and so this scale becomes even more useful to us. Let's look at some examples, using the illustration on the next page.

Here are three different groups of people, Witbank BaPedi in South Africa, the Senoi in West Malaysia and factory workers in Hong Kong.

The people in the first group are almost all Christians. Only a small percentage are still back in that category of having not moved beyond some knowledge of the gospel (-5). Approximately 45 percent of them have been incorporated into a fellowship of Christians (+2). This is a *reached* people.

The Senoi are at the other extreme. As best we can tell, about 80 percent of them are absolutely unaware of any existence of Christianity. True, there is a very small church (+2) but there is very little movement towards Christ.

The factory workers of Hong Kong, on the other hand, are surrounded by Christian symbols. Large numbers of them

EXAMPLE OF THE USE OF
THE ENGEL SCALE

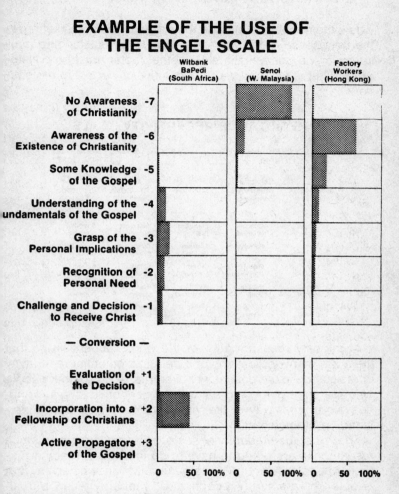

		Witbank BaPedi (South Africa)	Senoi (W. Malaysia)	Factory Workers (Hong Kong)
No Awareness of Christianity	-7			
Awareness of the Existence of Christianity	-6			
Some Knowledge of the Gospel	-5			
Understanding of the undamentals of the Gospel	-4			
Grasp of the Personal Implications	-3			
Recognition of Personal Need	-2			
Challenge and Decision to Receive Christ	-1			
— Conversion —				
Evaluation of the Decision	+1			
Incorporation into a Fellowship of Christians	+2			
Active Propagators of the Gospel	+3			

have an awareness of Christianity (-6). But the church is very small, although it appears that there are numbers of people who are moving towards Christ.

Now the advantage of these descriptions of people is that it helps us to *tailor our message*. We are much like the manufacturer of a product or a provider of a service. They have to know

29

THE UNREACHED AND HOW TO REACH THEM

where the people are in order to do a good job of marketing. In the best sense of the word, we want to be outstanding marketers of the gospel! But still another factor must be considered. What is the *potential receptivity of a people to the gospel?*

RESISTANCE/RECEPTIVITY SCALE

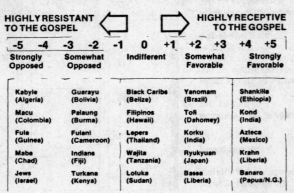

HIGHLY RESISTANT TO THE GOSPEL						HIGHLY RECEPTIVE TO THE GOSPEL	
-5	-4	-3	-2	-1	0	+1	+2	+3	+4	+5
Strongly Opposed		Somewhat Opposed		Indifferent		Somewhat Favorable		Strongly Favorable	

Strongly Opposed	Somewhat Opposed	Indifferent	Somewhat Favorable	Strongly Favorable
Kabyle (Algeria)	Guarayu (Bolivia)	Black Caribs (Belize)	Yanomam (Brazil)	Shankilla (Ethiopia)
Macu (Colombia)	Palaung (Burma)	Filipinos (Hawaii)	Tofi (Dahomey)	Kond (India)
Fula (Guinea)	Fulani (Cameroon)	Lepers (Thailand)	Korku (India)	Azteca (Mexico)
Maba (Chad)	Indians (Fiji)	Wajita (Tanzania)	Ryukyuan (Japan)	Krahn (Liberia)
Jews (Israel)	Turkana (Kenya)	Loluka (Sudan)	Bassa (Liberia)	Banaro (Papua/N.G.)

Missionary research all over the world has shown us that there are many indications of a people's potential receptivity or resistance to the gospel. For example, we know that people who are undergoing a great deal of economic stress, or upheavals in their way of life, are more open to a new understanding of the world.

The resistance/receptivity scale helps us know how much research we are going to have to do in order to reach a particular people. Although it is a generalization, we can say that people who are highly receptive will probably respond to almost any evangelistic method, while people who are highly resistant are going to need a great deal of special care.

Underneath the scale, we have listed peoples in these various categories. There are tremendous opportunities for the gospel around the world! Here are a few:

PEOPLE KNOWN
TO BE OPEN TO THE GOSPEL

Country	Group	Population	Percent Christian
CHINA (TAIWAN)	HAKKA	1,750,000	(1%)
INDIA	KOND	900,000	(3%)
PHILIPPINES	COTABOTO MANOBO	10,000	(1%)
THAILAND	LEPERS OF NORTHEAST	390,000	(.5%)
BENIN	BOKO	20,000	(2%)
ETHIOPIA	SHANKILLA	500,000	(1%)
KENYA	FISHING TURKANA	20,000	(4%)
GERMANY	KOREANS	10,000	(8%)
U.S.A.	RACETRACK RESIDENTS	50,000	(10%)
MEXICO	AZTECA	250,000	(2%)
BELIZE	BLACK CARIBS	10,000	(1%)
COLOMBIA	COREGUAJE	500	(1%)
GUATEMALA	QUICHE	500,000	(7%)

This is just a *partial* list of the peoples who have been researched and recorded from all over the world. What excuse do we have in the face of this kind of information? Yet, in the main, there are few missionaries attempting to reach these people.

How do we find the unreached?

As of January 1978, the Strategy Working Group was working on 102 countries of the world, compiling *Status of Christianity Profiles.* They had listed 2,928 people groups, 700 of which have been described in enough detail to become part of a directory of unreached peoples. These country profiles are compiled and stored on a computer for easy availability and updating. Each profile contains five sections: a description of the country, a description of the people of the country, a description of the church within the country, a description of the force for evangelism attempting to reach the people within the country, and a general analysis of the status of Christianity.

THE UNREACHED AND HOW TO REACH THEM

Unreached peoples surveys are carried out as part of the status of Christianity research using a survey questionnaire developed by MARC and the Strategy Working Group. A computer program is used to store the information as it is received on these questionnaires.

In addition to the work being done by MARC and the Strategy Working Group, there are some very significant Christian researchers who are making major contributions to this project. One of the most notable of these is the Unit of Research under the direction of Dr. David B. Barrett. Dr. Barrett is the senior editor of the forthcoming *World Christian Handbook,* which collaborators all over the world have been cooperating on since 1968. The information gathered on Christian churches of all ecclesiastical traditions and persuasions, as well as the religions of the world, comprises a very large databank that will be the foundation for future studies in world evangelization for years to come.

Another source of information on strategies for reaching unreached peoples are congresses and conferences. The first evangelical conference on world evangelization was held in Berlin in 1966. This was followed by regional and national congresses and conferences all over the world. The second major congress was the International Congress on World Evangelization held at Lausanne in 1974, out of which emerged the Strategy Working Group.

In addition to the *World Christian Handbook,* which concentrates on countries, the Strategy Working Group is compiling this annual directory.

This book, to be updated each year, will be yet another basic ongoing resource for all of those concerned with reaching the world with the good news of Jesus Christ.

The Status of Christianity Profiles, Unreached Peoples–1979, and the *World Christian Handbook,* give us basic information about the world, the countries of the world and the unreached peoples of the world. But we need to go further than that. We need to understand how to reach them. The basic tool being developed and tested by MARC and the

Strategy Working Group is the workbook *Planning Strategies for Evangelism.* This 32-page workbook leads the potential missionary through a series of questions which will hopefully lead him or her to a better understanding of God's strategy for a particular people.

HOW DO WE GO ABOUT IT?

Planning Strategies for Evangelism

We begin by *defining our mission.* What is it that God wants us to do? What is the biblical mandate for what we are about?

The next step is to describe the people as best we can. The questionnaire that has been developed, as well as questions in *Planning Strategies for Evangelism,* give a preliminary understanding (see Appendix A).

Frequently we move on to means and methods too quickly.

THE UNREACHED AND HOW TO REACH THEM

First we need to *describe the force for evangelism.* By "force for evangelism" we mean potentially the entire Christian Church. There are Christians all over the world, who, because of their concern, can bring to bear their prayer, their resources, and themselves to reach a particular people. We must decide what parts of the Church can be brought to bear on this particular people.

Next we come to *examine means and methods.* We realize for every people there will be old means and methods that can be reforged with new insights to tailor a program for reaching this particular people. It is very much like designing a unique key to unlock the hearts of a special people. We need to see that each lock is different, and although there will be similarities, we need to assume that God has a special way of reaching what to him is a very special people.

This, then, will lead us to *define an approach,* or to develop a strategy. We can now state how we intend to go about reaching this particular people.

But God intends that we have results. We need, therefore, to *anticipate outcomes.* We need to try to imagine what we believe God is going to do in the lives of this particular people if we carry out this approach.

Too often we automatically assume because we have a concern for a particular people that we are the ones who should be directly involved in reaching them. This is not always the case. Some of us are gifted in one direction, some in others. We need to *decide our role* before moving ahead. Assuming that we have decided to move ahead, we then need to *make plans.* In faith we need to anticipate what God would have us do. Any statement about the future is a statement of faith. The larger our faith, the greater our plans. Plans will require that we *gather resources.* There will be need for people, for funds, for facilities, for many different things. These need to be prepared.

Then we can *act* to carry out our plans.

But as we act we need to *evaluate.* Things seldom go completely as we anticipate them. Plans will go awry. Situations

34

will change. The Holy Spirit will lead in new paths. We should not slavishly follow plans but stay in tune with him. When we have carried out all our plans, we need to begin the cycle again and again *define the new mission*.

So *Planning Strategies for Evangelism* is a repetitive process, one that is useful for reaching any people. It is not tied down to any particular means or method. It does not make any assumptions about people. Rather, it attempts to keep us in tune with what the Holy Spirit might be saying to us by leading us through a thoughtful process.

Edward R. Dayton is the founder and director of the Missions Advanced Research and Communication Center (MARC), a ministry of World Vision International. Mr. Dayton worked in various engineering and management positions within the field of aircraft and space electronics for sixteen years. After receiving a M.Div. degree from Fuller Theological Seminary in 1967, he devoted himself to helping the church develop more effective strategies for evangelization. He has written books in the area of missions and management. The most recent include *Tools for Time Managment, Strategy for Living,* and *The Art of Management for Christian Leaders.* He is editor of the eleventh edition of the *Mission Handbook.* He is currently the director of the Evangelism and Research Division of World Vision International and adjunct professor of missions strategy at Fuller Theological Seminary.

Penetrating the New Frontiers

by Ralph D. Winter

The Second World War was one of the major hinges of history. Before that time, different parts of the Western world had long dominated the rest of the globe—a result of a trading and colonizing process that had begun four hundred years before. But in World War II, the West was locked in a massive, internal conflict for the second time in forty years. Then, once Germany was put down as a belligerent, the incipient tension between Russia and the capitalist world broke out into new and harrowing competition which has continued to the present. And new powers such as China and the Middle Eastern nations have emerged since World War II to complicate further the outlook in our time.

It is no wonder, then, that during the past thirty years the chief thinkers within the traditional missionary apparatus of the Western world have by and large considered it sufficient merely to hold on to or to consolidate work that had been initiated earlier. This preoccupation with our relations to the "younger churches" also arises as a result of the relative decline of the West. That decline allowed not only the somewhat chaotic emergence of independent nations in the non-Western world, but introduced massive turbulence among the national churches as they have grown toward independence. Western guilt feelings as colonial empires gave way flowed over into the arena of mission empires. In many cases Western mission leaders have bent over backwards to avoid an ungenerous or ungentlemanly or "paternalistic" stance toward the younger churches. A honeymoon era ensued which has only recently begun to fade as the younger churches have been seen in a more realistic light and both their strengths and limitations taken into account.

At this point, let me make clear that although I'm writing primarily for a U.S. audience, the term *younger churches* could just as easily apply to new churches planted cross-culturally by other younger churches. People "back home" are not necessarily Western Christians but those Christians, wherever they are, whose missionaries have established new churches cross-culturally. These mission efforts are merely more recent continuations of those by Western Christians— who are themselves simply converted savages from the forests of Europe a thousand years ago.

INTRODUCTION

The January 1971 issue of *International Review of Mission* carried an article I had written (Winter, 1971) on the rise of new missions from the soil of the younger churches. Edwin W. Kortz, executive director of the Board of Foreign Missions of the Moravian Church in America, was one who responded to that article. Among other things, he highlighted the need for the withdrawal of missionaries where national leadership takes over. My reply to him stressed the necessity of shifting our attention from the needs and concerns of the national Christians to the needs of a vast world far larger than can ever be reached by the capacities of the present national Christians. Kortz was shortly later to play an important role in the development of a consultation, The Gospel and Frontier Peoples, organized by R. Pierce Beaver in December, 1972. Earlier that same year (1972) Luther Copeland, the outgoing president of the Association of Professors of Mission, had proposed for 1980 a successor to the 1910 Edinburgh Conference. The 1910 meeting was notable (and to missionaries in Latin America, notorious) for its exclusion from its purview all missionary activities carried on within either Christian or nominally Christian areas, thus defining *mission* classically as work where there is no other witness. In 1974 twenty-four professors followed through to formulate a "Call" for such a meeting to be convened in 1980. This Call refers specifically to cross-cultural outreach, and the intended name of the 1980 meeting, World Missionary Conference (deliberately identical to the 1910 meeting) carries foward the concept of missions as they were conceived in 1910, e.g., "not efforts for renewal within the church, not local outreach in the same cultural sphere of existing churches." (This quote is taken from my own analysis of that Call (Winter, 1976).

Just a few days after the formulation of the Call, the mammoth International Congress on World Evangelization (ICOWE) took place in Lausanne, Switzerland. There I was given the privilege of stating in a plenary address the case for cross-cultural evangelism. I was asked also to write the introductory chapter of a book on unreached peoples, published especially for the Congress by World Vision's MARC division. And, an earlier paper (Winter, 1974) I had written entitled "Seeing the Task Graphically" provided some of the statistical base for the opening audio-visual at Lausanne, "The Task Before Us," which was developed by Waldron Scott (Scott, 1975). An update and refinement of those statistics was already built into my plenary address at the Congress, "The Highest Priority, Cross-Cultural Evangelism" (Winter, 1975). A further statement and refinement of this analysis was presented in the opening address I was asked to give at the joint IFMA-EFMA executive retreat in 1976, "The Grounds for a New Thrust in Missions" (Winter, 1977), bringing the population data up to July 1977.

Meanwhile, many other forces have begun to focus on the fact that in missions today we have perhaps worked ourselves out of many jobs, but not *the* job. For example, the General

THE UNREACHED AND HOW TO REACH THEM

Assembly of the UPCUSA (perhaps encouraged by the announced interests of the newly formed United Presbyterian Center for Mission Studies, which is focused especially on cross-cultural mission) appointed a committee in 1974 called "Strategy Development Committee for Reaching People Who Are Without the Gospel."

The problem is that despite this upswing of interest in new frontiers, the legacy of previous mission education in the churches has gone so far that by now what most of the people in the pews know is simply that there are "national" churches out there. While this pleases them, it often leads to lowered concern and to less involvement wherever the true scope of the still unfinished task is not brought into the picture. As a result, the very first and foremost strategy for reaching unreached people must be a massive new and urgent effort simply to expand the perspectives of the people back home.

In other words, over these thirty years, virtually all of us have become accustomed to thinking that where a mission is there is also a national church, and in that place pioneer methods are no longer appropriate. We think this way mainly because most of us have not been in touch with the continuing experience of penetrating still new frontiers that make our work identifiably parallel to the classical past. No wonder we still hear it said that the era of the pioneer missionary is past, that we have worked ourselves out of that kind of job!

Therefore, the first strategy we must develop is, surprisingly, not directly related to the task to be performed. It is as though "we have sighted the enemy, and the enemy is us." Alas, the non-Christian world, even including China, is more open and more reachable today than it has been for most of the history of missions. If it weren't for the massive contemporary misconstrual of the actual situation, we could probably go right ahead to get on with the task of strategizing for direct involvement with the unreached people. But the prior strategy is that we must give at least some thought to rebuilding the foundations themselves. Without that renewed foundation, other strategies will never be implemented.

STRATEGY I: REBUILD PIONEER MISSION PERSPECTIVE

To talk about missions in certain of the better informed quarters of the American church today conjures up the following scene. Picture a vast auditorium filled with the delegates to a church convention, wearied and tired after lengthy debates and strenuous dialogues of many kinds. The final item on the agenda is concluded and the meeting is gavelled into adjournment. People are streaming for the doors engrossed in conversation with one another. But now a small lady with a weak voice stands up in the podium and cries out shrilly over the microphone, "Wait, the meeting isn't over. We still have work to do." At first her voice isn't heard over the noice of the people. But finally the hubbub dies down and the startled delegates hear the message, "The job is not done!" Disbelief, weariness and disinterest flood the hearts of the vast majority. "This is no time to talk about an unfinished task. No one told us earlier. We were led to believe that adjournment was now appropriate. Don't lay on us this new task, saying it is the old task, unfinished." A church official gently leads the earnest woman away from the microphone, and the crowd continues to move out the exits. How could a whole auditorium of church leaders be wrong?

So long as the people back home feel they have completed the pioneering task, they will feel the situation can be normalized. They are not easily reprogrammed. They may say, "Just as the great industrial producers of tanks and guns in wartime shift over to automobiles and sewing machines in peace time, so the classical mechanism of missions now can be retooled for a new program of peace time aid to sister churches across the world." Many thus feel that there is no longer a spiritual crisis constituted by vast millions that are beyond the reach of existing churches. In part, it is this kind of thinking that allows a New York church executive to speak of the "end of the era of missions." The end indeed! It's only the end of pioneer efforts in merely those places where the church is well established. This line of thinking is (ironically but understandably) most prominent among those church people whose past efforts across the world have been most successful. The faster the national church grows, the more its needs, wants (and mere desires) grow up like high grass to restrict the view of the people back home from the needs of the regions beyond. But isn't it silly for a mission that has worked in the center of India for a hundred years to pull out and go home just because a tiny, 25-mile radius sphere has finally had some stable work established? This is not entirely silly. The work in that place has for a long time been not pioneer "missions" but "interchurch aid." The gradual shift to interchurch aid has inevitably selected other than "pioneer missionary" personalities and quite naturally favored the useful technicians of school and hospital, who are sensitive people, good people with spiritual insight, but people not at all prepared to be recast in pioneer roles. A friend of mine has long championed the phrase "disengage to re-engage." Magnificent logic, but really not very practical after the long transition has taken place. Himself a second-generation missionary, he just happens to have the pioneer mentality.

In view of this transition, we are no longer doing the nineteenth-century outreach despite the fact that there are now more non-Christians than ever before who are beyond the range of the normal evangelism of any national church. There is still a great deal of nineteenth-century work to do. The main difference in this century is that strong Christian churches are no longer to be found just in the West. There are now millions of Christians in the non-Western world. The problem is, the existence of younger churches in the non-Western world is in effect distracting and deflecting the mission mechanisms from their original purpose. The fact that new churches exist in the non-Western world should occasion new obligations and relationships on the part of the churches back home. But this new dimension must not replace the earlier purpose of continuing mission to new populations. Church leaders back home, having gotten wind of the existence of churches overseas, tend to identify more easily with national church leaders than with any continuing pioneer mission effort. And the people we now send overseas, whether or not we call them missionaries, no longer arrive in pitch darkness but are today usually welcomed by the smiles and genuine affection of true Christians. Quite naturally, in a foreign country, today's missionaries are glad to live and work among Christians and find the non-Christian world both less visible and less appealing.

As a result, almost all the older boards and agencies are today almost entirely involved overseas with the kind of work which in this country is normally called *nurture* or *home missions*. For example, an American missionary in Africa, should he not be involved in a school or hospital, is at best merely helping a national church do "local evangelism." Meanwhile, the precious product of our missions, the overseas national churches, remain for various reasons far less aware of the meaning of the Great Commission than do churches in North America. They are more likely to ask help with political oppression, just as we would in their place. Even the missionaries often do not recognize the distinction between (1) learning a foreign language to help (foreign) local Christians do local outreach (or fight hunger, poverty and oppression), and (2) learning a foreign language to reach people beyond the local outreach of the overseas national churches.

This is not to conclude that the vast flurry of activities of thirty-seven thousand missionaries shouldn't be. It is rather to emphasize that what we are now doing in missions is extremely and uneasily different from what has always been intended by the classical missionary movement. Indeed, the only justification for the present state of affairs would seem to be the total absence of the "regions beyond." But the regions beyond are still there, and they're massive.

The answer is not to try to turn this situation around. It is not as though what we're doing is wrong. Most of $700 million per year of American money going into missions is all to the good. To rebuild pioneer missions perspective does not require us to tear down interchurch aid perspective. The difference in role between the pastor and the missionary is so great that neither can displace the other. *The problem we face is really very different from what some people see as a tension between social action and evangelism.* Some of the most courageous social action and the most large-minded community development has been the work of early pioneer missionaries. And it is not at all mainly a distinction between mainline denominational boards and "faith missions." Today there is very little difference in the major focus of activity of an agency of mission, whether it is the United Methodist church or the Sudan Interior Mission. In both cases the preponderance of personnel are in church development, education, and health. With the exception of Wycliffe Bible Translators and Regions Beyond Missionary Union and a few other highly specialized agencies, virtually all missionary boards with more than twenty-five years of effort behind them are by now focused primarily on the care and feeding of existing Christian communities. The development of these beachheads to the point of safe disengagement of expatriate personnel is a good goal, but it is not good enough. The classical task remains.

To gain a proper impression of how tough it will be to rebuild pioneer mission perspective, take a lesson from my own church.

In a desperate effort twenty years ago to safeguard a continuing mission to fulfill this original, classical, unfinished task, the United Presbyterian Church in the United States of America endeavored to distinguish between interchurch aid (with which "fraternal workers" would be involved) and the continuing classical mission to non-Christians (with which "missionaries" had always been involved). I can recall vividly a crucial point in one of the plenary discussions of the WCC's new Commission on World Mission and Evangelism in Mexico City in 1963 when missionary statesman John Coventry Smith was pressed to account for the distinction reflected by this novelty in terminology. But then as now, the increasingly loud voices of the younger churches, loyally amplified by the proud or cowed parent bodies, spoke louder than the unstated needs of unrepresented non-Christians. Some may have feared that going into interchurch aid as a new venture separate from classical mission would mean giving up both the name and the vast support base which for a hundred years had focused primarily on the winning of non-Christians. Many may have felt that the new and worthy "mission" of interchurch aid could not so readily or so quickly develop its own roots as it could demand to eat from the classical mission trough. Thus reception to United Presbyterian honesty about maintaining this distinction was cool or confused, and not only at Mexico City.

Despite the cool response, my own agency, which had been simply a "foreign mission board" when I was commissioned a missionary in 1956, proceeded resolutely to divide its very name in order to allow for the distinction we are highlighting. It now became the United Presbyterian Church's Commission on Ecumenical Mission and Relations— *Relations* referring potentially to interchurch relationships, and *Mission* potentially to the traditional "unfinished task" of reaching non-Christians, now, of course pursued "ecumenically" (e.g. in cooperation with the younger churches and other church groups). Unfortunately, the people at the pew level in the church in the U.S. merely got the idea that all overseas workers should now be called "fraternal workers." This for them was the new day. And unfortunately, many of the very overseas workers who insisted on still being called missionaries were, in fact, as much interchurch workers as anyone. And before things could be straightened out, the whole issue was bypassed when the agency's name was again changed and the very word *mission* removed and appropriated by the central denominational apparatus to be reapplied as the purpose for all fund-raising of all kinds. In any case, the awesome thing is that, faced with most of the same basic circumstances, most boards, whether liberal or conservative, denominational or interdenominational, ecumenical or independent, have followed the same pattern. Thus, while the apparatus of mission has in most cases been successfully readjusted to "the emerging task" presented by the fruits of

45

earlier mission work, the classical "unfinished task" is still there, is still mammoth, but is no longer within even the *aim* of most present agencies, no matter what well-intentioned gestures are made toward "mission" and "evangelism" in the flow of promotional literature. Today such phrases are simply vestigial remains of a nearly extinct earlier vision.

But the classical task cannot and must not be that easily forgotten. The facts are too blunt. They are not, in fact, hidden in a corner, but are available to all who will stop to reconsider.

Before moving to a second strategy which will deal with the facts, let us note that pioneer mission perspective must be rebuilt across the entire spectrum—the people back home, the mission executives, the missionaries themselves, and even overseas church leaders. All these sectors either have lost sight of, or have not yet clearly confronted, the awesome scope of the unfinished task. Much less have they come to terms with the fact that a high proportion of non-Christians today are beyond the reach of the usual type of evangelistic strategy. The tactics whereby this strategy can be undertaken will be dealt with after mentioning other essential strategies.

STRATEGY II: REDISCOVER THE HIDDEN PEOPLE

At the risk of repeating some things published earlier, it will be well to try very briefly to restate the broad categories of unreached people in order to zero in upon what we shall define as the Hidden People. Precise figures are not necessary to reconstruct the overall contours. By going from country to country and roughly dividing Christians into two groups and non-Christians into two groups, all the while trying sincerely not to exaggerate the size of *the remaining task* (and therefore more likely to exaggerate the number of Christians), we still come up with some imposing world totals for each of four categories, as below. The explanation of the categories is as important as the resulting numbers.

● 219 million *Active Christians*. These people definitely possess a genuine personal faith and are capable of winning others to that faith. They do need Christian nurture, and many missionaries are involved in this task. The constant danger has always been that their own nurture will soak up all their own energies plus those of expatriate missionaries.

● 1,000 million *Inactive Christians.* These people are culturally within the Christian tradition but hardly qualify as committed Christians. They need "renewal" via an "innermission," or *E-O Evangelism,* if you will, since there is a zero cultural barrier to their vital participation in the life of the church. Most evangelism and mission effort (in India one report has it 98 percent) is focused on this group. Again, the danger is that what efforts may be left over beyond the nurture of the first group will be completely absorbed here.

● 500 million *Culturally-Near Non-Christians.* These are those whose cultural tradition and social sphere have already been penetrated by the Christian faith. Thus, for these people there now already exists, culturally near at hand, some Christian congregation or denomination where they can readily fit in linguistically and socially. While they may not actually live geographically near such a Christian church, they are culturally near. Thus, certain existing churches have the potential to reach out to them without crossing any cultural barriers other than the *one* "stained glass barrier" that lies between them and the believing communities. Sensitive E-1 evangelism is needed to cross the mono-cultural barrier. Note: missionaries who are "helping national Christians to evangelize" are often not working across this one barrier, but rather are working mainly with inactive, nominal Christians.

● 2,500 million *Culturally-Distant Non-Christians.* These are the Hidden People. These are individuals and groups of people who, whether geographically near or far from Christian outreach, are sufficiently different linguistically, socially, economically, or culturally so that they are simply not realistic candidates for membership in existing Christian churches. They are "hidden" or isolated by an invisible but significant caste or class barrier. One example is the 97 percent Muslim population of Pakistan which is isolated from the Hindu-background Christian communities in that country. Another example is the group in the book of Acts called the "devout persons" who as Greeks did not fit well into the Jewish synagogues Paul visited. Some of these Hidden People are *somewhat similar* in culture, but are yet too far to fit in reality. E-2 evangelism must take into account a second barrier beyond the stained glass barrier. E-2, unlike E-1 evangelistic tactics, cannot depend on existing congregations, but must create new congregations. (These may or may not be closely associated with existing congregations.) Note that E-2 necessarily brings into play traditional missionary techniques. Peoples close enough to existing congregations so that normal E-1 evangelism is effective are *defined* to be in the previous (E-1) category. *People who for whatever practical reasons cannot be effectively brought into existing congregations are defined to be in the Hidden People (or E-2, E-3 category.)*

E-3 evangelism, more difficult still, is required where cultural differences are nearly total. For simplicity in this paper, we are lumping together E-2 *(similar-*but-not-*same-*culture) and E-3 (very different culture) because unlike E-0 and E-1 evangelism, E-2 and E-3 are (1) both rarely accomplished apart from the specialized efforts or organizations such as mission societies or Catholic orders, (2) they are both beyond the reach of virtually all existing efforts and even beyond the present strategy of most mission agencies, and (3) E-2 begins a continuum that ends at E-3. The following diagram and table below are based on the four-fold breakdown we have just made. Note that the Hidden People (which are in the fourth column in the table and add up to 2,500 million people) constitute 83 percent of the total non-Christian population of the world. Yet columns 7, 8, 9 show the small mission force and the enormous linguistic and cultural diversity posed by the Hidden People in Column 4!

One or two cautions are in order. Some of the peoples in the 83 percent category are very difficult to reach: Chinese in mainland China, women in a harem in a remote Saudi Arabian village, etc. The point, however, is that *this entire category* is not seriously being dealt with today, by either Western or

WORLD POPULATION (IN MILLIONS), MID 1978

CHRISTIANS		NON-CHRISTIANS	
219	1,000	500	2,500
	(E-0)	(E-1)	(E-2 and E-3) The "Hidden People"

WESTERN WORLD	CHRISTIANS (Committed)	(Nominal E-0)	NON-CHRISTIANS (Within reach E-1)	(Beyond E-2, E-3)	TOTALS*	N. AMER. MISSIONARIES WORKING WITH Columns 1, 2, 3	4	DIVERSITY IN COLUMN 4 (Languages)	(Subgroups)
USA, Canada	69	144	17	12	242	—	—	80	300
Europe, Latin America, N.Z., Australia	55	698	185	147	1,085	15,018	1,000	480	950
NON-WESTERN									
Chinese	2	1	40	819	862	1,217	100	50	2,000
Hindus	5	10	30	492	546	950	50	200	3,000
Muslims**									
Asia	.11	.05	20	489	509	100	50	300	3,500
Africa	—	—	—	165	165	—	50	280	500
Other Asians	43	63	159	282	547	7,077	1,600	2,500	4,000
Other Africans	45	84	40	94	263	9,338	500	1,500	2,500
TOTALS	219	1,000	500 17%	2,500 83%	4,219	33,700 91%	3,350 9%	5,390	16,750

*Population Reference Bureau, Washington, D.C.

**Note: an additional 26 million Muslims live in the Western world

non-Western Christians *or their missions!* There are hundreds
of millions in this column who can more easily be reached
right now by known methods than ever before. But if we really
decide to put our shoulders to the task, we will, I believe,

49

discover that these 2.5 billion, now receiving only a tiny proportion of existing church or mission efforts, could effectively use at least as much as our entire present outreach, and our present board and agency structures would be the first to applaud this expansion and labor incessantly to implement it.

In a recent book (Winter, 1977) I have a chapter which describes and breaks down this fourth column in some detail. Here there is space only to mention one other caution. Some would question the value of the distinction between the heavy mission involvement with Christians (interchurch aid) and the relatively scant involvement with non-Christians (traditional mission work). Many missionaries today, even though they are working with an overseas church, will insist that they are *indirectly* reaching non-Christians by virtue of helping and equipping overseas Christians to do that job. What could be better than to get the overseas Christians, who speak the language as their mother tongue, to do the work the missionaries first came to do? Thus it may be alleged that this entire distinction is false because helping overseas churches is, it is said, the most efficient kind of mission. Indeed, more and more U.S. congregations are so eager to see "native missionaries" do the job that several organizations exist primarily to transmit funds directly to overseas Christians. Nevertheless, as the population bar graph shows, only 17 percent, or 500 million, of the non-Christians could conceivably be reached even if all the existing churches were to get busy and win all the people within their own social sphere.

Thus, as we have noted, the vast bulk of missionaries are not directly concerned with such outreach at all, and the average church overseas is no more likely to make strenuous efforts to establish congregations speaking languages other than their own than is the average church in the U.S. likely to be working diligently *as a congregational initiative* to set up new congregations for Chinese or Korean immigrants. Both in the U.S. and in the non-Western countries, specialized offices and agencies are necessary for such tasks. Whether the non-Christians are near or far, next door or in another country, there is no structure better designed for outreach than the traditional mission. Unfortunately, our present missions are so deeply involved with the nurture and the E-O and E-1 outreach of the national Christians they have little time left over to develop in the overseas national churches the appropriate mission knowledge and awareness. They're even further from being able to create the necessary national mission structures necessary to justify the idea that working with Christians overseas can be counted as a contribution toward reaching the 83 percent column, the 2,493 million culturally-distant non-Christians.

Even though the percentage of Christians is higher today than ever before in virtually every country of the world, the unfinished task of the nineteenth century is still very much with us. But the task has been virtually abandoned because the mission agencies of today are extensively converted over to the very different task of interchurch aid. Despite the flurry of discussion about the role of the present churches in society, no one has invented a better mechanism for penetrating new social units than the traditional mission society, whether it be Western, African or Asian, whether it be denominational or interdenominational. Indeed, the new fact of our time is the emergence in some force already of the so-called Third World missions. Some suggest that this is the answer.

But the central burden of Strategy II is not to decide who is to reach the Hidden People but to describe their existence in operational terms. This will be further elaborated in the section on Class II tactics.

STRATEGY III: REEVALUATE ALL PREVIOUS APPROACHES

David Liao in his book *The Unresponsive: Resistant or Neglected?* (Liao, 1972) suggest that while large blocks of people (in his case study, the Hakka Chinese) may for practical purposes be characterized as unresponsive, the fault may be as much ours as theirs. My personal opinion is that to speak precisely we must never use the word *resistant* to apply to a large group of people. The root word *to resist* more accurately describes the reaction of an individual person. But even where a family or small group seems to unite in resistance to a particular method, generalizing the term to any entire category of people (such as 700 million Muslims) is where the word *resistant* begins to lack justification. It is more honest to say that what we have tried hasn't worked. *Resistant* may throw the blame prematurely on the people we have not yet reached.

Lyle Vander Werff, in a book published in December of 1977, tries to summarize all the Christian approaches to the Muslim world by the Anglican, Presbyterian, and Congregational traditions up to 1938. While he does not emphasize reevaluation, his research does provide the necessary background of what has been done before. Recent articles in *Missiology*, notably the special issue on Islam in July of 1976, are pushing forward the task of reevaluation. See also John Wilder's "Some Reflections on Possibilities for People Movements Among Muslims" (*Missiology,* July, 1977). David Liao's book concentrates on ancestor "worship" in just the Chinese tradition. Bernard Hwang's article "Ancestor Cult Today" in *Missiology,* July, 1977, pursues the subject in an even broader context. But these references are just a few illustrations of the kind of foundational reevaluation that is necessary.

In one sense, the recent emphasis upon contextualization provides some helpful insights for reevaluation. But we must understand that mere reevaluation of our message and our theology is not sufficient. We do not merely preach a message which must be made relevant to each new context. The gospel cannot be disembodied. We not only proclaim a *message,* but carry and extend, modify, or create a social *mechanism* that is essential as a carrier vehicle for the gospel. The medium is not the message, but it is part of it. In the Muslim world, the structure of the Western church and of the Muslim mosque collide head on. The Fellowship of St. Andrew, on the other hand, has survived without any such conflict ever since

Samuel Zwemer first implanted it early in this century.

Class III tactics will be noted further on.

STRATEGY IV: RECONSECRATE OURSELVES TO THE WARTIME, NOT PEACETIME, LIFE-STYLE

The Queen Mary, lying in repose in the harbor at Long Beach, California, is a fascinating museum of the past. Used both as a luxury liner in peacetime and a troop transport during the Second World War, its present status as a museum three football fields long affords a stunning contrast between the life-styles appropriate in peace and war. On one side of a partition you see the dining room reconstructed to depict the peacetime table setting that was appropriate to the wealthy patrons of high culture for whom a dazzling array of knives, forks, and spoons held no mysteries. On the other side of the partition the evidences of wartime austerity provide a sharp contrast. One metal tray with indentations replaces fifteen plates and saucers. Bunks, not just double, but eight tiers high, shows how the peacetime capacity of 3000 could give way to 15,000 people on board in wartime. How repugnant to the peacetime masters this transformation must have been! To do it took a national emergency, of course. The survival of a nation depended upon it.

The essence of the Great Commission today is that the survival of many millions of people depends on its fulfillment.

But obedience to the Great Commission has more consistently been poisoned by affluence than by anything else. The antidote for affluence is reconsecration. Consecration is by definition the "setting apart of things for a holy use." Affluence did not keep Borden of Yale from giving his life in Egypt. Affluence didn't stop Francis of Assisi from moving against the tide of his time.

Curiously enough, while modern Protestantism has no significant counterpart to the Catholic orders (unless we think of the more recent campus evangelistic organizations such as Inter-Varsity, Campus Crusade, and Navigators), nevertheless the entire Protestant missionary tradition has always stressed a practical measure of austerity and simplicity as well as a parity of consumption levels within its missionary ranks. Widespread reconsecration leading to a reformed life-style with wartime priorities is not likely to be successful (even in an age of increasing awareness of the life-style issue itself) unless Protestantism can develop patterns of consecration among the people back home that are comparable to what has characterized the Protestant missionary movement for nearly two hundred years. Several possibilities will be mentioned under Class IV Tactics.

TACTICAL CONSIDERATIONS

Our entire discussion thus far has concerned general strategies which are larger than and at least partially beyond the scope of most existing Christian institutions. Most strategizing takes place on the level of the mission society, and therefore whatever task is inherently beyond the scope of any one mission society has fallen by the wayside. It is terrifying when you stop to think of it how many things ought to be done that will not get done if merely the existing structures are expected to work cooperatively for their achievement.

An example is the Missionary Research Library. When it was finally given over to the National Council of Churches' Division of Foreign Missions and thus became the responsibility of all mission agencies under the Division of Foreign Missions, the move was thought to be a beautiful solution. The decline of the Missionary Research Library is one of the great tragedies in modern mission history. All the valiant efforts of Union Theological Seminary may do not more than to put portions of it into a holding pattern. The vigorous further development of a collection of contemporary documents is an unlikely burden for a single theological seminary to carry successfully.

Thus, in mentioning various tactics that can fulfill the four strategies we have outlined, we must resist the inclination to talk only in terms of what existing organizations can do. Edward R. Dayton's workbook, *Planning Strategies for Evange-*

lism, outlines eleven steps which a specific mission agency may follow in order to evangelize a specific non-Christian people. The Strategy Working Group of the Lausanne Committee for World Evangelization is suggesting this eleven-step process for the use of existing agencies. They realize, however, that in order for existing agencies to follow these eleven steps, certain other things have to be done. They have encouraged conversation about the need for a Consultation on Muslim Evangelism sponsored by the North American Lausanne Committee for World Evangelization. They are proposing that regional and national seminars be held to identify and train key research leaders. They hope that in the normal course of preparation for congresses and crusades there will be special efforts at research leading up to those meetings. Thus we see the interplay of existing forces and incremental additional procedures, plans, and activities that can be built upon the present foundations.

It would be a gross and artificial modesty on my part were I to suppress the information that a vast new center of strategic studies and activities is in the process of development in Pasadena, California. Thirty acres of property and 430,000 square feet of buildings comprise the campus and off-campus housing that is the base of this new organization—the U.S. Center for World Mission. This center is one of a planned worldwide network of similar centers. The South India Center for World Mission is one overseas sister organization; the East West Center for Mission Research and Development in Korea is another. There is also the Hong Kong Center for Frontier Missions. Recently a second center in Korea has been announced. Many of the tactics referred to in this section will be attempted through this network of centers insofar as other agencies are unable to perform them. Not the slightest duplication is intended. Furthermore, the exclusive focus of the center is upon the Hidden People as we have defined them above. Thus 95 percent of the work related to present mission agencies is outside of the scope of the concern of these centers. Penetrating the remaining frontiers is their sole emphasis.

Let us go on then to produce what will for lack of space be basically a check list of subordinate tactics which would seem to lead to the fulfillment of the four major strategies we have outlined above.

CLASS I TACTICS

Class I tactics are those specific plans or programs which can aid in the success of Strategy I: Rebuild Pioneer Mission Perspective. It is clear that this strategy cannot be accomplished overnight. It is equally clear that it is not an altogether uphill task. There is an innate sense among the people in the pew that allots higher priority to pioneer missions than to any other. This is not mere old-fashionedness, but may in good part be an awareness of the meaning of the lost coin, the lost sheep, and the lost son in the parables of Luke 15. How else can we account for the fact that the Wycliffe Bible Translators have grown enormously in the last twenty-five years while in the same period the established denominational and non-denominational missions that have not emphasized the penetration of new frontiers show no similar dynamism whatsoever?

Nothing less than a top-to-bottom revamping of the church and its peripheral institutions is required by this strategy. Sunday school materials have got to be rewritten; the story of the church has got to be reanalyzed as a missionary advance; Christian colleges must reemphasize "new frontier" missions as being one of the more fundamental activities of history.

Many different sectors of the Christian movement must be revamped. Let us single out just four and enumerate tactics that would be appropriate in each case.

1. *Rebuilding Pioneer Mission Perspective in the Home Church.* "The local church can change the world" is a brilliant phrase devised by World Vision in a series of attempts to amplify mission understanding at the local level. The phrase acknowledges the central importance of the local church as a source of grass roots initiative. As a womb for the nurture of

future missionaries, the local church is potentially unexcelled. What does or does not happen at that level profoundly and gravely affects what can or cannot be done at any other level. When World Vision gave over *The Local Church Can Change the World Seminar* to the Association of Church Missions Committees, the latter employed those materials in its national conference in 1977 and has sent back seminar materials to member churches for their use at the local level. The ACMC is struggling to serve both nondenominational and denominationally related churches—not an easy task—and has already stimulated mission giving measurably. The increased giving to missions, resulting in its own impact on member churches, is running over twenty times as much as the ACMC funds required. Eventually there will have to be denominational adaptations of the ACMC mechanism that will cooperate closely or perhaps be part of the ACMC itself. The United Presbyterian Center for Mission Studies is an example of such a denominational agency; the Episcopal Church Missionary Community is another. Both the UPCMS and the ECMC are member organizations of the U.S. Center for World Mission. It is expected that in each country where there is a Center for World Mission of this genre, a characteristic feature will be a series of offices reflecting the various strata within the evangelical presence in that country. It is as important in the rebuilding of pioneer mission perspective to work along denominational, confessional, and cultural lines as it is to be sensitive to the cultural mosaic of a population first being offered the gospel of Christ.

The theme of the national conference of the Association of Church Missions Committees in 1978 was the unreached people, and one-third of its emphasis given to the work of missions in E-0, E-1, E-2/E-3 areas respectively, one-third therefore being on the Hidden People—people who can only be incorporated into Christian fellowship by E-2 and E-3 techniques.

The spectrum of ACMC interests underscores what I believe to be a crucial factor: pioneer missions are not necessarily

57

encompassed by general missions enthusiasm. And any strategy will mainly fail to reach the hidden people if "missions in general" is the broad mandate. The Mission Renewal Team, Inc., for example (also a U.S. Center member), puts on a day-long seminar that is much heavier than the seminar program mentioned above, and focuses primarily on what we have called the Hidden People. The MRT seminar is called "A Day of Discovery" and is designed for a group of 25 or 30 of the key leaders in a congregation. It takes place in the context of the church, rather than a city or region. It presents ten very carefully hammered-out themes, and trains the group to carry on for the next ten weeks studying one theme each week. The home churches need Sunday school materials, tourist caravans, and even special programs which have specifically pioneer mission emphases.

There ought to be available, for example, seven-minute video cassettes for multiple usage in the various programs of the local church. Something like the monthly "Church Around the World" bulletin insert could focus exclusively on pioneer missions. Why not a pioneer missions *National Geographic*? How about a national lay committee on pioneer missions? Certainly, to challenge a million people in America to pray regularly for the Hidden People is a worthy goal. In order literally to reach a million people, a simple do-it-yourself seminar kit is available which allows any local church or group within a church to put on its own "World Awareness Seminar" emphasizing the hidden people. This is produced by the U.S. Center for World Mission. This seminar leads to and builds upon a sound process of "registration" of "World Christians"—people who are willing to boraden their concern deliberately to include the Hidden People in increased study, prayer, giving, and sharing.

2. *Rebuilding Pioneer Mission Perspective Among Students.* The enormous growth of higher education in the U.S. has virtually separated millions of younger citizens from the mainstream of society. Their isolation is mainly an evil, but

cannot be remedied easily, and we are indebted to campus organizations like Campus Crusade, Inter-Varsity, and Navigators—Young Life, Youth for Christ (Campus Life) on the high school level—for the establishment of surrogate church congregations in the new communities of the university world. Curiously, despite many fine achievements, these campus organizations are hardly more successful than the local church in implanting or maintaining mission vision of any kind, much less pioneer mission perspective. These surrogate student-world denominations, like the regular denominations, have superb internal communication channels. But Campus Crusade leaders are very discouraged about the percentage of their students and staff who are ever recruited for overseas work. Crusade at least incorporates its own mission agency in its Agape Movement. Inter-Varsity at least has its triennial Urbana Missionary Convention. But even the Urbana Convention is in some ways a muted challenge in regard to pioneer missions. The development of the program each time is usually the result of a tug of war between the many contemporary definitions of mission. Not desiring to slight any of the mission agencies, only a small slice of the Urbana program focuses exclusively on pioneer mission perspective.

Students themselves, however, have certainly responded. The statistics are well known that in 1970, 8 percent of the twelve thousand students gathering at Urbana signed cards indicating their willingness to be led overseas; 28 percent of fifteen thousand did so in 1973; and 51 percent of seventeen thousand did so in 1976. Part of a pitifully small counter response on the part of the adult missions world has been the Summer Institute of International Studies, which, since 1974, has carefully disguised basic mission orientation in the form of credit-bearing courses in sociology, philosophy of religion, etc. This is a small, carefully-controlled program not trying to expand, but it can readily be duplicated, constituting as it does a superb model of what can and must be done if open-hearted young people are ever in any number going to get the solid knowledge necessary to make an intelligent and spiritually valid decision about their life work. A similar program during the academic year called simply the Institute of International Studies opened in January 1978 under the auspices of several West Coast colleges and hosted by the United States Center for World Mission.

Some students have taken the initiative to launch highly successful Student Conferences on World Evangelization (SCOWE). Thousands of students between Urbanas have been exposed to high quality pioneer mission orientation in these conferences, but as with all things ran by students, leaders graduate and replacement leadership does not always develop.

Beyond the Urbana, SIIS-IIS, and SCOWE "events" there needs to be a nurture mechanism which will not leave nor forsake the students who earnestly seek to know the Lord's will about possible overseas service. Thus was born the Fellowship of World Christians. As a result, small groups of students in many parts of the U.S. are praying together and studying some of the excellent materials produced by the FWC. Among other things in its quiver, the FWC offers a credit-bearing independent-study course called *Understanding World Evangelization* which involves an introductory cassette, a 200-page study guide, a 500-page specially edited reader, and three other books. Westmont College gives undergraduate credit and Conservative Baptist Seminary at Denver offers graduate credit.

A major new trend in the last twenty years has been the eager involvement of young people in a short term abroad. Intercristo has been invaluable in helping young people find their way into such experiences. This may actually be the single most important new source of missions to emerge in the past five years. In some ways, however, exposure overseas to the typical behind-the-lines work that missions are now occupied with is no more successful in the development of pioneer mission perspective than are the booths of those same mission agencies at Urbana. Thus we are once more impressed that present mission involvement often acts not so much as a channel to the Hidden People as it becomes a barrier to them. The mission agencies, if they do not take care, will continue on to be their own worst enemies. This leads us to our next point.

3. *Rebuilding Pioneer Mission Perspective in the Mission Agencies.* In view of the blunt significance of the Great Commission, which allows no stopping point short of reaching the entire world, in view of the sentiments of the people in the pew who are inclined to give more generously to pioneer work than to anything else, and in view of the actual preference deep down of many missionaries themselves to be involved in pioneer work, it is a foregone conclusion that the mission agencies are relatively alert on the subject of the Hidden People. Indeed, in our introductory remarks we have sketched a number of events that show the keen sensitivities of mission agencies to the mission to frontier peoples. Professor Beaver found only one board out of ninety contacted that disclaimed any interest and concern in the Consultation on Frontier Peoples which he organized in 1972. The matter of mission interest in the frontiers does not even need to be further discussed. The interest is there. The problem lies elsewhere. Mission agencies, in general, labor along with so many millstones around their necks in the form of vested interests, hardened structures, established institutions and responsibilities, rampant inflation, consuming personnel problems, and increasingly difficult recruitment and fund raising, that to speak of hidden peoples and new approaches requiring additional personnel and funds is like changing a tire on a Mack truck rolling downhill. Even missions founded for the sole purpose of reaching unevangelized areas soon find themselves enmeshed or "homesteaded," to use George Peter's phrase.

G. Thompson Brown, in a recent paper (Brown, 1977), has put us all in his debt by beautifully summarizing and elaborating with helpful diagrams the phenomenon Peter Wagner has termed the "church development syndrome." He points out that a church-to-church relationship between a sending church and receiving church, or even a healthy two-way flow between a "home church" and an "overseas church" is fundamentally inadequate, and he turns our eyes once more to the frontiers. This kind of thinking produced by a top mission executive and taken to heart in mission circles today could rebuild perspective all across the board. Would that it were as easy to conceive of the same thing happening among church leaders overseas.

4. *Rebuilding Pioneer Mission Perspective in the Younger Churches*. Many of the things we have said above about the need to build pioneer mission perspective in the home church can apply just as well to the overseas younger churches. One staggering difference results from the curious fact that missionaries across the decades have in many instances hardly ever mentioned (except on furlough) the idea that all believers everywhere are under the Great Commission. Few national churches today are as poor as those believers that backed William Carey when he went to India. If anyone anywhere suggests that a national church here or there is too poor to send missionaries, he should take a close look at the Friends Missionary Prayer Band of South India, which sends eighty missionaries to north India, has refused all gifts from abroad (it was offered one million dollars in one instance), and subsists with simple and stern dictum that every believer must either "go or send."

What can Westerners do to rebuild pioneer mission perspective in the overseas church? There continues to be many ways in which Western leaders and non-Western leaders can encourage each other. One or two examples out of many others would be the amazing series of pastors' conferences held all over the world by World Vision. More recently John Haggai has endeavored to encourage evangelism among Asian leaders. The Lausanne legacy continues to spur a great deal of healthy interchange. The World Evangelical Fellowship now has the missions commission. And, of course, the

World Council of Churches provides a discussion forum of a sort between the East and the West. Few of these influences, however, have dared to give proper stress to pioneer missions. We have all felt good about the development of the so-called Third World Mission Agencies, and at least two new books have recently come out on the subject (Nelson, 1976; Nelson, ed., 1976). But few of us have dared to press the point that most third world agencies are not in cross-cultural missions, and that even where they are, they are not often reaching the Hidden People, within whose cultural spheres there is no witness. This is one reason why there must be on the world level a consultation drawing together mission agencies for both East and West, North and South who are actively and specifically concerned about missions beyond where Christ is named.

CLASS II TACTICS

Class II tactics are those specific plans or programs which can aid in the success of Strategy II: Rediscover the Hidden People.

It must be clear by now the Hidden People of my definition are only part of the unreached or non-Christian people (individuals) in the world. According to the bar chart earlier in this paper, 1,000 million nominal Christians and 500 million non-Christians are unreached, but are *not* part of the Hidden People: there are another 2,500 million others in the Hidden People category. How, you might ask, can you justify excluding the first two groups from this strategy? Indeed we are not suggesting here any strategies for reaching them at all! Most existing missions and evangelistic agencies are interested in the full spectrum of evangelistic needs in the world. What they *intend* leaves out no non-Christians of any kind. Nevertheless, their actual outworking in practice is predominatly and admittedly a stress upon what is necessary to reach the E-0 and E-1 categories, that is, the nominal Christians and the "within-range" non-Christians. After all, the E-0 and E-1 categories consist of 1,000 and 500 millions of people respectively, roughly 1.5 billion together, and it is no wonder that these magnificent organizations do not often work beyond the horizons of such a large mass of authentic spiritual need. But once again, how can we avoid the evidence that *whenever an organization aims to minister to both Christians and non-Christians, the latter group easily becomes hidden from view and grossly underemphasized.* The fact is that a very small percentage of North American missionaries are working within cultures where there is not yet any national church.

There is a second reason why for strategic purposes some agencies must focus exclusively on the Hidden People. Pastors, for example, are usually working with E-0 and E-1 evangelism, but now and then bump into people who are sufficiently strange culturally so as not to fit into their congregations. So long as they have no clear idea what it takes to win such people, they may simply cross them off as "resistant." But let us imagine an inner city Baptist church around which has grown up a Polish ghetto. The church is holding on to a few elderly Anglos whose parents before them probably paid for the building in which they worship. But so long as a sharp distinction is not made in tactics of evangelism between reaching E-1 Anglos who need Christ and the very different task of reaching E-2 Polish, what may happen is that the people in the congregation may get depressed and not even try to win the remaining Anglos. Or, even if they win huge numbers of Anglos and keep their church building full, the Polish will still be hidden from their eyes as much by their very success as by their unanalyzed inability to reach them.

The apostle Paul in effect entered upon his revolutionary ministry by reason of his awareness of the existence of a Hidden People, namely the Greeks. The Jews in the synagogues he visited may or may not have accepted the gospel he preached, but in any case, most of them continued to have "people blindness." They didn't quite realize that the handful of Greeks in the back rows of their synagogues (despite the nice names given to them—the "devout persons" or the "God fearers") really constituted a different people, and that as long as the Jews ran the synagogue, there would never be more Gentiles than a few Greeks in the back rows. The most revolutionary strategy in the New Testament was when Christians began to look for those beyond their own cultural background as people who need the gospel.

We, too, must look beyond those fortunate people who at least have a church nearby that fits their cultural tradition, people who are already targets for the new impulses of evangelism that are widely promoted by agencies ranging from the Billy Graham Evangelistic Association to World Vision's pastors' conferences to John Haggai's workshops. The very existence of all such good work among people that we can already see may continue to blind us to the existence of the Hidden People. In order not to be blind, we must be determined to rediscover today *the people among whom there is not yet any culturally relevant organized Christian fellowship, our Hidden People.* By doing so, we are merely doing what William Carey and Hudson Taylor stressed in their own eras by the ample use of statistics.

Nor was Paul embarrassed by all the good work his mandate excluded. He acknowledged (Gal. 2: 7) that Peter was called to work among the circumcised (E-0 and E-1) but that he, Paul, was apparently intended by God to ignore such people, being himself sent to the uncircumcised. Imagine the strategic confusion if Paul (and all the other missionary bands) were *forced* by some faulty theological consideration to include both circumcised and uncircumcised in every move! It seems clear that if Paul had not assumed the complete legitimacy of focusing exclusively upon the uncircumcised, he would have had even greater difficulty than he had trying to please both groups. Thus, the Hidden People today must be isolated in our strategy. Whatever resources of personnel and funds that are focused upon their redemption need to be separated from resources focused upon those who are within the reach of churches. Otherwise I don't believe we can do either job properly.

To see how such a distinction in strategy can affect the

cause of missions, we must reflect for a moment upon the immense impetus in modern times resulting from Hudson Taylor's sensitivity to the Hidden People of his time. It bothered him profoundly that some people were without any witness at all. As a result of his new departure, the entire modern "faith mission" movement emerged, its most important emphasis being by no means the element of faith in its fund raising, but rather the relentless emphasis upon the "inland" peoples. Thus arose the China Inland Mission, the African Inland Mission, the Sudan Interior Mission, the Unevangelized Fields Mission, the Heart of Africa Mission, the Regions Beyond Missionary Union, the New Tribes Mission, etc., etc. The statistics Hudson Taylor worked with and the "ever accusing map" drove him to his knees and to bold moves that his retiring nature would never have suggested. How we need many new Hudson Taylors today! They must arrive from both East and West to befriend and help to rediscover by maps and statistics the vast groups of Hidden People today, far more vast than those within view, to whom are directed the bulk of $700,000,000 per year of U.S. mission effort.

Of all the functions of the U.S. Center for World Mission, its "strategy institutes" are accorded the highest of all its priorities. Each institute will also function as a department of the William Carey International University, which is the sister corporation to the USCWM. Five of the six institutes now have at least an acting director. They will be autonomous and have a life of their own and can grow as large as seems necessary. The three that focus on the Chinese, Muslims and Hindus respectively need to be fairly large because of the immense sectors of humanity they represent. Each institute will try to keep track of all research being done in its area, sharing in both a giving and a receiving relationship with its counterpart institutes in the sister centers around the world.

Lest there be any confusion in our research activity about what is intended by the phrase *the Hidden People,* let me reiterate that these are *the* people *of the world who cannot be drawn by E-1 methods into any existing, organized Christian fellowship,* e.g., church or redemptive sodality).

Let me illustrate. When I was in Guatemala, I had to study both the Spanish Language and an American Indian tongue. In Spanish I was working at an E-2 distance. In the Indian language, I was at an E-3 distance. But neither group would be part of the Hidden People category we have defined here, since in both groups there were many solid believers and believing fellowships. The gospel has now successfully penetrated these two cultures, and thus *by E-1 methods any of the non-Christians in either group can be drawn by local E-1 activity into existing Christian fellowships.*

Are there then any Hidden People in Guatemala? The descendents of the Maya speak thirty-three different mutually unintelligible dialects. The group with which my wife and I worked numbers today about 400,000, and there are at least five significantly different subdialects for this one of thirty-three dialects. All five of these subdialect areas by now have believing fellowships within them. Yet there are still some (but not very many) *areas where a new believer could not be incorporated into an existing, believer fellowship.* People in such areas are Hidden People.

We hope that soon there will be a Center for World Mission in Guatemala that can collaborate with us in determining all the places where Hidden People of that sort are, how to get to them, and whether any additional help is needed from any foreign country in the world. Meanwhile, the U.S. Center for World Mission must undertake to pinpoint the Hidden People in the U.S. Some of whom may be Navajo. It may be that Guatemalan Indian believers might be more successful than U.S. citizens in reaching Navajos.

The Hidden People in Guatemala, however, are not all tribal people. *Any linguistic, cultural, or sociological group defined in terms of its primary affinity (not secondary or trivial affinities), which cannot be won by E-1 methods and drawn into an existing fellowship, are Hidden People.* They may be Russian Jews in the capital city or wealthy Asian families within whose social milieu there simply is not yet any opportunity to hear the gospel and be carried forward in discipleship by an existing Christian fellowship. Note that we are not counting as Hidden People the masses of nominal Catholics who, while they may be unreached and needing E-0 evangelism, are not *hidden* by culture barriers so as to require E-2 and E-3 techniques. We do not unfeelingly exclude them. The great masses of truly hidden people are not spiritually higher in priority. But for some people somewhere, they must become *highest priority* lest we continue to put the bulk of all our efforts into rewinnning nominal Christians in Europe and Latin America while truly hidden, unreached people cry out for even a minimal witness.

Why should there be more U.S. missionaries in Austria than in all of North India? Per capita, we have sent ten times as many missionaries to Kenya as to Indonesia. Yet the few pioneer missionaries in Kenya get relatively little support from either the missions or the national churches. There are intrepid missionary pioneers in Irian Jaya (former West New Guinea), but the bulk of missionaries in Indonesia are assisting settled Christian communities, which evangelize their own kind, but seldom reach out to cross new frontiers.

The tactics necessary to rediscover the Hidden People must be developed in close coordination with existing churches and missions, especially missions arising inside the same political boundaries as the Hidden People. Ultimately, however, the Hidden People belong to God, not to man, and we must all recognize the need to obey God rather than man in fulfilling the biblical mandate to seek and find those who sit in darkness. An overemphasis on "partnership in mission" is stagnating many potential efforts.

CLASS III TACTICS

Class III tactics are those specific plans or programs which can aid in the success of Strategy III: Reevaluate All Previous Approaches.

I have spent ten years evaluating many aspects of the whole

history of the expansion of Christianity, and I am aware that a brief subpoint in this paper cannot properly deal with all the necessary tactics under this strategy. We can at least insist that there is much to be gained by disciplined reflection upon past experience. Have we learned all we should from the movements of Jewish and Christian merchants in the early centuries, and the importance of a relatively simple process whereby a synagogue or a church can be founded? Or the significance of the involuntary cross-cultural transmission of the gospel to or from captured peoples? Or the gospel-spreading effect of exiled church leaders? Or rigorously-committed communities devoted to the transmission of the Bible? Or charismatic mendicants who flooded Europe with their simple but devout enthusiasm? Or the austere Moravian missionaries who transplanted whole village economies into wilderness outposts? Or disciplined orders that impressed emperors with their scientific knowledge? Or breathtaking attempts to build upon and to extend the Vedic literature into the full light of the gospel? Or puzzling proposals for maintaining respect but not worship of ancestors?

Nowadays the quest for satellite communication in the major world languages is merely one evidence of our modern impulse to find shortcuts without carefully reviewing the record of the past.

Indeed, the characteristic passion of the missionary tends to impatience. To review all previous approaches is the last thing the activist wants to do. Even more troublesome, however, may be the appalling ignorance of missionary principles and practices among the masses of evangelicals to whom all appeals for funds must make sense. It is an inherent problem that work at a cultural distance will not only be difficult for the missionary to fathom, but doubly difficult for the people back home to digest. William Carey finally gave up on the people back home and organized his own self-support on the field. Hudson Taylor in an 1888 consultation suggested approaches to polygamy with which even his followers today would have great difficulty. Even the apostle Paul found the

THE UNREACHED AND HOW TO REACH THEM

bulk of the Jewish believers unable to comprehend the strategies he employed in dealing with the Hidden People of his day—the Greeks, Barbarians, and Scythians.

The opposite side of the coin is the tendency to uncritically project on foreign fields the methods and techniques that work in the U.S., assuming they will work in profoundly different situations. This is the bane of many new mission organizations. One of the most tragic weaknesses has been the American (not so much the European) tendency to establish institutions—schools, radio stations, hospitals, seminaries, and in some cases, even churches—that are *seemingly designed to function only if there is perpetual subsidy from abroad.* "Freely we have received, freely we must give" is the misused phrase that has undercut a transition to what may be called the "developmental approach."

The essence of the developmental approach is recognizing that external resources are limited. Thus, the spending of resources must wherever possible somehow have a multiplying effect, developing in the process a self-sustaining phenomenon that will go on generating new resources, eventually functioning without continuing aid but mere intercommunication.

For example, it is possible to calculate even for the most traditional missionary effort a dollar per dollar return. If you measure all the dollars poured into missionary salaries and work budgets over a period of time and compare this to the dollars represented by the national leaders' time—both volunteer and paid—and all the money raised in the development and growth of the national church, you would find that after twenty-five years of church planting activity in a given situation many a mission could say with verifiable justification that every dollar spent has produced $2 or $10 or perhaps even $100. Today the offerings of many a younger church greatly exceed current mission subsidy. Mission work is really not a bad investment! This reminds us of the developmental significance of the parable of the four soils and the parable of the talents.

But it is also a widely known dictum in the management of

human affairs (notably as Parkinson observed it) that *expenses always rise to meet income.* Accountability and measurement of results are needed. It is unlikely that any private business trying to establish itself in a foreign country would become self-sustaining even in a thousand years if its income steadily arrived from the home office with no questions asked about the development of income in the overseas branch itself. Yet many missionaries work year after year with income from home that is not related to observable results. In such a case, the fact that even half of all missionaries are as successful as they have been is a magnificent tribute to the quality of intuition, the integrity of purpose of the traditional missionary movement, and the inherent, unrestrainable power of the Word of God.

Nevertheless, previous approaches must be reevaluated with developmental perspective. We understand that laws are already on the books in India which, if implemented, would cut off all foreign funds destined to religious institutions. Some village congregations appear to be too poor to provide for a pastor without outside funds. (This is doubtful unless missionaries have forced city-trained professionals upon them.)

But congregations need not only to support a pastor but also to send missionaries across new frontiers to reach the Hidden People. This may indeed take economic development within the church and the surrounding community.

One missionary is training tribal people to set up and operate as retail merchants in jungle outposts, thus displaying a development perspective as well as a tent-making missionary strategy.

Only careful, God-directed evaluation will enable us to build responsible, mature bodies of believers.

CLASS IV TACTICS

Class IV tactics are those special plans or programs which can aid in the success of Strategy IV: Reconsecrate Ourselves to a Wartime, not Peacetime, Life-Style.

THE UNREACHED AND HOW TO REACH THEM

There will only be a way if there is a will. But we will find there is no will

● so long as the Great Commission is thought impossible to fulfill;

● so long as anyone thinks that the problems of the world are hopeless or that, conversely, they can be solved merely by politics or technology;

● so long as our home problems loom larger to us than anyone else's;

● so long as people enamored with Eastern culture do not understand that Chinese and Muslims can and must as easily become evangelical Christians without abandoning their cultural systems as did the Greeks in Paul's day;

● so long as modern believers, like the Hebrews, get to thinking that God's sole concern is the blessing of our nation;

● so long as well-paid evangelicals, both pastors and lay people, consider their money a gift from God to spend on themselves rather than a responsibility from God to help others in spiritual and economic need;

● so long as we do not understand that he who would seek to save his life shall lose it.

America today is a save-yourself society if there ever was one. But does it really work? The underdeveloped societies suffer from one set of diseases: tuberculosis, malnutrition, pneumonia, parasites, typhoid, cholera, typhus, etc. Affluent America has virtually invented a whole new set of diseases: obesity, arteriosclerosis, heart disease, strokes, lung cancer, venereal disease, cirrhosis of the liver, drug addiction, alcoholism, divorce, battered children, suicide, murder. Take your choice. Labor-saving machines have turned out to be body-killing devices. Our affluence has allowed both mobility and isolation of the nuclear family. As a result our divorce courts, our prisons, and our mental institutions are flooded. In saving ourselves we have nearly lost ourselves.

How hard have we tried to save others? Consider the fact that the U.S. evangelical slogan "Pray, give, or go" allows people merely to pray, if that is their choice! By contrast the

Friends Missionary Prayer Band of South India numbers 8000 people in their prayer bands and supports eighty full-time missionaries in North India. If my denomination (with its unbelievably greater wealth per person) were to do that well, we would not be sending 500 missionaries, but 26,000! In spite of their poverty, those people in South India are sending fifty-two times as many cross-cultural missionaries as we are! This fact reminds me of the title of a book, *The Poor Pay More.* They may very well pay more for the things they buy, but they are apparently willing to pay more for the things they believe. No wonder the lukewarm, non-sacrificing believer is a stench in the nostrils of God. Luis Palau in a new book speaks of "unyielding mediocrity" in America today (Palau, 1977). When will we recognize the fact that the wrath of God spoken of in the Bible is far less directed at those who sit in darkness than it is against those who refuse to share what they have?

How hard have we tried to save others? The $700 million per year Americans give to mission agencies is no more than they give for chewing gum. Americans pay more for pet food in two months than they spend annually for foreign missions.

A person must overeat by at least $1.50 worth of food per month to maintain one excess pound of flesh. Yet $1.50 per month is more than what 90 percent of all Christians in America give to missions. If the average mission supporter is only five pounds overweight, it means he spends (to his own hurt) at least five times as much as he gives for missions. If he were to choose simple food (as well as not overeat) he could give ten times as much as he does to mission and not modify his standard of living in any other way!

Where does this line of reasoning lead? It means that the overall life-style to which Americans have acquiesced has led us to a place where we are hardening our hearts and our arteries simultaneously. Is our nation not described by Isaiah?

My people are like the dead branches of a tree. . . . a foolish nation, a witless, stupid people. . . . the only language they can understand is punishment! So God will send against them foreigners who speak strange gibberish! Only then will they listen to him! They could have rest in their own land if they would obey him, if they were kind and good (Isa. 27:11; 28:11, 12, TLB).

Or, hear Ezekiel:

They come as though they are sincere and sit before you listening. But they have no intention of doing what I tell them to; they talk very sweetly about loving the Lord, but with their hearts they are loving their money . . . . My sheep wandered through the mountains and hills and over the face of the earth, and there was no one to search for them or care about them. . . . As I live, says the Lord God . . . you were no real shepherds at all, for you didn't search for them (my flock). You fed yourselves and let them starve. . . . Therefore the Lord God says: I will surely judge between these fat shepherds and their scrawny sheep. . . . And I will notice which is plump and which is thin, and why! (Eze. 33:31; 34:6, 8, 20, 22b).

We must learn that Jesus meant it when he said, "Unto whomsoever much is given, of him shall much be required." *God cannot expect less from us in our struggle to save Hidden People than our own nation conventionally requires of us in wartime.* This means that we must be willing to adopt a wartime life-style if we are to play fair with the clear intent of Scripture that the poor of this earth, the people who sit in darkness, shall see a great light. Otherwise, again Isaiah, "I faint when I hear what God is planning" (Isa. 21:3).

The essential tactic to fulfill Strategy IV is to build on the pioneer mission perspective that will be the fruit of Strategy I, and to do so by a very simple and dramatic method. Those who are awakened from the grogginess and stupor of our times can, of course, go as missionaries. But they can also *stay home and deliberately and decisively adopt a missionary support level as their standard of living and their basis of*

74

life-style, regardless of their income. This will free up an unbelievable amount of money—so much in fact that if a million average Presbyterian households were to live within the average Presbyterian minister's salary, it would create at least two billion dollars a year! That happens to be only one seventh of the amount Americans spend on tobacco. But what a mighty gift to the nations if carefully spent on developmental missions!

In order to help families shift to a wartime life-style, two organizations are proposing a six-step plan that will lead gradually (with both education and coaching) to the adoption of the salary provisions of an existing mission agency, the remainder of their income, at their own discretion at every point, being dedicated to what they believe to be the highest mission priority. The United Presbyterian Order for World Evangelization is a denominational sister of the general Order for World Evangelization. The two-fold purpose of each of these organizations is (1) to imbue individuals and families with a concern for reaching the Hidden People and (2) to assist them in practical ways to live successfully within the limits of expenditure as defined by an agreed-upon existing mission structure.

Even missionary families need help in staying within their income limitations, but ironically, no more so than people with twice their income. These organizations believe that families can be healthier and happier by identifying themselves with the same discipline with which missionary families are coping. For two hundred years it has been the undeviating pattern of all Protestant missionary agencies to establish a single standard for all their overseas personnel, adjusted of course to known costs of living and for various kinds of special circumstances. Some boards extend this system to their home office staff. No agency (until now) has gone the one logical step further—namely, to offer to the donors themselves this unique and long-tested system. In view of today's widespread concern for a simple life-style, it would seem that this is an idea whose time has come.

THE UNREACHED AND HOW TO REACH THEM

We have Weight Watcher Clinics. We have Total Woman Clinics. Why not mission-focused Family Life-Style Clinics? How much more significant these clinics will be with ends as noble as the Great Commission!

To reconsecrate ourselves to a wartime life-style will involve a mammoth upheaval for a significant minority. It will not go uncontested any more than did the stern warning of Isaiah and Ezekiel. But we do not need to defend our campaign. It is not ours.

Bibliography

Beaver, R. Pierce, ed. *The Gospel and Frontier Peoples: A Report of a Consultation, December 1972.* Pasadena, Calif.: William Carey Library, 1973.

Brown, G. Thompson. "Possible Directions for the International Mission of the Church in the Next Decade: A Study Paper." Available from the United Presbyterian Center for Mission Studies, 1605 Elizabeth, Pasadena, Calif., 1977.

Liao, David. *The Unresponsive: Resistant or Neglected?* Chicago: Moody Press, 1972.

Nelson, Marlin L. *The How and Why of Third World Missions: An Asian Case Study.* Pasadena, Calif.: William Carey Library, 1976.

Nelson, Marlin L. ed., *Readings in Third World Missions: A Collection of Essential Documents.* Pasadena, Calif.: William Carey Library, 1976.

Palau, Luis. *Time to Shout.* Portland, Ore.: Multnomah Press, 1977.

Scott, Waldron. "The Task Before Us," slides and script. Pasadena, Calif.: William Carey Library, 1975.

Winter, Ralph D. "The New Missions and the Mission of the Church." *International Review of Mission* 60 (1971): 237, pp. 89-100.

Winter, Ralph D. "Seeing the Task Graphically." *Evangelical Missions Quarterly,* January 1974.

Winter, Ralph D. "The Highest Priority: Cross-Cultural Evangelism." In *Let the Earth Hear His Voice,* edited by J. D. Douglas. Minneapolis: World Wide Publications, 1975. Available also in booklet form—entitled *The New Macedonia*–from the William Carey Library with an introduction by Dr. Donald A. McGavran.

Winter, Ralph D. "1980 and that Certain Elite." *Missiology: An International Review,* April 1976, pp. 145-159.

Winter, Ralph D. "The Ground for a New Thrust in Missions." *Evangelical Missions Tomorrow,* edited by Wade T. Coggins and Edwin L. Frizen, Jr. Pasadena, Calif.: William Carey Library, 1977.

Rev. Ralph D. Winter served for ten years as a Presbyterian missionary to Guatemala where he was involved in leadership development among Mayan Indians. He has served as executive secretary of the Latin American Association of Theological Schools, Northern Region (ALERT). He was a professor of missions at Fuller Theological Seminary for ten years and continues at present as an adjunct professor of the historical development of the Christian movement. He is general director of the Center for World Missions in Pasadena, California. He is author of numerous articles and was a major presenter at the Lausanne Congress on World Evangelization. He holds a Ph.D. in linguistics and cultural anthropology from Cornell University and a B.D. from Princeton Theological Seminary.

Unreached Peoples: An Indian Perspective
by George Samuel

The term *reaching the unreached* is familiar these days among Christians who are concerned with sharing the Good News. Reaching involves giving individuals and groups a valid opportunity to accept Jesus Christ as Lord and Savior and serve him in the fellowship of his Church. The large majority of the people in India remain unreached even though Christianity in India is almost as old as Christianity itself. The working definition for unreached people is a group that contains less than 20 percent practicing Christians. In India, only 2.6 percent of the total population of 623 million are called Christian, whether Protestant, Catholic, or other denominations. Not all among this 2.6 percent (16 million) can be called practicing Christians.

UNDERSTANDING THE EXISTING CHRISTIANS
It is traditionally accepted that the apostle Thomas visited South India in A.D. 52 and that the St. Thomas Christians are descendants of those who turned to Christ centuries ago. In A.D. 345, Christians from Syria emigrated to Kerala to engage in trade and to strengthen the early church. The descendants of this ancient church in Kerala are called Syrian Christians.

But this church, though not swallowed up by Hinduism, became like any other caste of India.

Many Nominal Christians

The modern missionary movements sent missionaries to India before any other country. The Danish Halle mission sent their missionaries to Tranquebar near Madras in 1706, and William Carey came to India in 1792. Scores of missionary-sending agencies of the West have sent their missionaries to India since then. One tangible result is most of the total community of 16 million Christians. Out of this, about 2 million can trace their spiritual ancestry to the ancient church, largely resulting from biological growth during these centuries. Fourteen million are the net outcome of all the activities of the modern churches and missions. Many among them are second (or later) generation Christians.

A large majority among the existing Christians are not born again. We can say, however, that these 16 million are related to the Christian church. They celebrate Christmas, a good number attend the church service at least on Good Friday, and most of them attend marriage and funeral services. They claim Christianity as their religion, even though there are atheists among them. They are the reservoir for the many activities involving Christian participation as well as the target of most of the evangelistic efforts in the country. Somewhat more than half are Roman Catholic.

Because of the great spiritual need among the Christian community, the evangelistic efforts are mainly geared to church members, particularly those who attend Christian gatherings. Those not within the reach of such gatherings and those outside the Christian community continue to remain unreached. While some efforts are being made to reach those outside this community, they are only a small part of the effort.

Large Majority in South India

These 16 million Christians do not represent a cross-section of Indian languages and cultures. There are seventeen major languages and over 840 mother tongues. Hindi is accepted as the national language. Forty percent of the Christians of India are living in Kerala, a state where they speak Malayalam, one of the major languages. About 21 percent of the Kerala population are Christians. Even in Kerala the Christians are not a cross-section representing all the ethnic and cultural units found in the state. In spite of the existence of Christianity in Kerala from the first century, the movement to Christ touched only a few ethnic units. Many of the ethnic units remain unreached.

Another 40 percent of India's Christians are in Tamil Nadu, Andra Pradesh, and Karnataka. That means 80 percent of the Christians in India are in the southern part of the country. About 10 percent are concentrated in northeastern India, particularly in Meghalaya, Manipur, and Nagaland. The remaining 10 percent are scattered throughout the rest of India.

Since the majority are Christian in name only, it will not be wrong to estimate that there is but one believer to witness to 700 nonbelievers in South and Northeast India; in North India, there are about 22,000 unbelievers to be reached by one believer! Even more sobering is the fact that the 700 in the south and the 22,000 in the north are in different lingustic, cultural, and religious backgrounds. The existing Christians belong only to certain languages and cultures. Many of the 840 language groups are yet to be reached. Even gospel records are available only in about 270 languages.

Christians Only From a Few Ethnic Groups
Only some castes responded to the call to receive Christ and became Christians. In certain areas a large number of people turned to Christ from the same caste. They made their decision to follow Christ along with their family and friends in mutual affection. Such movements to Christ are possible in people-conscious societies where they are interdependent. Though each person decides for himself or herself, decisions for Christ are registered in multi-individual fashion. Most of the large denominations are the result of people movements

to Christ. Members belonging to the same tribe, caste, class, or lineage became Christians without separating themselves from their own people. In modern India, no less than 70 percent of the Roman Catholics and Protestants are converts in people movements or descendants of such converts. In some districts the percentage is as high as 95.

UNDERSTANDING THE UNREACHED PEOPLE

According to Donald McGavran, only twenty-one out of three thousand castes, ethnic units, tribes, or social groups have had major movements to Christ. Minor movements have occurred in about fifty other castes. Since the number of people who became disciples of Christ were relatively small, they did not have much impact on their own people or on the general population. Only in those twenty-one castes do Christians form any considerable proportion of their total caste population. By this estimate, there are practically no Christians in more than 2900 castes. There may be one or two from some of these castes who joined the church and were ostracized from their people. Such occasional converts find it very difficult to go back to their own people and win them to the Lord. So there are more than 2900 groups which will require Christians to cross linguistic, cultural, geographic, and social boundaries to communicate Christ.

People-Conscious and Culturally Different People

Even if the language of those to be reached is the same as ours, their culture may be different. Customs, values, view of God, of man, of salvation, heaven, and hell are all influenced by culture. We need to consider the total life ways of a people in order to give them the gospel. Certain customs and practices of North India are totally different from those of the South. People groups follow different life ways even in the same state.

It is impossible for communication to take place outside culture. When we communicate we are wrapped up in our own culture. The non-Christians who are wrapped up in their own cultures will see first the cultural wrappings around us before they understand the gospel. Learning their culture will help us to communicate as we want to. People may be geographic neighbors, but be cultural strangers. Two cultural factors in India are ethnic background and caste. Caste differences, especially, separate one people from the other and often cause barriers to communication.

Caste differences have ancient Hindu religious sanction. Nowadays, the government and other agencies are trying to eradicate caste. Yet certain degrees of caste feeling can be seen in all people, including Christians and Muslims. It is tragic to know that in certain areas two people of the same religion are not allowed to sit together and eat due to caste differences. Some of these castes feel more at home with their counterlarts in other religions than with fellow members of their faith. People are very alert in tracing their ancestry and taking pride in their caste.

People must be seen as they are, as speaking a particular language, belonging to a particular caste or community, doing a certain kind of work. These characteristics are important to deal with in reaching them with the gospel. It is one thing to evangelize a group of church members who come to our evangelistic programs and understand our jargon. It is quite another to reach the people who are linguistically, religiously, and culturally different from us.

Often an individual can be identified as belonging to a particular group by looking at his surname. For example, the surname *Patil* will always indicate a Marathi-speaking person belonging to a particular community, whereas *Patel* indicates that he is Gujarathi speaking, belonging to a Gujarathi community. I learned that one must be careful while addressing such people. One friend looked at me in an unpleasant mood and raised his voice when I mistakenly called him Mr. Patil instead of Mr. Patel, not knowing the difference. The surname sometimes indicates the district or town from which they come or the kind of work they or their forefathers were doing. Sometimes people may have the same surname, but are proud of what kind of Singh, Mehta, or Panicker they are, particularly if they belong to an upper caste.

Because the language differences are obvious, the usual way of identifying the group to which a person belongs is in terms of that language, whether it is Malayalee, Tamilian, Bengali, Marathi, etc. The next question is to identify the ethnic background—what kind of Malayalee or Tamilian a person is.

Caste is sometimes denied and not taken into account, but it continues to color and influence everything. Urbanization, the impact of Christianity, and efforts for national integration have made the idea of caste unpalatable. It is distinctly poor taste to ask an educated person about his caste. The word is avoided in polite society. Nevertheless, since the caste feeling is still in the minds of people, a synonym, *community,* has become popular. "What is your community?" is the decent way to ask the question. *Communal feeling* is a synonym for *caste feeling.*

Caste organization remains qualitatively the same in both village and city. What variation exists is mainly due to the exigency of the urban situation. Professional and employer loyalties supplant the power system of caste in the city. In urban areas the caste system is gradually eroding and is being replaced by a class system. People of various castes working in industrial establishments congregate during lunch break. Restaurants, lodging houses, recreation centers, public transporation, and intercommunity activities have encouraged a considerable degree of interdining and mingling with other castes. But intermarriage is very rare even in cities— despite all modern outlooks. One sample survey indicated that intercaste marriage is found in one family unit out of 1,040 interviewed in the cities, one out of 631 interviewed in the town, and only one in 2,249 interviewed in the villages. Also there are people who live two lives in this respect—one in the village where the feeling is strong and another in the town where it is not shown in public life.

Caste differences are deeply rooted in the mind and very

few individuals have renounced it. Though caste feeling is not being expressed openly in public life and dealings, some higher caste people in cities take pride in their caste superiority and express it outwardly, even when their economic or social status is low.

Language Groups

Each state has its own official language, and the country is divided mainly on the basis of regional languages. India's 623 million are not in a truly multilingual situation. Most people live in monolingual situations, except in some big cities where migrants from other states and languages live nearby.

Migrants, after spending a considerable period in a new place, adopt the local language. Their children start speaking the language of that area. In certain cases the migrants settle in the new place after retirement. Children brought up in such homes face a bilingual situation. At home they speak the language of their parents, and at school they follow their peers in social life and parents in family life. With very few exceptions, migrant parents look for someone from their own community when their son or daughter is to be married.

In their settlements, migrants continue to speak their mother tongue. Some of the cities are congeries of language settlements. Over ninety-six languages are heard in Bombay, and the government is conducting schools in ten languages. Yet certain wards are predominantly monocultural. The members of certain housing societies are from the same background. Some landlords rent apartments only to those of their own background. Eating houses serving a particular kind of food also can be seen in places where people of a particular background live together.

Thus in the heterogenous urban situation, homogenous units continue their hold over life-style. People like to keep their identity, speak their beloved mother tongue and enjoy their favorite food. Affinity brings people together and keeps them in sociological groups even in urban areas.

THE UNREACHED AND HOW TO REACH THEM

The Accessible Unreached

Often people think of the unreached as those who live in remote places. Perhaps they are tribal people not exposed to modern civilization. In mission planning, the main object of concern is generally people who live in "unreached areas." Promotional materials and prayer letters of sending agencies give prominence to these people. It involves a great deal of sacrifice to reach these areas, learn the languages, and live in substandard conditions. Foreign missionaries have worked among some of these people and now Indian missionary-sending agencies are also focusing on such people.

Though it is difficult to take a census of such people, it is estimated that between 70 and 90 million people live in such areas.

But the vast majority of the 623 million unreached live in areas easily accessible with ordinary transportation. In our own cities, towns, and villages, right at our door step, there are people who have never heard the gospel. It may be that the city headquarters of a missionary-sending agency is housed in the same compound where there are thousands of men and women who never had a valid opportunity to receive Christ.

Social Change in People-Conscious Societies

While people try to maintain their identity as a particular group and hold on to their customs and practices, they cannot avoid a certain degree of social change. The rural-urban relationship along with exposure to mass media and new ideas cause changes in values, work, and relationships. Because of the necessity of accommodating people of different backgrounds, social tolerance increases. Competing in the economic field to improve social status is becoming predominant. New social positions arise from new occupational opportunities that depend on the skill of the individual rather than previous caste status.

Personal and familial disorganization is also a by-product of rapid social change. Division of the extended family into single family units is the most typical change. Each individual family becomes a self-governing entity. The son is not likely to follow the same occupation as his father. Family members no longer have a single unifying work interest, but each member works in a field about which other members know little.

Change is also taking place due to the desire of climbing up in the social ladder. Those who are termed "scheduled castes" show the tendency of rising to the upper levels. They certainly need not remain low caste when equal status is guaranteed by the Constitution. The attitudes of the upper castes need to be changed to accept these others in a new status. Though people are strongly conscious of their ethnic backgrounds, practically all communities want to adopt new ways of life which promise them a better life.

Religious beliefs and practices are also affected by social change. With the introduction of scientific knowledge and technology, superstitious beliefs start disappearing. Old gods fade away along with the ghosts the people feared. Erosion of faith is a common phenomenon among educated people. Yet people are still aware of spiritual needs.

Eight percent of the population still lives in rural areas. Yet the influence of the cities reaches out into many rural areas. Previously isolated villages are now in touch with the outside world. Residents of almost every village have relations or neighbors living in at least one of the cities or towns. When urbanites visit their home villages, they take with them new ideas, as well as city clothes.

SEEKING STRATEGY TO REACH THE UNREACHED

A strategy for reaching the unreached must focus on the 600 million non-Christians rather than the nominal Christians who've been on the receiving end of so much mission strategy already. The best way to reach each group is by the witness of individual Christians who can communicate with people of their own background. In order to accomplish this there must be Christians from each background who have come to faith in Christ. As mentioned earlier, the existing 16 million Christians belong to only 110 ethnic units and less than 100 languages.

Reaching people of the same language and same culture is called near-neighbor evangelism. Through near-neighbor evangelism we can presently reach only 5 percent of the non-Christian population of India. Ninety-five percent can be reached only by cross-cultural evangelism. Christians who have come to faith in Christ in a particular language and culture must cross such boundaries in order to get the message to peoples of a different language and culture.

We cannot afford to import Christians from other countries to reach these 600 million people. The existing Christians will have to make a conscious, persistent attempt. If we receive believers from other lands, particularly those trained to reach people of a different culture and language, we can make use of them. But we know there are many problems associated with this in the present decade. We therefore must make the best use of our existing Christians.

Mobilizing the Existing Christians

Soul winners must be produced from among the 16 million Christians. The nominal Christian must be revitalized and revived. If the believers among the 16 million pray and work effectively, this can become a reality. The believers must be trained, inspired, and mobilized to reach their own church members who are still nominals (and there are many). When the believers are able to reach their own church members, they can make use of these revived members for reaching more people by doing it together. Moreover, the new believer must be given some opportunity to work. We have found that the newly born again people from the nominal Christian background have great initial enthusiasm. We must sustain this enthusiasm by giving them opportunities to be involved in the ministry. We can deploy them depending on their talents, gifts, and abilities. They are eager to share the new life they have experienced in Christ. They must be encouraged as they are good channels to reach the other nominal Christians. Also they need to be trained to share Christ with their non-Christian friends in the course of their daily work.

There are good, keen, dedicated Christian men and women in our churches. They want to be used by the Lord in reaching others with the gospel. But the social situation and the cultural environment is such that they are limited in their involvement in persuading non-Christians to receive Christ. Due to the poor testimony of the existing Christians and due to community feelings, even keen Christians are not bold enough to begin discussing the topic. Most non-Christians have not yet seriously considered becoming disciples of Christ.

With the constraining love of Christ as the motivating factor for going to the non-Christians, the Christian must try all means to get the message across. Each individual may be different in his potential to be effective among certain kinds of non-Christians. This *evangelistic potential* of the Christians must be considered and they must be mobilized *depending on the population to whom the existing Christians will be effective.* About 70 percent of the population is illiterate, and we need people who can really communicate to such people. We also need people who can communicate to the highly educated. There are segments of these groups that are responsive to the gospel. Whether illiterate or educated, we must be willing to obey the Lord in communicating to the unreached.

Effectively Communicating the Good News
The nature of evangelization is the communication of the Good News. The effectiveness will differ if we try to communicate with the non-Christians in the same way we preach to the Christians. The non-Christians who are aware of the existence of Christianity may have wrong impressions about Christianity. This can cause communication barriers. Those who have hostile attitudes to Christianity may have other wrong concepts. Whatever the understanding or misunderstanding of the non-Christian, the gospel must be addressed to them in the least confusing and most appealing form.

In the minds of many educated non-Christians, Christianity

89

is thought to be only for the lower strata of the society. Christianity's association with Western culture and habits, reflected through certain converts, has also caused problems. Actually Christianity does not need the atmosphere of the Western world to be successful. Many non-Christian segments of the population, instead of thinking of receiving eternal life and sharing the glories of Christ in heaven, associate Christianity with certain despised tasks or habits. We have to surmount the many social obstacles to discipleship if we are really interested in reaching the non-Christians.

Because of wrong approaches in the past and the poor testimony of existing Christians, barriers exist in the minds of the people who are to receive the message of the gospel. These barriers must be surmounted. Moreover, we must communicate the gospel truths in understandable terms through the language and thought forms of the people. Here both the verbal and non-verbal aspects of communication must be considered. In our day to day living and witnessing, much is communicated non-verbally. According to Ray Birt Whistall, 65 percent of our communication is non-verbal—that is, our *being* and *doing*—and only 35 percent is verbal. As we communicate the beauty and qualities of Jesus in our being and doing, we also earn the right to speak. Radiating the beauty of Jesus through our life depends on our relationship with our Lord.

Understanding how people relate to each other in the society will help us make our communication effective. Communication is people oriented. It never takes place in a social vacuum, but always between individuals who are part of a total social context. We must also realize that the meaning of a message is what the people put into it. Meanings are in people and not merely in the words we use. The message may be very meaningful to us, but the listener need not give the same meaning as we give to the words used. They identify the word symbols by relating these to things already in their experience and thus interpret the message. The meanings are sometimes distorted even by people who speak the same language. The chances of distortion are much greater when we learn a different language and communicate to a linguistically and culturally different people. It depends not only on *what* we speak, but also *how* we speak.

People's minds are not empty vessels. Every person is subject to the culture of his society. God's revelation of truth comes to and through the "culture-bound person." The biblical message is couched in ordinary human language, identified with human cultures. Coming through the Hebrew and the Greek cultures, the original revelation became meaningful and relevant; and being inspired of God, the writers were restrained from the errors and mistakes of these ancient cultures. Though subject to the distortions of culture, sin, and man's finite capacity to grasp the truths, God's revelation is adequate to the purpose for which it is intended—to bring about a faith response to God.

As we communicate the same unchanging message of the gospel to people of other cultures, we need to recognize their cultural context. God desires to meet everyone in his own culture. We must understand this fact if cross-cultural communication is to be effective. Even our communication method must be the method of the culture. We have to develop and use indigenous media. Our task is effective communication of the gospel to the receptive segments of each sociological group with the conscious purpose of incorporating the responsive into the Body of Christ.

Helping the Responsive Become Disciples

After we communicate effectively and give a valid opportunity to receive Christ, we also have the responsibility of helping the responsive become disciples of Christ who serve him in the fellowship of the church.

Various stages in the process of religious change take place in a people-conscious society. When the gospel truths are presented in understandable terms, the receptive people, hearing the Word of God, become aware of their need. This is called a *period of awareness*. Following this there will be a *point of realization* at which the prospective convert will begin to balance his old religion against the new ideas of the gospel. Then he has to decide whether he should accept or reject the new idea of the gospel. This is called the *period of decision-making*. Individuals often make decisions through interaction, so families and groups will be involved in the decision instead of just an isolated individual.

As he makes the decision he faces a precise *point of encounter*. Here he turns his back completely on his old ways and turns to God. He may even demonstrate it by the act of burning the fetishes and the like. It is the real point of commitment. "Old things are passed away, and behold all things are become new." Yet many social problems may be involved. He may have to follow certain customs that are used as social control measures in his society. Here the new believer, cut off from the old ways, has to be made to feel at home in the fellowship of other believers. This is the *period of incorporation*. The new disciple is incorporated into the church. He has to discover the resources of God's promises and the new values in sharing the Christian life. He has to find an active role as participant in the fellowship of believers.

If we fail at some of these points and periods, it's usually at this one. Here, more than at any other stage, the Westernism (or any other ism!) of a missionary or evangelist can impose itself on the new group of believers. Actually the language, music, worship forms, the type of buildings, and many other things should be determined by the new converts themselves. A foreign congregational structure (which does not fit into the local culture) is likely to hinder the congregation. The Bible is our norm for faith and practice—not the elements of a particular culture or subculture. Here the sound teaching of the Word of God will help them to understand the total gospel. This is the *point of confirmation* when they are established in faith.

Then following this is the *period of maturity* during which believers grow in Christlikeness. The application of biblical truths to all aspects of life helps them in preventing pagan customs (which are contrary to the Word) from being brought into the church. We have a responsibility to devise proper spiritual diet, care, nurture, and methods of spiritual reproduction to keep on winning new generations for Christ.

In view of the social situation in India, we need to propose a discipleship that is realistic in light of the various ethnic units. We must take care not to insist that they must follow any of the patterns of the existing congregations. New disciples can form congregations of Bible-obeying Christians while remaining in cultural harmony with their own people. Since a very large number of sociological groups remain undiscipled, we must think in terms of helping each of them to become Bible-believing, Bible-obeying and Christ-honoring Christians in their own cultures. Instead of following a foreign culture, whether Western or non-Western, they should develop social structures which are more in harmony with God's will according to the Scripture.

Hundreds of culturally different groups can be identified in many villages, towns and cities. There is great need to unite the people divided by language, caste, class barriers. Communal feelings and class distinctions have divided the people. But only when people are united in the love of Christ can they really love across linguistic, ethnic, or class lines. There will be true integration in the society as people experience the oneness of Christ which surpasses all class, caste, and racial barriers. We can try in the power of the Holy Spirit to bring Christ into every language, tribe, caste, and sociological group so that these thousands of unreached people will no longer remain strangers and sojourners but will be "fellow citizens with the saints and members of the household of God, built upon the foundation of the apostles and prophets, Christ Jesus Himself being the cornerstone in whom the whole structure is joined together and grows into a holy temple in the Lord" (Ephesians 2:19-21, RSV).

George Samuel, B.S. (chemistry and physics), M.S. (physical chemistry), M.S. (nuclear physics), M.A. (missiology), is currently researching and teaching evangelism, missions, and church growth. He is chairman of the Devlali Continuation Committee—a follow-up of the All-India Congress on Mission and Evangelization—and a member of the LCWE Strategy Working Group. He directs the Counselling and Training Centre, Tiruvalla, Kerala, and teaches at the Indian Missionary Training Institute in Nasik. He is also a radiation health specialist and nuclear medicine consultant. He formerly worked with Bhabha Atomic Research Centre (Trombay, India), Harbor General Hospital (Torrance, California), and Bay Harbor Hospital (Harbor City, California). His education and training are from the University of Kerala, University of Bombay, Bhabha Atomic Research Centre, University of California School of Medicine, Los Angeles, and Fuller Theological Seminary School of World Mission, Pasadena, California.

PART 2
Case
Studies

The Unreached People of Kau

by David B. Barrett

By definition, unreached peoples are those about whom we have scant information. They are hidden people, as Bob Pierce puts it, "hidden behind the closed doors of culture . . . sealed off from our Christian witness." This is particularly true of the yet pagan or animistic tribes in Africa who still rarely see foreigners.

It is startling, therefore, when the secular world presents us with a detailed photographic portrait of the life of a primitive people still completely unreached. Two large glossy volumes, entitled *The Last of the Nuba* (Harper & Row, 1974) and *The People of Kau* (1976), provide just such a portrait—a superb color photographic record of the lives of two separate Sudanese peoples in the southern part of the Nuba mountains. The first book describes the Mesakin Nuba, an isolated and self-sufficient people. The second describes an even more remote people, the Kau Nuba (or South-East Nuba), 125 miles to the east. Both volumes are the work of Leni Riefenstahl, a German woman who was 73 years old when she visited the Kau Nuba for sixteen weeks in 1975. She was accompanied by a professional film director and documentary photographer. Her extraordinary series of photos gives us, unintentionally no doubt, a vivid picture of what it is like today for a people to be totally unreached by the gospel.

Of the numerous unreached Nuba peoples, this case study will deal primarily with the Kau Nuba.

THE NUBA

The name *Nuba* does not refer to a single people or language, but is used to designate over 100 Negroid tribes living in the Nuba Mountains in the Kordofan province of northern Sudan. Driven into the hills long ago by Arab incursions and later slave raids of the seventeenth to nineteenth centuries, they now have a general cultural affinity. They speak over 100 Kordofanian languages of the Chari-Nile family, most mutually unintelligible. Among the best-known are the Katcha; Katla; Koalib, including the Heiban (25,000), Moro (40,000), Nirere (50,000), Otoro (28,000), and Nyaro; Mesakin (10,000); Tagali; Talodi; Temein; and Tumtum, including Krongo (25,000) and Kadugli. Altogether, a total Nuba population of 990,000 live in the hills, surrounded in the plains by Baggara Arabs. As well as their own language, they speak Arabic as their *lingua franca*. They have long had a military reputation; the Nuba are to the Sudanese army what the Gurkhas were to the British empire's armies.

The whole of this region is studded with rugged granite hills rising sharply from the wide clay plain. The Nuba are agriculturalists, using terraced fields, hoe cultivation, crop rotation and fallowing. Their main crops are sesame, millet, sorghum, maize, okra, gourds, groundnuts, peppers, beans, onions, tobacco and cotton. Their livestock include cattle, sheep, donkeys, goats, and chickens. Most also still retain neolithic pig culture. Kinship descent is usually matrilineal in the south. Marriage payments are made in livestock or weapons. Polygamy is widespread—in most tribes, over fifty percent of all married men have plural wives. In remoter areas men go naked, and women wear only beads.

A number of Nuba pockets still have little or no contact with the outside world. In the extreme southeast corner of Kordofan province, three of the most remote villages among the South-East Nuba are Nyaro, Fungor and Kau, with a population of 3,000. These "hidden people" are so hidden that even government census takers are unable to get accurate statistics. (Although these peoples have lived in Nuba for probably a thousand years, the 1955 Sudan census listed the population of Kau and Nyaro as two!)

Their future is not bright. J. C. Faris predicts, "The South-East Nuba represent a unique and entirely self-contained society whose traditions will undoubtedly become extinct within a generation."

Kau Nuba Personal Art and Sport

The Kau Nuba differ in temperament from other Nuba tribes. Whereas the Mesakin are described by Riefenstahl as gentle and friendly, the Kau Nuba are described as wild and passionate, yet timid and hostile in the presence of strangers. The most startling cultural feature about this people, preserved over the years by their extreme isolation, is their highly-developed art of face and body painting, a form of personal embellishment probably more highly developed among the Kau Nuba than anyone else in the world. Each day, each man oils his face and paints on a unique personally-designed facial mask, often asymmetric and of striking beauty, using a different design from one day to the next. With these on, the men then engage in sports, consisting of wrestling and fights with sticks or knives. Knife-fighting (*zuar*) is a ferocious but fair sport in which blood flows freely. All men between the ages of 18 and 28 participate.

Nuba Religion

The Kau Nuba are pagan animists. Nuba animism revolves around charms, amulets, shamans, agricultural priestly experts carrying out rites for grain and simsim, animal sacrifices to placate the ancestors, and the like. Most of the other Nuba tribes are animists also, though several have a thin veneer of Islamic teaching, especially those living in the townships.

CASE STUDIES

One Nuba tribe, the Tagali, has been exposed to Islam for 400 years and is now 100 percent Muslim. There is little Muslim interest in converting the Nuba, but a number of Sudanese and Egyptian members of the Muslim Brotherhood work among the Koalib, and a small but steady trickle of converts are won by offering gifts of tea and sugar or bolts of cloth. On the whole, Islam scarcely touches the traditional agricultural life of the Nuba. Likewise Islam has yet had no effect on any Koalib customs, whether marriage, inheritance, burial, or circumcision. Shamanism remains the primary belief among the Koalib and the other Nuba pagan tribes.

Across the Sudan there are numerous pockets of animists similar to the Kau Nuba. When Anglican missionaries first arrived in 1899, animists in the Sudan numbered around 2,077,000. By 1970 they had increased to 3,378,000, due to rising birth rates, and by 1978 to 3,655,000. Huge tribes such as the Dinka and Nuer are still over 95 percent animists, and the Kau Nuba are typical of a multitude of smaller peoples.

The First Christian Missions

Christianity entered the land now known as the Democratic Republic of the Sudan in the fourth century after Christ, and for a thousand years there were strong and powerful Christian kingdoms on the Nile. In the fourth century, the king of Axum in Ethiopia, newly converted through Frumentius of Syria, knew of the existence of the Red and Black Nuba, but no attempt was ever made to evangelize them until 1920 when the Australian branch of the Sudan United Mission (SUM) settled among various Eastern Nuba tribes. They entered Heiban in 1920; Koalib, 1923; Krongo, 1930; Moro, 1933; and Otoro, 1936. Over the years SUM missionaries produced the first Nuba Scripture translations, including in the Heiban language (Gospel 1931, New Testament 1966), Krongo (Gospel 1934, New Testament 1963), Moro (Gospel 1951, New Testament 1965), Nirere (Gospel 1937, New Testament 1967), and Otoro (New Testament 1966). By 1954 the SUM had nine mission stations, including a leper colony.

61740

Around 1935 the Church Missionary Society (CMS) began work among the Western Nuba. Their main station was at Katcha. North of there, in Kadugli they opened and expanded schools until they were taken over by government after the 1959 Independence.

PRESENT STATUS OF CHRISTIANITY

In 1962, SUM missionaries were expelled, but their work continues as the Church of Christ in the Nuba Mountains. Members are mostly from the Koalib, Moro, Otoro, Labu, Heiban, and Shwai tribes, and number about 20,000. Among the Moro, the church today is growing relatively fast. CMS work is now under the province of the Episcopal Church of the Sudan, with about 3,000 Nuba members among the Nyima, Dilling, and Tumtum tribes. In the Sudan the Episcopal Church is divided into four dioceses. In one of these (Omdurman) the bishop, Butrus Shukai, is himself a Katcha Nuba. The Roman Catholic Church has very little work among the Nuba, with only small churches among the Dilling and the Kadugli.

Although there are large and active Christian communities among the Koalib, Moro, and Otror of the northern and central Nuba, these dwindle as one travels south. Writing of the Mesakin as late as 1973, Riefenstahl could observe, "No missionaries have disturbed them." Farther to the southeast, there are no Christians among the Kau Nuba either.

With the expulsion of foreign missionaries throughout the Sudan in 1962, a vast reservoir of anthropological and linguistic expertise was lost, not to mention their concern for reaching the yet unreached. For churches without the necessary resources, these peoples today are simply too hard to locate or reach.

Receptivity

Observers who know anything about the South-East Nuba describe them as highly resistant to Christianity. The pagan Nuba are the northernmost unevangelized tribes in Africa

101

from Nigeria to the Red Sea, and are now surrounded by a sea of Islamized peoples. Their receptivity to the gospel, small as it is, will probably decrease markedly in the coming five or ten years as Islam encroaches further.

THE TOTAL FORCE FOR EVANGELISM

The resources available for the evangelization of the Kau Nuba may be described as at four different cultural distances, and at correspondingly vast geographical and political distances also.

First is (1) the *Nuba church* itself, with its 24,000 or so members. It is the closest culturally to the people of Kau, and, given sufficient encouragement, training, and outside aid, it might well undertake this venture. This has long been their aim: "The main hope of the fuller evangelization of the Nuba is a witnessing Church, and an increasing number of evangelists and teachers" (Maxwell 1954: 326). As a minority church, however, and one faced by both a religiously hostile Muslim society and a mildly hostile political administration, it faces enormous difficulties. Simply to physically reach the area of the Kau Nuba is impossible by vehicle during the six-month rainy season, when the ground becomes an impassable morass. And during the dry season, travel is extremely expensive over more than a hundred miles of appallingly rutted roads. The photographer Riefenstahl was only able to travel and survive because she hired a large and powerful lorry and then traveled with a vast amount of equipment—tents, water filters, water, provisions, tinned foods, medicines, cooker, photographic apparatus, ropes, tools, vehicle spares, etc.—in order to camp and survive in such a hostile climate.

The second force for evangelism is (2) the *Sudanese church*—the 1,500,000-strong Protestant, Anglican, and Roman Catholic churches among the Nilotic peoples in southern Sudan. The nearest to the Kau Nuba, living 70 miles to the southeast, are Presbyterians and Catholics among the

Nilotic Shilluk along the Nile below Malakal. However, the capital and heartland of these vast churches is over 400 miles south, in Juba. As with the geographical distance, the cultural distance between the Nuba and the Nilotics is immense.

Thirdly, there is (3) the *African church* itself—180 million black Christians, almost all under dynamic African leadership and with a strong concern for evangelization. To date, however, the vast geographical and cultural distances have meant that these massive churches—Protestant, Catholic, Angelican, indigenous—have sent scarcely any missionaries to the Sudan. The handful of those who have gone—an Anglican priest from Nigeria, two or three Ugandan clergy, a layman from Kenya, et al—have all been asked to serve in strong Christian centers in Nilotic areas, and not in unreached areas. Several have had very difficult times; one Ugandan pastor who worked for a time at Rumbek was very badly treated. Even if such African volunteers could be found to reach the unreached peoples, and even if the exceptionally difficult languages and problems of logistics were overcome, it is highly probable that at the last they would be refused entry visas on political or religious grounds.

Finally, there is the force for evangelism that originally began the evangelization of the Sudan—missionaries from the Western world. In (4) the *European and American churches,* there are today over one billion Christians. These churches still produce 95 percent of all foreign or cross-cultural missionaries in the world. Unfortunately, however, not only is their cultural distance from the South-East Nuba the greatest of all, but also such Christians are nowadays virtually unacceptable as evangelists to unreached tribes; unacceptable to the local church and certainly unacceptable to the state. As a force for evangelism in the Sudan, therefore, European and American Christians have had their golden era—the period of 1900-1962—and are unlikely to be of any further direct use.

A POSSIBLE STRATEGY

We come finally to the key question. With so many un-reached peoples remaining in the Sudan, what form of strategy for their evangelization can be evolved?

In the first place, we should realize that of our four forces for evangelism just enumerated, the first is too weak and impoverished to undertake such a task unaided, and the last two are at too great a cultural, political, and geographical distance to have any prospects of success. This leaves only the second, the Sudanese church. Today this church has become a formidable force for evangelism, composed as it is of some 1,300,000 practicing Christians and with 1,800 clergy, ministers, and other full-time church workers (1,520 Sudanese, 280 foreigners). This church already has a certain commitment to foreign mission—it has sent out some sixty Sudanese clergy, ministers, and laypeople to serve in other countries, Uganda, Zaire, and the Central African Empire in particular. If it has little concern for unreached peoples in its own nation, then this is because the needs of these peoples have not yet been placed before it vividly enough by linguistic and anthropologically-minded authorities competent to describe them.

Perhaps the best strategy would be (a) to document the situation of all such unreached peoples as the Kau Nuba, with emphasis on their languages, population sizes, and cultural features; (b) to place this information officially and formally in the hands of the most effective local force for evangelism (in this case the Sudanese church); (c) to offer to such authorities courses of specialized training in cross-cultural unreached-people evangelism; (d) to evolve selection methods to enable the local church itself to select and train suitable volunteers and link them to specific unreached peoples; (e) to assist in the motivation of volunteers for such work; and lastly (f) to then offer the church the necessary management and logistic support to work out the practical details, including the cost of sending and placing a few national Christians among unreached peoples.

In the case of the Kau Nuba, perhaps a single evangelist willing to live among the people for a year or two would be all that is needed. The Sudanese church could be aided in the search for a dedicated Christian—a person at the smallest cultural distance from the people of Kau, if possible, a person from one of the other Nuba tribes. But such a volunteer would not be able to offer his services until this specific need has been widely made known and the multitude of practical difficulties have first been faced and overcome.

BIBLIOGRAPHY

"A Study of Shamanism in the Nuba Mountains," S. F. Nadel, *Journal of the Royal Anthropological Institute*, LXXVI (1946), 25-37.

Half a Century of Grace: A Jubilee History of the Sudan United Mission, J. L. Maxwell, London: SUM, n.d., 1954.

Nuba Body Painting, J. C. Faris, London: Duckworth, 1972.

"Some Aspects of the Spread of Islam in the Nuba Mountains," R. C. Stevenson, in *Islam in Tropical Africa*, I. M. Lewis (ed.), London: OUP, 1966.

The Last of the Nuba, Leni Riefenstahl and Max Planck Institute, Munich, New York: Harper & Row, 1974.

The People of Kau, Leni Riefenstahl and Max Planck Institute, Munich, London: Collins, 1976.

"Two Nuba Religions: An Essay in Comparison," S. F. Nadel, *American Anthropologist*, LVII (1955), 661-679.

David Barrett studied aerodynamics (B.A., M.A.) at Cambridge University, then theology (B.D.) and the sociology of religion and missions at Union Theological Seminary, New

CASE STUDIES

York (S.T.M.) and Columbia University (Ph.D.). From 1948-52 he was a scientific officer at Britain's Royal Aircraft Establishment, Farnborough, and a pilot in the Royal Air Force. Ordained in 1954 as a minister in the Church of England, he joined the Church Missionary Society and served as a pastoral missionary among the Luo of western Kenya. He is now married, with two children. In 1965 he began an interdenominational research center in Nairobi that produced over fifty published studies on evangelization, indigenous churches, *et alia*, including the *World Christian Handbook*. Since 1960 he has visited almost all countries in the world collecting data on evangelization.

The Evangelization of the Fulani

by Gerald O. Swank

PART ONE: ORIGINS AND DISTRIBUTION

The Fulani stand in striking contrast to their Negro neighbors. Their narrow noses, thin lips, bronze skin, wavy hair, tall stature, and unusual language have led to much speculation about their origins. The Fulani themselves say they originated from Ukbatu, an Arabic-speaking Greek or Roman from Egypt who married Bajjomaggu, daughter of the King of Malle. Bajjomaggu, according to the legend, is the mother of all Fulani. The Fulani call themselves Fulbe and their language Fulfulde. Others call them Ful, Peul, Pular, Fula, Fulani, Pulo, Felata, Fila, etc. We will use the designation *Fulani* for both the language and the people since it is the designation commonly accepted by the British from the Hausas of Nigeria.

Linguistic and anthropological data place the earliest concentrations of Fulani (prethirteenth century) in the Futa Jalon area of what is now Guinea and the Futa Toro area of what is now Senegal. The Fulani language resembles the Wolof, Serer, and Jola of Senegal-Gambia-Guinea more than any other sub-Saharan language. Here is a conservative estimate of the Fulani statistical distribution.

Mauritania	12,000
Senegal	450,000
Mali	600,000
Benin	54,000
Guinea	1,200,000
Niger	269,000
Ivory Coast, Upper Volta	600,000
Chad	24,000
Central African Empire	28,000
Cameroon	305,000
Nigeria	3,630,000
Gambia	58,000
Ghana	5,500
Portugese Guinea	36,500
Other	20,000
Total	6,744,000

From Futa Jalon, Futa Toro and Macina the Fulani spread eastward mainly in search of good pasture for their cattle. They avoided the rain forest and other areas because of the tsetse fly. By the eighteenth century they had spread into Chad and Oubangui covering an area over 2,500 kilometers long and 800 kilometers wide.

Precolonial History: The Jihads

The Fulani are basically cattle herdsmen. Their search for good pasture made them extremely mobile and nomadic. Their penetration into the already-settled areas of sub-Saharan Africa was generally peaceful. From as early as the fourteenth century they were being Islamized, though large groups remained pagan. The nomads, having little time to settle down and practice Islam, were not offensive in their propagation of the faith. In spite of their relatively poor status, they considered themselves superior to the surrounding races, and Islam enhanced that feeling of superiority.

As some of them became more affluent and sedentary, they took their religion more seriously. Several were instructed in the centers of Muslim learning in Arabia and Egypt, and many achieved the title of *Al Haj* by making the pilgrimage to Mecca. By the end of the eighteenth century the stage was set for the Fulani to become the dominant force in sub-Saharan West Africa.

The three names that stand our in the "Fulanization" of West Africa are Usman dan Fodio of Sokoto, Shehu Ahmadu of Masina and Al Haj Umar of Senegal. All three were known for their piety and learning. All three conducted holy wars for the purification of West African Islam and for the reduction of animist groups to Islam.

Usman dan Fodio was proclaimed King of the Muslims in 1804 in Gobir (now northern Nigeria). He declared a holy war (*jihad*) against enemies of Islam and eventually extended his rule over nearly two-thirds of Nigeria.

Shehu Ahmadu was a Muslim teacher of repute in the early nineteenth century in Mali. Through successive military victories over the Bambara, Tuareg, Dogon, and neighboring peoples, Shehu Ahmadu and his son Hamadu Shehu established the Fulani empire of Masina.

Al Haj Umar Saidu Tal was born in 1797. In 1827 he made his pilgrimage to Mecca and observed the reform movement in Sokoto and Masina and was well received upon his return to his own country. He was most successful in his holy war in Guinea and eventually extended his influence into Masina.

An additional Fulani reformer should be mentioned: Modibbo Adama who received the flag of holy war from Usman in 1805 and proceeded to conquer eastern Nigeria and all of northern Cameroon.

Sedentaries and Nomads: The Colonial Period

Reactions to the Fulani empires varied under French and British administration. Colonialization was a boon for the Sokoto empire since the British worked through the Fulani emirates that they found, and the Fulani became firmly established politically. But the British encouraged Hausa as the official language of northern Nigeria, so culturally the sedentary Fulani began to lose their distinctiveness and adopt Hausa ways. The more numerous nomadic Fulani, however, carried on the characteristics of the race. They were more isolated from the Hausa cultural influences and intermarriage was strictly forbidden.

In French territories, the Fulani did not fare as well politically, though their refined manner and relatively highly developed culture impressed French authorities. The French would countenance no official African language, so Fulani were not significantly affected by other African cultures. In northern Cameroon, Fulani became the semi-official language since it was the language used in the market place. The distinction between sedentary and nomadic Fulani was not nearly so marked in northern Cameroon and other French territories as in Nigeria.

The purity of tradition and language of the nomadic Fulani is maintained by their strong clan fidelity. A Fulani of the Wodaabe clan in central Cameroon, for instance, is much closer in tradition and language to the Wodaabe of western Niger than to his neighboring Jafu-en brother.

Religious conservatism of sedentary Fulani has retarded their incorporation into modern life. The normal Fulani head of household is dismayed at the incursions into traditional Muslim life by the influence of public schools. Traditionally a boy would study at least four years with a Muslim teacher, learning the Koran by rote, and the traditional Muslim attitudes. As colonial powers and later independent states began to make education compulsory, the father would choose one son— often the youngest or the least promising, or the son of a concubine or woman slave—and send him to public school in token compliance with the government regulation. The boy who was sent to "white man's" school was considered as good as lost to Islam. This has fast been changing as these "rejects" begin to assume responsible positions in the nations. Now nearly all boys go to public school, and the

Koranic school has been reduced mainly to an extra-curricular activity, or is carried on within the family.

In spite of the late start, Fulanis hold positions of importance in nearly all nations where there is a sizeable number of them: Senegal, Guinea, Mali, Upper Volta, Niger, Nigeria, Cameroon. Until the recent Biafran revolt, Fulanis had virtual control of Nigeria. The late Ahmadu Bello, Sardauna of Sokoto was not only the political leader, but was a leader of world Islam. It is reported that he was one of the few Muslims in the world permitted inside the Ka'aba, the sacred temple in Mecca. The Nigerian civil war altered the influence of the ruling Fulani class. On the other hand, the position of the Fulani nomads remains virtually the same.

Cameroon is perhaps unique in that Fulanis retain both political and cultural denomination of the northern half of the country. A non-Fulani has some chance for high government office if he declares himself a Muslim, but he is in a much better position if he is Fulani. Because of their dominant position, Fulani is progressing as a language in North Cameroon.

PART TWO: THE EVANGELIZATION SITUATION

Churches and missions are awakening to the strategic place of the Fulani in the evangelization of sub-Saharan Africa. In spite of nationalistic attempts to revive it, animism is discredited as a viable religious expression in emerging Africa. Without any doubt, the major religion that Christianity faces is Islam. Some see Islam as Christianity's major world challenge. This is certainly true in West Africa. And historically the Fulani have been the most effective champions of Islam in West Africa. They can present Islam as the black man's religion even though they are not originally Negro themselves.

Approximately 400 Fulani are known Christians. Of those, 300 are in Benin, 70-80 in Nigeria, 10 in Cameroon, and a few in other countries (1974 estimates). Rev. H. O. Watkins has been working among the Fulani of Guinee for some 35 years, but so far the conversions have been practically nil. Others have been working among the nomadic Fulani in the area of Kano, Benin, Cameroon and also in the Zaria area, south of Kano. Two missionary families are working among the Fulani in Niger. A number of young Fulani men have been trained in Bible schools and are now working among their own people, but those who have given themselves for this work are extremely few compared to the vast numbers of people to be reached.

Until recently the Fulani remained aloof and distant toward any who appeared to want to help them. This included messengers of the gospel. They resisted efforts to put their youth in schools—it just didn't fit into a shepherd's life. But today there is a change in the attitude of the Fulani towards the new culture, and as noted above, a few have made decisions to follow Jesus Christ as Lord and Savior. With this new receptivity, particularly among the young people, we need to develop a suitable strategy to reach the Fulani and to overcome the barriers of their nomadic character and distinctive language.

In November 1969 and again in December 1970, conferences were held in Kano for all Christian missions and churches interested in reaching the Fulani. Since then it has become an annual affair. Some of the goals of those conferences were: (1) a short-term (one or two weeks) Fulani institute; (2) a Bible school for Fulani workers and preachers; and (3) a Fulani training center, which would include language instruction, customs and orientation study, literature development, and radio program production. It was also suggested that missionaries and national pastors and evangelists be set aside for Fulani evangelism, an information center to begin circulation of prayer requests is a priority item, and it was convenanted to ask the Lord for hundreds of family groups to turn to Christ.

Ways and Means

Radio broadcasts in the Fulani language have been extremely useful and should be considered a high priority in continued outreach to the Fulani people. A half-hour daily broadcast had been aired regularly for several years from the RVOG, Addis Ababa, Ethiopia. With the recent closure of that station, however, the radio ELWA of the Sudan Interior Mission in Liberia has taken up this opportunity of broadcast to the Fulani. The Sawtu report indicates that there is not only a faithful regular audience, but there is virtually no other broadcast in Fulani. Radio is an effective tool for the church of Christ to reach the Fulani people as a group.

Adequate follow-up, however, of these radio broadcasts must be instituted as quickly as possible. The two-step theory of mass communication is helpful in defining the task of Fulani broadcasting. According to this theory, each society has its leaders and followers, its innovators and imitators, its thinkers and reactors. The large majority of people in a given society belong to the second part of each of these designations. The leader-innovator-thinker types are those who influence the direction taken by the whole society. They are the key people to reach since they are the ones who influence the masses. It just so happens that among Fulanis, it is generally the leaders, innovators, and thinkers who own radios. In-the-field research reveals that 82 percent of the listeners are Muslim. There is a very low literacy rate among the Fulani and therefore letters received are about 50 percent from Muslims and 50 percent from Christians. Fulanis have a strong desire to have news broadcast in their language. Christian stations can meet this need.

Besides radio, another means of reaching the Fulani is through local village believers. Fulani graze their cattle herds near farming villages and towns. The farmers appreciate the fertilizer, and the cattle enjoy the grain stalks.

The cornstalk-grass domed huts of the Fulani may be seen dotting the countryside throughout northern Nigeria. This means that in many areas they are within easy reach of groups of believers who buy milk and butter in exchange for grain and bran.

CASE STUDIES

PART THREE: A WORKING PROGRAM

Objectives

1. To evangelize the Fulani people so that all will have an adequate opportunity to know Jesus Christ

2. To help them find suitable ways of worship within their cultural structures with minimal disturbance to their life-style

3. To establish Fulani churches wherever advisable (It may be on the back of a cow)

4. To mobilize the believers throughout northern Nigeria to carry out the necessary steps to accomplish this

Personnel

1. Coordinator in charge of the program. Rev. Yakubu Yako, ECWA evangelist and one with long experience in New Life for All.

2. District coordinators for each ECWA district, full time, to provide instruction, encouragement, and understanding among the local churches.

3. In each local church train eight to ten team members for organized teaching and witness in the Fulani camps on a weekly basis.

4. Local pastors or lay leaders may serve as instructors and coordinators of mobilization, giving encouragement and advice at local church level.

5. All believers take part in prayer cells and showing kindness and love to Fulani.

Multi-Media Program

1. The handbook, *Let's Help the Fulani* contains twenty-two Bible stories for pre-evangelism, all slanted toward the shepherd culture. Fulani cultural characteristics are defined, suggested ways of showing love are given, and a sample gospel message is presented—"New Shepherd—New Life." This is meant especially for the teams but serves to clue everyone in on the program of outreach.

2. Door/window cards to announce neighborhood gather-

ings for weekly prayer meetings specifically for Fulani. These prayer cells should involve as many people as possible in prayer support for the ministry.

3. Promotional literature. Posters for churches.

4. Radio Programs. Two stations, ELWA and RVOG have already broadcast in Fulani. Programs are being prepared using the twenty-two Bible stories in both Hausa and Fulani. The Hausa programs will aid the Fulani believers (who are all Hausa-speaking) so that they can better use the stories when witnessing.

5. Tracts for non-readers. Perhaps 99 percent of Fulanis cannot read. A four-panel cartoon strip has been designed for wide distribution. The believer uses this as illustrative material as he witnesses to Fulani.

6. Four or five teams in each local church, trained to use the handbook, will visit Fulani camps weekly over a period of a year or more. This is a ministry of pre-evangelism and each session builds on previous ones. The objective is to keep Fulanis listening to the Word of God so that they learn what God says about man, God, sin, and Jesus Christ. There will be a concerted effort to win households and clans to the Lord.

The Strategic Medium—the Cassette Player

1. In every local church we want to place a cassette player and a set of six tapes with the twenty-two Bible stories recorded in the Fulani language. This equipment would be used by the teams who have been trained for Fulani visitation and witness. Each team will be assigned to a Fulani camp where they will make a weekly visit. They will seek to set up a relationship of confidence and mutual trust between themselves and the Fulani elders, and gather a group every week for a Bible story and discussion. This will usually be done in the Hausa language.

These stories are being put into Fulani language in dramatic form and recorded on cassettes by a Fulani evangelist. It is proposed that each church have a set of six cassettes (C-60) which could be used in rotation by the several teams of that church. In any area there are usually three to five Fulani camps. Each story would be 14-15 minutes long and would be structured to encourage further discussion and questions.

2. The unique role of the cassette player.

● The Fulani must depend on oral transmission of the message.

● Very few non-Fulani understand the Fulani language, which means a second language must be used. There are only a few scattered Fulani believers, and they are mostly babes in Christ.

● Since the Fulani are a strong ethnic group their language is a matter of extreme pride and joy to them. They must know that God speaks Fulani.

● No other tool in our hands can overcome this communication block as well as the cassette player.

● Once the message is recorded, it never changes. The nomad will hear the same message even at widely separated places.

● It lends itself to repetition, which is extremely important in this culture where news is passed on orally.

● Follow up sequences on tape can be used later.

The foregoing strategy is now being implemented in Central Nigeria with a number of local churches. It is too early to assess the progress that has been made or the benefits received, although there is a continuing high interest among the Fulani. And some local churches have a real desire to reach out to them. Only as the local churches take up this outreach in a serious way will the difficulties posed by a nomadic people be overcome. This strategy should be easy to duplicate in any part of West Africa where there are local believers.

Gerald O. Swank has lived and worked with Sudan Interior Mission in Nigeria since 1940. He directed the Kagoro Bible Training School in Central Nigeria for seventeen years. In 1963 he founded the New Life for All movement and directed it for five years. He was the first secretary for evangelism and church growth for the Evangelical Churches of West Africa.

He is author of *Frontier Peoples of Central Nigeria and a Strategy for Outreach* (William Carey, 1977). Rev. Swank is currently the director of overseas ministries for the Sudan Interior Mission. The background material for his article was drawn from a paper prepared by the staff of Sawtu Linjila in Cameroon for the Lutheran World Federation Broadcasting Service Board.

The Unreached Gabbra: A Plan to Reach a Nomadic People

by Bishop David Gitari
Rev. Stephen Houghton
Gordon R. Mullenix

Under God's sovereign guidance and timing, three dreams converged to fuel a plan to evangelize a nomadic Kenyan tribe—the Gabbra. The three visions were:

● Christians around the world praying for and witnessing to people who are unreached by Christ's message.

● A church diocese where missiological insight guides evangelism to unreached people.

● People responding to the Christian witness of a family member who lives as an example of Christ's pattern of love.

The resulting evangelistic strategy is not the only effort to reach the Gabbra, but it is unique in emphasizing a nomadic ministry by a Gabbra evangelist. That plan is described here.

THE GABBRA

Most of the Gabbra[1] live in Marsabit District in northern Kenya. They occupy land from Lake Turkana on the east to the border of Wajir District on the west. The Ethiopian border forms the northern boundary to their territory. The southern boundary is a line from the middle of Lake Turkana to Marsabit.

The land is extremely dry and sparsely populated. It is volcanic and is crossed by dry stream beds. Rainfall is limited—between 1.5 and 12 inches yearly. Most of that falls within the March-May or October-December periods. In some places the water table is 800 to 900 feet deep. Wells are unreliable, and the shallow wells require great human effort to lift water to the surface. There are only about twenty springs or dry weather wells within Gabbra territory.

The latest census (1969)[2] of Kenya indicated that there were 16,108 Gabbra in Kenya. The remoteness of many camps made accurate assessment very difficult.

There are five Gabbra divisions, each with its own name, political leaders, and legal authority. Each of these divisions traditionally use certain pastures and water supplies (although access to water and pasture cannot be denied Gabbra of other divisions).

Ceremonial and political functions for each of the five divisions are conducted by a council *(Ya'a)*. This council settles disputes and performs sacrifices. They regulate the social organization via the important age-grade system. Age grades are organized in eight-year cycles. They regulate the responsibilities and privileges that each man assumes.

The most visible unit of social organization is the group of families that share water, grass, and labor. Each group will move several times during the year in search of water and pasture. They are each governed by one man appointed on the basis of reputation to serve as an administrative officer.

The Kenya government administers the Gabbra using agents, who are appointed after consultation with the tribe. These agents see that government regulations are communicated to the Gabbra. They have little authority within traditional Gabbra life.

The eldest man of each family controls access to family herds. The oldest son inherits the bulk of his father's herd and continues to control its use until his death. The man's family obtains their food from the animals and his unmarried sons care for his herd. They rely upon him to provide the animals that will make their marriage possible.

Marriage arrangements begin when the young man is circumcised at about age eighteen. The father tries to obtain a girl from a family with a reputation for successful animal breeding and large numbers of children. A girl may be betrothed by her father when she is only four years old. Girls commonly marry at about age sixteen. Their husbands are often thirty years old. They live with the husband's father because he controls the herd from which they will get their food.

Children make an important contribution to the family labor force. When they are about seven years old, they begin animal herding. They learn the necessary methods from older children and their parents.

Until the age of nine, girls tend to spend time with the boys herding animals. Later they spend less time with the animals and begin preparing for their marriage. They care for younger children, help their mothers obtain household water and prepare food.

The tent that the Gabbra use for shelter is considered the property of the women. They are responsible for its maintenance, transportation to new sites, and assembly. These are difficult and time consuming tasks.

Among the Gabbra, polygynous marriages are infrequent, probably not involving more than 10 percent of the married men. Likewise, divorce is not common among the Gabbra.

The Gabbra depend on herds of camels, goats, sheep, and some cattle for food and ritual requirements. Perhaps the major result of Gabbra dependence on animals is the necessity to move homes about once each month, or whenever an area can no longer supply the grass and water to maintain the herd. The Gabbra have learned to match animal requirements to the water and forage resources in different locations during various seasons of the year. Since camels tend to require less water than other animals they range further from water supplies. Cattle are the most difficult to manage on limited water and therefore are confined to higher elevations with more water.

Cooperative herd management is a major feature of Gabbra pastoralism. A single family could not provide the labor force to water and herd all the animals. Animals belonging to several families are herded together in order to efficiently use the labor force.

Camels supply the major portion of milk and blood consumed by the Gabbra. Sheep and goats provide meat. Each herd owner wants his herd as large as possible in order to survive raids by neighboring tribes, disease, and drought. In recent years the Gabbra have experienced severe drought, and today the herds are relatively small.

Gabbra religious beliefs are inseparably interwoven with their herds. Animals not only provide their food but are necessary as sacrifices to ensure fertility, health, and cooperation. Of all the animals, camels play the most important religious role. Goats, sheep, and cattle are also used for sacrifices but do not have the mystical power possessed by camels.

The head of each family acts as the ritual leader. He organizes ceremonies to ensure the health and productivity of his herd. These ceremonies occur several times each year. Other religious events are marriage, the birth and naming of children, and death of family members. On each of these occasions animals are sacrificed.

Members of a senior age-grade act as priests at all major ceremonies. They are thought to possess special power and are treated with respect. The Gabbra hold ceremonies on auspicious days. They have an elaborate calendar which is consulted by the ritual leaders. This calendar determines the schedule of age-grade ceremonies as well as lesser events in Gabbra life.

STATUS OF CHRISTIANITY

Christianity is known among the Gabbra. Catholic, Anglican, and African Inland missionaries have worked in the area.

By placing Christian witnesses at the water supplies, some contact has been established with perhaps 80 percent of the Gabbra. However less than 5 percent have modified their behavior to conform to their understanding of Christian teaching.

A small number of Gabbra have received Christian teaching during their stay in boarding school. But child labor is such an important part of Gabbra survival that schools do not attract significant number of Gabbra children. Christianity is thus not penetrating Gabbra life significantly through school children.

To increase the penetration of Christianity into Gabbra society it must be established that the Gabbra Christian will not necessarily leave his pastoral life. If Christianity remains linked to education and urban employment, it will be a threat to the survival of the family and will not be considered by elders who cannot leave their traditional responsibilities.

Christianity may always remain a minor factor in Gabbra life until an evangelist is able to demonstrate that acceptance of Christ does not adversely affect the fertility of animals. The Gabbra believe that the fertility of their herds is related to the proper conduct of worship. In traditional life this is done through a series of sacrifices. The Christian evangelist will be challenged by the need to relate the Christian message to Gabbra concern for their animals. He will need to articulate a "Theology of Herd Management."

Receptivity

The Gabbra are probably best described as indifferent to the Christian message. The willingness of people to accept a new religious message is related to their willingness to change other areas of their life. The Gabbra have faced situations in recent years which have stimulated changes in their life.

Two noticeable religious changes are (1) the acceptance of Islam by town-dwelling Gabbra, due to social reasons, and (2) thirty years ago demon possession seems to have begun, possibly as a result of contact with neighboring Ethiopian tribes. As a result, some Gabbra have sought Christian prayer and exorcism of demons. This provides a good channel for Christian witness.

During 1971-77 there was an extreme shortage of rainfall. This shortage made necessary several changes in Gabbra life. Because of the lack of rain the Gabbra were not able to maintain their usual diet of milk, blood, and meat. As their animals died they were forced to rely upon relief programs for food. This food was usually maize meal. Some of the Gabbra lost their entire herd, and some moved into towns to find employment. Some have been able to return to their former pastoral life. Others have taken up the sedentary town life.

Where water and grass is sufficient, the Gabbra appear willing to give up nomadic life. However, there is conflict between the need to find water and grass and the opportunity to receive medical care and education, which can be provided in settled populations.

Force for Evangelism

The force for Gabbra evangelism is partially expressed in the vision and determination of one young Anglican priest. This young Gabbra began his education at about age twelve because of a government decree that his people must send children to school. Before entering school he heard about Christianity in an Anglican church. During school holidays he was sometimes driven home by a missionary who stayed several days to preach.

He finished his primary education, trained as a teacher and taught school for two years. During this time at an evangelistic meeting he experienced a vivid call to evangelize his own people. Because of his call he has perhaps been a disappointment to his family who are sympathetic to Christianity, but not believers. They expect him to provide financial assistance. As a priest he cannot bear the financial load that would have been possible as a teacher.

It is also a significant sign of his determination that he resisted ordination. He was afraid that he would be assigned to a parish where his duties would make it impossible for him to work among the Gabbra. He agreed to ordination in 1975 only when the bishop convinced him that he would be allowed to follow God's call to the Gabbra.

STRATEGY

Based upon all of the criteria discussed above, it appears that the gospel will best be communicated to the Gabbra by someone who appears to them to understand their situation and has demonstrated that he shares their same life-style and world view. What is needed is an evangelist who lives and works and moves with the Gabbra—if you will, a "nomadic evangelist."

With the approval of the bishop of the diocese within which these people live, a strategy was constructed that includes the following elements:

An evangelist who can enter into the obligations of Gabbra life to demonstrate how Christianity can be lived as a Gabbra. Previous attempts to evangelize the Gabbra have largely been made by people who were unable to be nomadic. We now have an evangelist who can move as the poeple move and thus sustain contact with people long enough to demonstrate a Christian life.

Supported by a bishop who will encourage the expression of a Christian life in forms meaningful to the Gabbra. The evangelist will not be rigidly bound by church administration or tradition. The evangelist is encouraged to find creative solutions to problems that have overcome other evangelistic attempts.

The strategy then, is deceptively simple: a Gabbra evangelist will attempt to show how a Christian can live as a Gabbra and please Christ.

Since the Gabbra are a nomadic people, the evangelist will be nomadic. He will live within a Gabbra family group and depend, as they depend, upon their animals for transportation and food. He will own animals and therefore take part in the cooperative herding efforts. This will bring him into contact with traditional Gabbra ceremonies to promote the fertility of the herds. He will need to respond as a Christian.

Living as a Gabbra, the evangelist will assume the obligations of a family member. He will have the opportunity to suggest Christian responses to family problems. One such problem will be the maintenance of Christian family standards as adultery is widely practiced.

A base camp will be established at Bubisa where there is now a well. Since this is the only permanent water supply for many miles, large numbers of people come to Bubisa to water their animals. The evangelist will be able to travel from Bubisa with families that indicate an interest in Christian teaching.

Christian teaching will be greatly facilitated by the recent completion of the New Testament translation. For the first time the Gabbra will have a complete New Testament with which to encourage scripture memorization and teaching. This will provide a uniform text upon which oral teaching can be based.

NOTES:

1. The unpublished thesis of William I. Torry, "Subsistence Ecology Among the Gabbra Nomads of the Kenya/Ethiopian Frontier" (Columbia University, 1973) was an invaluable source of information supplementing Rev. Houghton's years of contact with the Gabbra.

2. Kenya Population Census, 1969 Volume I (Statistics Division Ministry of Finance and Economic Planning, November, 1970), page 69.

The Rt. Rev. **David M. Gitari** was born in a Christian home about 40 years ago. His father was the first to bring the good news of Jesus Christ to his home village. After graduation at the Universities of Nairobi and London he worked for the Bible Society of Kenya for four years and was consecrated bishop of Mount Kenya East in 1975. He is a member of the Strategy Working Group of the Lausanne Continuation Committee and the Theological Commission of World Evangelical Fellowship.

Stephen Houghton studied modern languages and theology (B.A., M.A.) at Cambridge University before training for the Anglican ministry. He was ordained in 1957 and joined the Bible Churchmen's Missionary Society in 1960 as a pastoral missionary among the Boran and Gabbra people in northern Kenya, where he worked until 1977. He was leader of the team that translated the Borana New Testament (1978). Currently, principal of St. Andrew's Bible School, Embu, he hopes to return to northern Kenya as coordinator-exegete of the team translating the Old Testament into Borana. He is married and has four chidlren.

Gordon R. Mullenix has worked in Africa for seven years as a consultant and teacher. He is currently the senior advisor for evangelism and research assigned to the Africa Regional Office of World Vision. He is trained as a sociologist and has had experience with a wide variety of development and evangelism programs in Africa. He is an occasional lecturer at St. Andrews Bible College, Embu, Kenya.

The Gujarati Indians of England and Wales

by David J. Reynolds

DESCRIPTION

The Gujarati people come from the western coastal state of Gujarat (area, 72,000 square miles; population, 23 million) in India. They have always been active as traders between India, East Africa, and the Arabian peninsula. During the period of British rule in India, many Gujaratis emigrated to East and South Africa as traders and workers. In East Africa particularly, the Gujaratis prospered greatly. As a consequence by the 1960s, restrictions were placed on them by these governments, forcing large numbers to emigrate to Britian. It has been estimated that 200,000 Asians have now come to Britain from East Africa. And 70 percent of those are Gujarati Hindus.

Apart from East Africa, immigration into Britain started immediately after the Second World War. Economic expansion and the resulting shortage of labor attracted immigrant workers from all over Europe, as well as many parts of the Commonwealth. The Asian migrants make no secret of the fact that they are economically motivated, and this is particularly true of the Gujaratis.

The Gujarati people have a distinct ethnic language that, like any language, has dialect variations. However, this in itself has not been the most important factor distinguishing them as a people. More important is the caste system, which though officially abolished, still represents the single most important factor in the distinctiveness of the group.

129

CASE STUDIES

There are four social classes and in each class there are many castes and subcastes.

Brahmins   (Priests)
Kshatriyas   (Warriors)
Vaisyas   (Merchants, Farmers, Craftsmen)
Sudhras   (Menials)

Each class is considered exclusive of the others. For many, intermarriage and social intercourse between classes is forbidden. Of the migrants to Britain, by far the largest number have come from the Vaisyas or merchant class, so that the name *Patel* (or *Patidar,* meaning landowner) is by far the commonest Gujarati name in England and Wales. Because of the large number from this class there are national associations of Patidars, Shahs, and Lohanas, as well as many more at a local level. These associations exist primarily to promote and encourage their Indian cultural heritage. Some breakdown of the old caste system has occurred in that Patidars do allow marriage to Shahs and so on. Even now, however, the number of marriages that occur outside of the family social and class system is very small.

As with most Asian groups there is a very close family and kin bond. The Gujaratis have been termed the "Asian Jew" not only because of their ability to succeed in business (their ability to own and run small shops successfully is well known) but also because of their close community. The joint family system is still very strong. Married brothers and their families, unmarried brothers and sisters, all live under the authority of the oldest male member—usually father or grandfather. Age is a mark of wisdom—youth a mark of inexperience. All orphans, widows, and aged members of the family are cared for by the others. The head of the family has authority over the other members, even those who are married and are themselves fathers.

Thus if someone marries his daughter, the Gujarati parent would visit her every week to make sure that she is happy, that her husband is looking after her, and that he is bringing up the children properly. If not, he would tell him what to do and expect him to comply! Any financial problem is not just the couple's problem, it is the father's problem, too. If the husband is out of a job, the father-in-law might buy him a shop.

The practice of giving dowries is still maintained, though to a lesser extent. In East Africa, a father would sometimes pay for a husband-to-be to come out from India and set him up in a job as the dowry. In England and Wales, sums of money are still demanded, sometimes as high as $10,000, particularly if the marriage is into a "well connected" family. However, "reverse dowries" are also worked. Hence for $1,500, for example, a man can come from Gujarat and marry a woman already in England!

Religion

The earlier Gujarati immigrants who settled in the Midlands, Lancashire and Yorkshire were mainly Muslims, with a smaller number of Hindus. The Muslims established their own Mosques and developed a normal Muslim life-style. Increasingly, however, larger numbers of Gujarati Hindus have joined them, so that there are now few towns or cities where the Muslims outnumber the Hindus. The Hindus have now built their own temples, although these are still few in number. Interestingly Carey Baptist Church in Leicester has now become the main Hindu temple in that city, something which is symbolic of the reversing situation being faced in Britain.

Because there are so few temples and those that exist are mainly attended by older women and young children, many Gujaratis, particularly the young people, have little to do with the outward worship. Many have become disillusioned with Hinduism, and are as irreligious as many of their English contemporaries. Without a doubt the women are the custodians of Hinduism and set themselves the task of bringing up their children in this faith. It is estimated that of the Hindu Gujaratis, nearly 80 percent are orthodox in their faith. Some women meet regularly in *Sat Sungs* for prayer and encouragement of one another. These are meetings in homes where thirty to forty women come together for worship.

131

CASE STUDIES

Literacy

Literacy among the Gujaratis is a question that is often ignored but is vitally relevant to the communication of the gospel. Many varied estimates have been made, but there has been no definitive research. The following information represents the sum of discussions with many language workers, missionaries and Gujaratis themselves.

Children and Young People. For those Gujarati children who have been educated here in Britain, there is no definable difference in their literacy rates, and those of the majority. The only difference is that most will speak Gujarati, but perhaps less than 5 or 10 percent will be able to read or write the language. Of those who were educated in East Africa and have arrived here since about 1970, English is still undoubtedly their main language. They may have an acquaintance with "kitchen" Swahili, and again will speak Gujarati. Very few, however, will read or write Gujarati.

Young immigrants direct from Gujarat, India are normally of a lower educational standard than those from East Africa. If they have the equivalent of a "school-leaving certificate" they will be literate in Hindi (now the official language of India), Gujarati, and perhaps even English. It would appear that the majority do not reach this standard. Many "brides" come straight to Britain able to speak only a few words of English and Hindi, although fluent in Gujarati. They are, however, often illiterate in all three languages.

Twenty to Forty Years Old. In 1978, the majority of the population was from this group. Their literacy depends on whether the people came from East Africa or India, and whether they are male or female.

	Literacy			
	East Africa		India	
Language	Men	Women	Men	Women
Gujarati	85%	50%	35%	20%
Swahili	20%	5%		
English	50%	20%	25%	10%

132

Over Forty. In this group literacy generally drops alarmingly due to (1) few even having more than a basic education, and (2) due to close family ties, little need to learn a new language.

Most will communicate verbally in Gujarati, but will normally use the children to communicate in English with a caller to the house. Just as there is little desire on the part of most children to become literate in Gujarati, so here the reverse trend is true, little desire to become literate in English.

Numbers and Locations

According to Desai, the total Indian and Pakistani population of the U.K. in the middle 1950s was 10,000 people. By 1960 the total had risen to nearly 100,000, and by the 1971 census, the total was 462,000. It has been widely suggested that this latter figure was underenumerated by up to 10 percent because of the large number of households where more than six persons were present. Hence a total of 500,000 born in India and Pakistan (including Bangladesh) would probably be more precise, and even this figure would not account for (a) those born in U.K., and (b) those born in East Africa.

The total Asian population is today reckoned to be nearly 1.2 million. This could be roughly broken down into the following groupings.

Pakistanis	250,000
Punjabi Sikhs	150,000
Punjabi Hindus	150,000
Bangladeshis	150,000
Gujaratis	300,000
S. Indians	
N. Indians	
Bengalis	120,000
Marashians	
Kerla	
Asians from American NCW	80,000

133

CASE STUDIES

From the above one can see that the total Gujarati population of England and Wales is estimated to be 300,000, out of a total population of 49,200,000, or 0.5 to 0.6 percent.

Of this number approximately half would live in the Greater London Council area, i.e. 120-150,000. By far the largest single concentration in the G.L.C. is in the Borough of Brent with probably 30-35,000 Gujaratis. Next in order would come:

Barnet	12-14,000
Newham	12-14,000
Harrow	10-12,000
Wandsworth	7-9,000
Redbridge	7-9,000
Croydon	6-8,500
Ealing	5-7,000
Harringay	4-6,000
Hounslow	3-4,000

The rest would all have less than 1,500.

In the rest of England and Wales, the general distribution of Gujaratis is centered around three major areas:

Leicester	25-28,000
Bolton	12-16,000
Birmingham	10-12,000

All other communities have a total Gujarati population of less than 10,000, but at the present time these have not all been precisely defined. It is important to note that in the areas mentioned, the Gujaratis are invariably concentrated in the towns and cities rather than in the outlying rural environment.

The population has been very mobile, and the obvious trends are to move out of the inner-city, low-grade housing areas to the more spacious residential areas. Hence in London we see moves out to Hemel Hempstead, Watford, Crawley, and Kent, all typical commuter belts. This trend will undoubtedly continue in the coming years. The Gujaratis are great house owners and there are undoubtedly a higher proportion of house owners among the Gujaratis than among any other single identifiable group.

STATUS OF CHRISTIANITY

The two predominant religions of the Gujarati are Hinduism (about 70 percent of the total) and Islam. These have dominated their thinking and life-style to such an extent that the impact of Christianity on the group is virtually nonexistent. In the whole London area, there are only fifteen to twenty-five Christian Gujarati families. All of these have come directly from Gujarat and not one has been converted in the United Kingdom.

The churches in London are slowly becoming aware of the need for reaching this group, but do not know what to do. There are signs of meeting "community leaders" in the Thornton Heath area and Brent, of holding out hands of friendship, but it seems an indictment against the churches that as far as can be determined there is not one Gujarati person who has become a Christian in England and Wales above age twenty-one. There were a handful in East Africa but none in this country.

In Leicester perhaps thirty youngsters and teenagers have professed Christianity, and there are a few Christian married couples. These attempt to evangelize among their own people, but normally worship in English since it is their "first" language. In essence the status of Christianity among this group is virtually zero. There are some groups who are working among the Asians, such as International Mission, Church Army, WEC, and BMMF. However, in the main these are "front post" assignments, often with little help from the indigenous church.

Receptivity

What work has been done so far among the Gujaratis has been almost exclusively among the majority Hindu population. This almost certainly is due to the fact that the Hindu is more outgoing than the Muslim.

Generally the Hindu is quite prepared to make friends and to invite others into his house. Friendship is certainly the start. Language workers have a particular entree, which gives them

CASE STUDIES

a privileged position as well as a special responsibility.

Experience over the past six years shows, however, that the receptivity of the average Gujarati Hindu adult is zero. They have little or no awareness of Christianity, and among those who have, few other than the youngsters have any knowledge of the fundamentals of the gospel. Many equate the lower moral standards and crime prevalent today with "Christian" England and are obviously reluctant to associate with this.

Receptivity among youngsters is greater. There is the natural rebellion of youth against parental standards. Even today, however, the pressures are for youngsters to conform to the established social pattern. For a teenager to become a Christian can mean being thrown out of the house and totally cut off by the parents. For a younger person it can mean being kept indoors, or being forced to Hindu temple worship. Naturally if a "friendship" contact has already been initiated with the parents, they are more likely to allow their children to attend Sunday school, youth clubs, etc.

Over the next few years the biggest problem to be faced concerning receptivity is the question of race relations. The National Front is undoubtedly causing grave concern to all coloured immigrant groups and as a result they are becoming more inward looking and less receptive to "outsiders."

Forces for Evangelism

The most prevalent means of evangelism so far has been among young people. These can be interested in Bible study/youth club activities, from twelve years old on up. However this depends on:

● Workers reaching out to the Gujarati youngsters and, if necessary, providing separate classes for girls and boys.

● The local church supporting the "work" and not objecting to the fact that the youngsters only go to the club and never a church meeting. (This is often due to parental limitation. The youngsters being allowed only one meeting a week).

● The church welcoming in Gujarati Christian converts.

● Involvement with the youngsters' families.

● Prayer and much perseverance.

When it comes to those over twenty-one, it is evident that new experiments need to be made, such as:

● Distribution of Gujarati/English Scriptures.

● Writing articles for local or national papers, particularly at Easter and Christmas. Most Gujarati papers would willingly include Scriptures and Christian material at these times.

● Local radio programs in Gujarati.

● Selling Gospels in shops, parks, door to door.

One means that has not yet been tried is to use Gujarati/Hindu sound tracks on films. The Gujaratis are avid cinema goers, as is evident from the large number of cinemas they have bought.

Each of these strategies need to be tried and evaluated. And new methods and means will likely be conceived as we become more deeply involved with the Gujaratis.

REFERENCES

1. *Indian Immigrants in Britain,* Rashmi Desai-Oxford University Press (1963)
2. *Ethnic Minorities in Britain* (statistical data), Community Relations Commission; Sixth Edition (1976)
3. *New Patterns for Discipling Hindus,* B.V. Subhanna, William Carey Library, California (1970)
4. *Between Two Cultures: Migrants and Minorities in Britain,* J.L. Watson, Blackwell (1977)

David Reynolds was appointed special assignments assistant to the Rev. Tom Houston, executive director of the British and Foreign Bible Society, in January 1978. He is responsible for preparing research reports. He graduated in 1967 from Southampton with a degree in chemistry, and two years later completed his Ph.D. He is currently involved in preaching and teaching in his local church. He is married and has a son and a daughter.

PART 3
Unreached Peoples— Expanded Descriptions

The following section contains expanded descriptions of eighty people groups in alphabetical order. Each group has is a data table giving basic information based on questionnaires completed by persons in the same country or otherwise knowledgeable about the people group.

In the data table, the most *common name of the people* group is given first, followed by the *name of the country* in which the group is located. A complete listing of all un-reached people groups currently identified in the MARC files in this way may be found in the Registry of Unreached Peoples section following these expanded descriptions.

The following is a summary of the remaining data categories:

marc id: An identification number by which information on that particular group is filed. Any correspondence sent to MARC dealing with a group, sending corrections, updates, additions, or requests for further information should refer to that number.

alt names: Any alternate names or spellings for the people group.

pop: Latest population estimate.

also in: Any other countries the group may inhabit. Many groups straddle national boundaries or are found in scattered parts of one or more countries. This heading lists any other countries in which the people group may be found. Note: The name *Democratic Kampuchea* (see the Brao people) refers to what was formerly known as Cambodia. All other country names should be familiar.

distinct: Distinctives that unify this group. Many different things may make a group distinctive or cause them to consider themselves a people. Often several factors give them some kind of affinity toward one another, or make them different from other groups. Respondents to the Unreached Peoples questionnaire were asked to indicate the relative importance of various factors in making the group distinctive. Those factors were: speaking the same language, common political loyalty, similar occupation, racial or ethnic similarity, shared religious customs, common kinship ties, strong sense of unity, similar education level, common residential area, similar social class or caste, similar economic status, shared hobby or special interest, discrimination from other groups, unique health situation, distinctive legal status, similar age, common significant problems, and "other(s)."

languages: Primary languages. Multilingual communities often use different languages in different situations. They may learn one language in school, another in the market, and yet another in religious ceremonies. Respondents were asked to indicate the major languages used by the group as well as the place or function of each language. These functions are indicated in code form under **uses.** The codes are as follows:

V—vernacular or common language

T—trade language or *lingua franca*

S—language used for instruction in schools

W—the language used for any current or past Christian witness

G—the language most suitable for presentation of the gospel

P—the language used in any non-Christian ceremonies
The percentages under the headings **speak** and **read** indicate respectively the percentage of the total group that speak and read the language(s) listed.

chr lit: Christian literacy. This indicates the percentage of Christians among the people (if any) over 15 years of age who can and do read in any language.

scripture: Indicates the availability of various forms of biblical literature in the languages of the group.

rate chg: Rate of change. This represents an estimate of the overall rate that cultural and social change is taking place in the group. Categories are: *very rapid, rapid, moderate, slow*, and *very slow.*

rlg chg: Openness to religious change. This is an estimate of how open the group is to religious change of any kind. Categories are: *very open, somewhat open, indifferent, somewhat closed*, and *very closed.*

att chr: Attitude toward Christianity. This is an estimate of the opennness of the group to Christianity in particular. Categories are: *strongly favorable, somewhat favorable, indifferent, somewhat opposed*, and *strongly opposed.*

religion: Religious composition. This indicates the primary religion(s) found among members of the group. The percentage shown under **adherents** estimates the percentage of the group who would say that they follow the religion(s) listed. The percentage under **practicing** indicates the number who *actively* practice the religion(s) listed (in the opinion of the researcher or reporter).

churches: Churches and missions. This indicates the primary Christian churches or missions, national or foreign, that are active in the area where the people group is concentrated. The figure under **members** is the approximate number of full members of this church or mission denomination from the people group. The figure under **community** is the approximate number of adherents (including children) to the denomination or mission from the people group.

profile: Evangelism profile. People tend to come to Christ in more or less well defined steps. This scale (based on a scale developed by Dr. James Engel of the Wheaton Graduate School) indicates the approximate percentage of the group who are at various levels of awareness of the gospel. The scale ranges from people with no awareness of Christianity to those who are active propagators of the gospel. A further explanation of this useful tool may be found in Edward Dayton's chapter earlier in this book.

nc: Not compiled. Whenever this appears in any category, it indicates that the information has not yet been received by the MARC computers. In future volumes of this series, information will be added as it becomes available.

Following the data table with the basic information about the people group are several paragraphs further detailing the characteristics and situation of the group.

AFAR   marc id: 21
Ethiopia

alt names:	Danakil
	Adal
	Afaraf
	Tseltal

pop:	300,000
also in:	Djibouti
distinct:	religion
	language

languages:		uses	speak	read
	Afar	V	100%	nc
	Arabic	T	40%	8%

| chr lit: | 20% |
| scripture: | nc |

| rlg chg: | somewhat closed |
| att chr: | somewhat opposed |

religion:		adherents	practicing
	Christianity	1%	nc
	Islam-Animist	99%	nc

churches:		members	community
	Roman Catholic	250	250
	Protestant	nc	nc

"It's a foul place anyway—hot, dirty, a no-man's land. It's time to go," said a French business man as he prepared to leave Djibouti at its birth as a nation in June, 1977. Djibouti, the last European colony in Africa to gain independence is a rock-strewn wasteland of volcanic and coral origin. At the time of independence, it had no attorneys or accountants, only three college graduates, and virtually no skilled labor. The only known resources were sand, salt, and a strategic location on the narrowest part of the strait between Africa and Arabia. The recent Ethiopian-Somalia conflict had made things even worse.

Djibouti and Ethiopia are the home of the Afar, a tribe of Ethiopian origin, and the Issas, of Somali origin—traditional fighting cousins. To be a virtuous Afar is to be tough, warlike, and quick to take revenge. Vengeance killing is the final proof of honor and the finest demonstration of manly virtue. The strikingly beautiful Afar women

EXPANDED DESCRIPTIONS

despise the suitor who has never killed a man, and long for the one with the iron bracelet indicating he has killed ten men.

Afar villages are tents surrounded by their camels, scattered seemingly without reason across the shadeless terrain. The men wear long flowing robes. Women often go bare-breasted. While most manage adequately in the desert, many Afar are now drifting towards the furnace-hot city of Djibouti. There is little chance, though, of their participating in the meager cash economy. Incredibly, almost 80 percent in the city are unemployed.

While nominally Muslim, Islamic orthodoxy is practiced only in the coastal regions. As with other groups in the horn of Africa, reaching the Afar for Christ may depend mainly on quality *oral* presentations of the gospel by trained but still semi-nomadic evangelists. Cassettes with simple Bible stories and music enjoyed by the Afar might be effective as it has been with nomadic Somali in Kenya.

```
AHL-I-HAQQ IN IRAN                                      marc id:   1237

alt names:   Ahl-i-Hakk

pop:         500,000
also in:     Afghanistan
             India
             Lebanon
             Egypt
             Turkey
distinct:    ethnicity
             religion

languages:                            uses      speak      read
             Kurdish dialects         VG        100%       25%
             Farsi                    TSW       60%        25%

chr lit:     25%
scripture:   portions

rate chg:    rapid
rlg chg:     somewhat open
att chr:     somewhat favorable

religion:                             adherents
             Islam                    100%

churches:                             members
             Kermanshah Evangelical   10
```

profile: 0% No awareness of Christianity
           90% Aware of existence
           5% Some knowledge of gospel
           4% Understand the message
           1% Personal challenge to receive Christ
           0% Decision to accept Christ
           0% In a fellowship
           0% Propagators of the gospel

The Ahl-i-Haqq, or People of Truth, are extensively dispersed in the Middle East with communities extending from Egypt and Greece in the west to Afghanistan and India in the east. They are composed of several ethnic groups. In Iran, they are mostly found among the Kurds, though several other tribal groups contain members of this sect. In Iran, they are found in the mountainous Kermanshah region and the western Khorasan Province (adjacent to Afghanistan). The men are physically distinguished by their large moustaches.

Iranian Ahl-i-Haqq number perhaps 500,000, although actual numbers are hard to determine due to the secretiveness of the sect. They have been mentioned in several mission articles as being particularly open to the gospel in Iran. However, very little work has been done.

The sect is derived from Shiah Islam as well as several other religious streams, including Christianity. They hold an incarnational view of God. Christ is accepted as a manifestation of God by some members of this sect. However, they hold to other non-Christian beliefs such as reincarnation and a pantheon of manifestations of God.

There has been some response to Christianity from members of this sect. Two of the best known evangelists in Iran are former members of this group. The Kermanshah Evangelical Church had a proposal to work among these people in 1975; but, it is not known whether this was done. They do allow free conversion from their group. Their secretive nature makes them a difficult group to penetrate, however, it might be possible to place workers in living situations among them.

AJURAN   marc id: 467
Kenya

alt names: Somali

pop: 17,098
also in: Somalia
            Ethiopia

EXPANDED DESCRIPTIONS

distinct: language
                ethnicity

languages:		uses	speak	read
	Somali (Ajuran)	V	100%	2%
	Boran		10%	nc
	Swahili		5%	nc

chr lit: 99%
scripture: Bible

rlg chg: somewhat closed
att chr: somewhat opposed

religion:		adherents
	Islam	99%
	Christianity	1%

churches: Roman Catholic
            Africa Inland
            Anglican

The Lenana 75 Conference in Nairobi indicated that "there is virtually no Christian work which is being done in the Northeastern Province (of Kenya) where most of the Somali live." The Ajuran are one of six Somali groups (including the Ogaden, Degodia, Gurreh, Hawiyah, and Gosha) who wander the dry pastureland of Kenya with little Christian attention.

Somali is derived from the Arabic words that mean "possessors of wealth." Like other Somalis, the wealth of the Ajuran consists of herds of cattle, sheep, and especially the highly prized camel. Damage for injuries, bride wealth, and ritual sacrifices are all evaluated in terms of camels and goats.

Most of the year is spent in herding camps with a few closely related families, moving about the countryside in response to available water and pasture. The Ogaden warfare has had a destabilizing effect on the Somalis of Kenya, but the former guerrilla warfare (ending in 1968) against the Kenya government to unite with Somalia has not reappeared.

Though they are strongly Islamic, few have a deep understanding of their faith. Women, though treated as inferiors, are not secluded. Though Somali scripture is available, literacy is too low to think scripture distribution would have a significant impact. Instead, experiments using field-developed cassettes are underway. Audience tests are made to ensure music preferred by the Somali is used and

Bible stories and scripture read which will acquaint them with Jesus Christ and arouse their curiosity for more.

The Mennonite Board of Kenya has taken interest in the evangelization of the Northeastern Province. So has the Mount Kenya East Diocese of the Anglican Church, which has established an evangelist training school at Embu. Already, the Anglicans are working with the nomadic Gabra and are developing methods applicable to the Ajuran. Converted Somalis, utilizing oral communication methods and living seminomadically would be the most effective evangelists.

```
AKHA                                            marc id:  609
Thailand

pop:        9,916
also in:    Burma
            Peoples Republic of China
distinct:   language
            ethnicity

languages:                      uses      speak      read
            Akha                 V         100%       1%
            Northern Thai        T          25%       nc
            Lahu                            40%       nc

chr lit:    95%
scripture:  New Testament

rlg chg:    somewhat closed
att chr:    somewhat favorable

religion:                       adherents
            Ancestor Worship        99%
            Christianity             1%

churches:                               community
            American Baptist               30
            Overseas Missionary Fellowship 100
            Roman Catholic                 70
```

The roots of the Akha are to be found in mountainous Yunnan in China where 60,000 continue to live. Pressured by the expansion of the Han Chinese, they have migrated into Burma, Laos, Vietnam, and Thailand. Their entrance into Thailand from Burma is recent, occurring about 35 years ago.

With them, they have brought a distinctive life-style focused on villages built near ridge tops in mountainous regions. They subsist on rice, maize, millet, tobacco, and other crops grown with the slash-and-burn method. Opium poppies are grown and its product sold to itinerant traders. Pigs and chickens are not only important protein sources, but crucial in the ritual sacrificial system. Hunting and fishing also contribute meat to the diet.

Village populations vary from 200-1500. Population estimates run as high as 30,000 in Thailand with an overall Akha population of 125,000. Households are composed of a man, his wife (or wives), and married sons with their families. This extended-family living pattern means the average household numbers ten persons.

Family, and ancestors are important in Akha religious life. Village gates are ritually decorated with male and female fertility figures and carved figures representing the eight powerful spirits to warn evil spirits not to enter. The family spirits are represented by a basket kept in the house or by a sacred post. Shamans and other religious practitioners deal supernaturally with illness. Physical medical techniques center on the use of opium and bloodletting.

Their language is related to Lahu and Lisu and many Akha are bi- or trilingual. General literacy rates are so low that scripture distribution in other than oral forms is relatively meaningless. When approached in a culturally sensitive way, they show interest in and appreciation for Christianity. Evangelism encompassing whole extended families and villages in multiindividual, mutually interdependent decisions for Christ will be the only mechanism by which the Akha will turn to Christ in large numbers.

```
ALAWITES                                        marc id:  1104
Syria

alt names:  Nasranies

pop:        600,000
distinct:   ethnicity
            religion
            sense of unity

languages:                      uses      speak      read
            Arabic              VTSG      100%       nc

chr lit:    50%
scripture:  Bible

rate chg:   slow
rlg chg:    somewhat closed
att chr:    indifferent
```

religion:		adherents	practicing
	Islam	100%	80%

profile:
- 0% No awareness of Christianity
- 90% Aware of existence
- 10% Some knowledge of gospel
- 0% Understand the message
- 0% Personal challenge to receive Christ
- 0% Decision to accept Christ
- 0% In a fellowship
- 0% Propagators of the gospel

Though Alawite beliefs predate Islam, they now consider themselves Muslims. They are not accepted as Muslims, however, by conservative Sunni Muslims, the majority religion in Syria. Indeed, some points in the Alawite creed are far from Islam—some are apparently borrowed from Christianity; some are entirely their own.

Most distinctive in their faith is their belief in a divine Trinity. Ali, the son-in-law of the Prophet Muhammed, is regarded as the incarnation of the Trinity and is known as "The Meaning". Muhammed, whom Ali is said to have created of his own light is known as "The Name". A figure known as Salman the Persian is called "The Gate". Thus, the Alawite catechism is expressed in the formula: "I turn to the Gate; I bow before the Name; I adore the Meaning". Their testimonial prayer says "there is no God but Ali."

Alawites also believe that all were at first stars in the heavens who fell to the earth because of disobedience. Faithful Alawites believe that after seven transformations they may again take their place among the stars, where Ali is the prince. However, those guilty of sin may be reborn as Christians among whom they will remain until atonement is complete, and those falling from the faith will be reborn as animals. Many of the other tenets of the Alawite faith are secret. They do not worship in mosques, and only the men take part in the worship.

The Alawites are Syria's largest religious minority and live chiefly along the coast in Al Ladhiqiyah Province where they form over 60 percent of the population. Their social and economic position is generally below that of the Sunni and many are tenants and sharecroppers working on Sunni land. When they do own land, it is usually inferior in quality.

It is apparent that there are analogies that may be drawn between the Alawite faith and Christianity. Obviously, too, there are immense

EXPANDED DESCRIPTIONS

differences and difficulties in approaching and communicating with these people on matters of faith. Converted Moslems and/or other Mid-Easterners might be most effective.

```
ASMAT                                          marc id:  205
Indonesia

alt names:   Manowey

pop:         30,000
distinct:    language
             ethnicity

languages:                      uses      speak      read
             Asmat                V        100%       10%
             Indonesian           T         10%        nc

chr lit:     5%
scripture:   portions

rlg chg:     somewhat closed
att chr:     indifferent

religion:                       adherents
             Animism               90%
             Protestant             2%
             Roman Catholic         8%

churches:                       community
             Agats Post Church          nc
             Evangelical Alliance Mission   100
```

Fifteen years ago, the Asmat were the fascination of the an-thropological world. They were "living museum pieces in a museum of early man." It was they who presumably killed, and possibly ate, Michael Rockefeller on his ill-fated expedition in search of Asmat wood carvings in 1962.

The bold Asmat carvings are symbolic of their very existence. Their legendary creator, Fumeripits, is said to have begun carving statues of people to fill the empty "house" that he had built. When it was full of statues, he carved a drum and when he beat it, the figures came to life and began to dance in the Asmat way.

Fumeripits is also said to have been the first to destroy life, killing a crocodile that threatened the house he had built. Thus, they be-lieved that in the creation of life, something must be destroyed. The cannibalism of former years was a means of ensuring that the essence of the victim's life was preserved.

The Asmat carvers are still at work. Every village, large or small, seems to have one. They know, of course, that however good their carving may be or however long they may dream, their figures will never come to life. They know, too, that death is a prerequisite to life. Most, though, still do not know the one who died once and for all that all might find in him life eternal.

Life has changed rapidly for the Asmat as for other groups in Irian Jaya. Secular and material influences flood in with education and development. They do not have the luxury of choosing carefully between the beneficial and the destructive elements of modern culture being thrust upon them. Now is the time for the gospel of Christ to fill their lives and shape their destiny.

```
AZTECA                                       marc id:   284
Mexico

alt names:  Nahuatl, Mexicano

pop:        250,000
distinct:   language
            ethnicity

languages:                        uses        speak
            Nahuatl, Hidalgo       V          100%
            Spanish                T           65%

chr lit:    35%
scripture:  portions

rlg chg:    somewhat closed
att chr:    strongly favorable

religion:                         adherents
            Christo-Paganism         85%
            Christianity              2%
            Unknown                  13%

churches:   Union of Evang. Mexican Chs.
            Baptist
            Pentecostal
            Roman Catholic
```

The Nahuatl-speakig people are the largest indigenous population of Mexico, totaling 1.25 million. The Azteca are a subgroup found in the east central area. The Nahua, or "los mexicanos" as they are known popularly, are also found in Veracruz, Puebla, Guerrero, Federal District, and Hidalgo.

In so large a group, it is to be expected that there are wide differences in the degree to which they have retained traditional patterns and remain monolingual (the largest such concentration is in Puebla) or have ladinoized and are bilingual. The vast majority live in small villages and towns surrounded by the fields cultivated by the Azteca men.

Family life is central and marriage tends to be stable. Households are usually made up of three generations, including grandparents and grandchildren, with authority held by the husband. Almost equally important in organizing life is the ritual kinship system (*compadrazgo*) that is entered into at the baptism of children. Godparents become lifelong friends who can be depended upon for financial and social support in times of difficulty.

In each village, the Catholic church, which fronts the central plaza, symbolizes the centrality of religion in life. The people believe in a system of saints and spirits, and seek favor from the supernatural. Each village has its chosen majordomos who are responsible in a given year to carry the financial and organizational responsibility to put on fiestas and pilgrimages honoring saints. Staggering financial burdens are assumed by individuals to fulfill these duties and ensure good luck and blessings for the village and thus gain the villagers' highest respect.

Evil eyes, shamans to deal with witchcraft and sickness, and a strong identification with the Virgin of Guadelupe make up the balance of their religious world. It is believed that the Virgin of Guadelupe is mother of all "mexicanos." Facing this mixture of Christian and non-Christian ideas, evangelization has an uphill challenge.

```
BAJANIA                                      marc id:  263
Pakistan


pop:          20,000
also in:      India
distinct:     language
              ethnicity

languages:                          uses      speak      read
              Gujarati dialect       V        100%        1%
              Sindhi                 T         90%        nc
```

Barabaig

```
chr lit:     1%
scripture:   none
```

```
religion:                           adherents
             Hinduism                 99%
             Christianity              1%
```

```
churches:    Church of Pakistan
             Pentecostal
             Seventh-day Adventist
```

The Bajania are part of the depressed class of people dubbed the Harijans, "People of God," by Ghandi. Considered untouchable and polluted by the strict caste Hindu, they have never been admitted to many of the privileges and courtesies of human life.

Located in the Sindh of Pakistan they have been affected by the troubles that led to the partition of the Indian subcontinent into Pakistan and India. Many of them chose to migrate to India rather than remain a tiny minority amid a sea of Muslims.

In the early 1940s, evangelism among this minstrel caste was carried out by Christ Church (Anglican), Karachi with notable success. Over 500 were baptized and a promising movement begun. However, whether because of the Hindu reform movement, Arya Samaj, the transfer of the Anglican missionary, or migration at the partition, no Christians are now to be found among them. Where did they go? Why was a good beginning not followed by a bringing to completion of this work? The answers are hidden in history.

It is apparent that scheduled castes such as the Bajania are among the more receptive groups in Pakistan. They are invited to join a church, the vast majority of whom are converts and descendents of other Harijan Hindu castes. Two current problems exist in terms of restarting the Christward movement that began in the 1940s. First, no one is trying—no laborers are giving their witness here. Second, a distinctive strategy to reach them has not been developed. Scripture in their everyday thought forms is important for their distinct identity as a people. The promising response in the 1940s gives hope that a similar moving of God could occur in this generation. But we'll never know until it is tried.

```
BARABAIG                                  marc id:   573
Tanzania
```

```
alt names:   Brariga
```

EXPANDED DESCRIPTIONS

pop: 49,000
distinct: language
enthnicity

languages:		uses	speak	read
	Tatoga	V	100%	nc

scripture: none

religion:		adherents
	Animism	98%
	Protestant	1%
	Roman Catholic	1%

churches: Elim Pentecostal
Evangelical Lutheran
Pallotine Fathers

Change is sweeping across Barabaig country. Limitations are being placed on the number of cattle they can own, which has been received just as we would accept limitations on the amount of money we can own. Cattle raiding is now forbidden and severly punished by the Tanzanian government. "Ritual murder," which formerly was a primary means of gaining status and respect, has recently been curbed by hanging the perpetrator and by rounding up young Barabaig men for national service as both punishment and reeducation.

There was a time when the Barabaig, a cattle-herding people just south of Lake Eyassi in Tanzania, were the scourge of the area. Cattle herds could be increased as fast as possible, through dispute settlements, dowry, raids, or other means. A man could be uniquely rewarded for killing either wild beasts or neighboring tribe members, both of which are considered "enemies of the people." For such a manly act, he could anoint his head with butter and travel with all his girlfriends from place to place singing his kill song, soliciting gifts of cows or ornaments, and being showered with butter from admiring households.

Such "honors" were rare in the difficult day to day life of the Barabaig. Syphilis, malaria, and dysentary have been distressingly common. The venereal disease and unsanitary birth practices—sometimes sitting on a small mount of cow-dung—have made childbirth and infancy precarious. Evil spirits, witches, and sorcerers are believed to plague them, necessitating all manner of precautionary and curative measures.

Christian missionary activity, begun in 1958, had little effect and

won few converts among the Barabaig until an African mission
teacher was speared and mutilated near his home in 1968. The government at that time took measures which have drastically altered the
Barabaig way of life. They have now been confronted with the social
and physical world beyond their borders and this had brought some
of the openness that characterizes peoples in transition.

```
BASOTHO, MOUNTAIN                                    marc id:  232
Lesotho

pop:        70,000
distinct:   residence

languages:                          uses      speak      read
            Southern Sesotho         V         100%       40%
            Fandgold                             80%       nc
            English                               2%       nc

chr lit:    80%
scripture:  Bible

rlg chg:    somewhat open
att chr:    strongly favorable

religion:                       adherents
            Animism                85%
            Protestant              1%
            Roman Catholic         13%
            Other Christian         1%

churches:                       community
            Roman Catholic        9,000
            Lesotho Evangelical     700
            Anglican                200
            Zionist                  80
            Mahon Mission            30
```

Travelers entering the little country of Lesotho pass under an
archway with the phrase *Kena Ka Khotso,* "enter in peace." But most
Basotho (pronounced bah-soo-too) have never known the only true
peace that comes from above.

Rugged, beautiful Lesotho ranges from five thousand feet in the
western lowlands to over eleven thousand feet in the Muluti and
Drakensberg ranges. It is often called the "roof of Africa." Snow
skiing, horseback riding, fishing in well-stocked streams, and
gambling in Maseru's casinos attract people and money from South

EXPANDED DESCRIPTIONS

Africa to this "Switzerland of Africa".

Apart from the tourist industry, however, the Basotho have few resources or wage-earning possibilities. This tiny country, completely surrounded by South Africa, is poor and overpopulated. Huge numbers emigrate to South Africa to work in the mines, causing hardships and disruption for Basotho families.

Lesotho has a long missionary history, the first missionaries arriving in 1833. Close ties were made early with the famous king and founder of the nation, Moshoeshoe I (pronounced mo-shay-shay), so Christianity made good progress. Education has played an important part in the missionaries' work, which has resulted in one of the highest literacy rates in Africa—almost 60 percent.

The Basotho have had the Bible in their language for seventy years. More than forty Christian agencies are or have poured funds and personnel into the country. Still, though there are signs of life, fewer than 15 percent of the Basotho are practicing Christians. The political situation in neighboring South Africa has bred a mistrust of the whites and successful ministry to the Basotho will probably require sensitive teams of blacks and whites or strongly committed Basotho Christians.

BHILS   marc id: 291
India

alt names: Dangis
             Adivasis

pop: 800,000
distinct: language
             ethnicity

languages:		uses	speak	read
	Dangi	V	100%	nc

scripture: Bible

rlg chg: nc
att chr: somewhat favorable

religion:		adherents
	Christianity	1%
	Animism	99%

158

churches: Christian & Missionary Alliance
             Methodist

The Bhils, India's third largest tribe, is one of the ancient tribal groups of India. Widely scattered through central India in Gujarat, Rajasthan, Maharashtra, and Madhya Pradesh, most occupy settled villages where they grow dry crops such as millet, maize, wheat, barley and pulses. Some work as laborers, watchmen, or sell grass and firewood for cash. Their traditional way of life, which included hunting and shifting agriculture, has given way completely to village life.

Most are viewed by neighboring populations as superstitious. They worship various dieties (including the tiger and serpent) and live in great fear of the evil eye. The evil eye is essentially a fear of jealousy, a feeling that some envious person might cast an evil spell and harm them or their family. Members of the same family may even eat in different corners of the house in order to avoid the evil eye. Shamans are called in for curing animals that are thought sick because of the evil eye. But all of this traditional religious belief exists in association with the Hindu practices which they have adopted. The worship of Hanuman is important.

There have been several Hindu sectarian movements. A strong Bhakta or devotee movement known as Bhagat occured in western Madhya Pradesh. Its followers practiced devotion to Rama and abstained from eating meat and wine. They now form the top of the three-caste tier with ordinary Bhils in the middle and Christian Bhils at the bottom in Madhya Pradesh.

A strong "original inhabitant" (*adivasi*) movement has developed which is strengthening tribal pride and self-identity. Assimilation to general Hindu culture is occuring but its speed has slackened in recent years as the *adivasi* movement has grown. Family respect is strong among Bhils and there is a sense of continuity of the living with the dead.

BLACK CARIBS IN BELIZE   marc id: 252

pop: 10,000
also in: Guatemala
              Honduras
distinct: language
              ethnicity

EXPANDED DESCRIPTIONS

languages:		uses	speak	read
	Moreno	V	100%	nc
	Spanish	T	90%	50%
	English		2%	nc

chr lit: 70%
scripture: portions

rlg chg: somewhat open
att chr: somewhat favorable

religion:		adherents
	Christo-Paganism	95%
	Christianity	1%
	Unknown	4%

churches:		community
	Plymouth Brethren	nc
	United Brethren in Christ	nc
	Mennonite	30

The Black Caribs of Belize (also Honduras and Guatemala) have a unique blend of African and Indian culture. Slaves from British and Spanish vessels were at times shipwrecked in the Caribbean. Others escaped or were liberated from their masters. Many of these slaves settled in St. Vincent in the early 1600s where they intermarried with the Carib Indians. By the late 1700s, the mixture of these two races totaled 5,000.

Because of their rebellious tendencies, they posed a threat to British authorities on St. Vincent. In 1797, the British deported them en masse to Roatan, 1800 miles away off the coast of Honduras. They migrated from there to Honduras, Belize, or Guatemala. A very important annual celebration for them is a reenactment of their landing on the coast of Belize. Today, about 25 villages are mostly Black Carib, including in Belize the towns of Stann Creek, Punta Gorda and three other villages.

While marriage patterns are informal—mostly common law—the Black Caribs are morally strict and families are strong except where employment problems have caused long separations. Most of the people still live on the coasts by fishing and small-scale agriculture. A loose and syncretistic Catholicism is practiced, but their primary religion consists of ancient rites and black magic which propitiate local spirits and the ghosts of ancestors. Shamans, trances, and excited dances characterize their worship of the all-important ancestors.

160

Protestant missions groups have found house visitation and Bible studies to be effective in ministering to them. Efforts to force them into Ladino (westernized, Spanish-speaking) cultures and the use of Spanish in the church services hinders evangelization. Scriptures are limited in Moreno and little effort has been made to extend the availability of scripture for the Black Caribs.

```
BRAO                                          marc id:  108
Laos

alt names:  Lave
            Love

pop:        18,000
also in:    Kampuchea, Democratic
            Thailand
distinct:   language
            ethnicity

languages:                        uses    speak    read
            Brao                   V       100%      nc
            Lao                    T        nc       nc

scripture:  nc

rlg chg:    somewhat closed

religion:                         adherents
            Animism                  99%
            Christianity              1%
```

The Brao are one of the 25-30 tribal groups that make up the Mon-Khmer people. The Mon-Khmer are thought to be the original inhabitants of Laos, conquered years ago by a wave of Tai-speaking Lao invaders. Most have been pushed up into the mountainous areas where farming is less productive.

Located in a wide area from northern Attopeu province south into Cambodia, the Brao have been subject to the almost constant warfare in Southeast Asia over the past 20 years. Some have migrated into northeastern Thailand across the Mekong river into lower-lying flatlands.

The Brao live in large, fortified round villages during the dry season for security reasons. Only in times of relative peace do these large villages split into 5-10 smaller villages due to internal conflict. During the rainy season, the Brao move out to their hillside plots of

EXPANDED DESCRIPTIONS

dry rice. There they occupy makeshift shelters and till their slash-and-burn fields until the harvest. Fishing provides a rather reliable source of protein.

Villages are organized as independent units. Each Village is governed by a headman but there are no further recognized lines of political authority that might unify this group. A large communal house serves as the central axis of village life, other houses being arranged about it like spokes of a wheel. Polygamy is practiced.

They have had very little contact with Christians or the gospel. When Laos came under control of the Pathet Lao, there were probably no more than a dozen Christians and no known continuing witness. The present political and military situation in Laos and Cambodia means evangelization will largely be accomplished among Brao in northeast Thailand. But it will require Christians who are willing to brave a difficult security risk and whose presence will be approved by the Thai government.

```
BUSHMEN (KUNG)                                    marc id:  562
Namibia

pop:        10,000
also in:    Angola
distinct:   language
            ethnicity

languages:                         uses      speak      read
            Xu                      V         100%       nc

scripture:  none

att chr:    indifferent

religion:                             adherents
            Animism                      90%
            Protestant                   10%

churches:   Evangelical Lutheran
            Evan. Luth. Ovambokavango
            Nederduitse Gereformeerde Kerk
```

The children are spell bound. They sit listening with rapt attention as the old man spins a tale about the ancient hunts. He gestures, immitating first the ostrich, then the elephant, then the hyena. The imitations are stunningly accurate, catching precisely the mannerisms and movements of the animals. Later, the group may break

162

into singing and dancing, both for fun and for ritual as they purify themselves for future hunts.

The Kung are one of many small tribes of bushmen who live in and around the Kalahari desert of Namibia and Botswana. They are essentially refugees who, as evidenced by their rock paintings, have historically moved down the African continent from the Sahara to South Africa. Under pressure of Bantu peoples in the north and Europeans in the south, they have squeezed into a land in which only nomadic hunters and gatherers can live.

The Kung move about in small bands of 20-60, the men doing the hunting and the women gathering wild vegetable foods. Their only personal property are their items of clothing, digging sticks, food scrapers and ornaments. There are no extended families and no chiefs, but older men act as leaders in determining migration patterns. Likewise, there is no government, no formal authorities, no system of laws or punishment. The Kung live by complex patterns of defined social relationships. Every Kung knows exactly where he stands in relationship to everyone else—even strangers—and how he should act toward them. The system provides psychological security and promotes peace. When grievances do occur, they are settled privately and violence is extremely rare among these gentle people.

Bushmen do not make a cult of their ancestors, but do believe in the continuing presence and importance of the spirits of their dead. The Kung believe in two supernatural beings: one is the creator of this world and of life, while the other is responsible for sickness and death. Other religious beliefs are kept as secrets and mysteries from all but the mature and initiated Kung men.

It is apparent that innovative strategies and nomadic life-styles are necessary for effective ministry to the Kung. Music, drama, and storytelling will very likely be the most important media for communicating the gospel to these people.

```
CHAMULA                                    marc id:  162
Mexico

pop:        50,000
distinct:   language
            ethnicity

languages:                      uses      speak     read
            Tzotzil (Chamula)     V        100%      10%
            Spanish               T          5%      nc
```

EXPANDED DESCRIPTIONS

chr lit: 10%
scripture: portions

rlg chg: somewhat open
att chr: strongly opposed

religion: adherents
              Christo-Paganism   99%
              Christianity   1%

churches: community
              Indigenous   300
              Roman Catholic   nc

John the Baptist looked high and low before finding so fair a people and beautiful a country in which to build his church. Chamula was his choice and now as its patron saint he presides over the saints and brings blessing and bounty when he is well served.

Chamula is the major center of a mountainous region where descendents of the Mayans continue an ancient way of life under a modern facade. Forcibly Christianized by Spanish conquest, the actual concepts and practices of present day life are strikingly similar to preconquest Mayan life.

Chamulans are maize farmers, cultivating both highland and lowland fields. The true owners of the land are believed to be the earth lords, supernatural beings that inhabit the caves and mountains. Safety and prosperity in "their land" requires offerings of "food" in the guise of candles, incense, and rum. Crosses are gateways into this world and are found in homesteads, waterholes, sheep pens, cornfields, and mountains where offerings are regularly made.

Most of the year is spent in vigorous labor in the fields in small hamlets scattered across the landscape. Market days and major fiestas bring Chamulans into the town that acts as a focus for the people as a whole. Here is located the civil and religious center. A municipio president is responsible for orderly life and he is assisted by 68 elders who carry the burden or "cargo" of responsibility for maintaining community life. Each "cargo" holder has specific responsibilities for a year, paying personally for the expenses of the office.

The fiesta cycle is run by these "cargo" offices and provides a colorful punctuation to the seasons of their yearly life. Most important are the duties to care for the "saints" in the church and Saint John the Baptist, their president. While the saints look like many of the images found in cathedrals everywhere, to the Chamulans they are earth

Chinese Hakka

lords who have chosen the church as home.

This fantastic syncretism with its strong and intimate connection to the Chamulan self and community identity is the chief problem in communicating the gospel. Bible translation, community decision for Christ, and witness by fellow Mayan Indians are keys to the evangelization of the Chamula.

CHINESE HAKKA OF TAIWAN   marc id: 746

alt names: Hakka Peasant
pop: 1,750,000
distinct: sense of unity
            language
            ethnicity

languages:		uses	speak	read
	Hakka	V	100%	nc
	Mandarin	T	75%	75%
	Taiwanese (Minnan)		nc	nc

chr lit: 75%
scripture: Bible

att chr: somewhat favorable

religion:		adherents
	Christianity	1%
	Traditional Chinese	99%

churches:		community
	Southern Baptist Conv	40
	Norwegian Lutheran	50
	Presbyterian	1,174
	Swedish Holiness	55
	Assemblies of God	nc
	Roman Catholic	nc

Descendants of northern Chinese with a long and remarkable history, the Hakkas ("sojourners") speak their own Chinese dialect and maintain a strong ethnic identity as a distinctive group. The majority of the Hakka continue to dwell in Kuangtung province of South China. Nearly three million live overseas in countries other than Taiwan, concentrated especially in Thailand, Malaysia, and Indonesia.

Traditionally they have been considered resistant to the gospel in Taiwan since they have a much lower percentage of Christians than other ethnic Chinese. David Liao's book, *The Unresponsive,* offers

165

EXPANDED DESCRIPTIONS

detailed proof that the Hakka are more neglected by the church than resistant. Their resistance has been to a Christianity which has come to them in other Chinese dialects and without deep sensitivity to their particular consciousness as a people distinct from the majority Minnan or the dominant Mandarin-speaking mainlanders.

Cultural conservatism still exists and ancestor worship is a problem which the church must face creatively if it is to shepherd these people. But by far the major problem has been the lack of incarnating Christianity into their own cultural forms. Churches and mission agencies have not designated much personnel or finances specifically to focus on reaching this Chinese dialect group. Also, the larger Minnan dialect church has been reluctant to acknowledge and permit the Hakka identity to emerge in church life and evangelism.

Modernization of social and economic structures is a fact of Taiwan's future. Old symbols of the Hakka culture are being exchanged for new ones. Secularization is making major inroads. This generation is crucial in determing whether the Hakka will find a new identity in Christ.

```
CHINESE IN UNITED KINGDOM                      marc id:   1225

pop:        105,000
distinct:   occupation
            ethnicity
            economic status

languages:                         uses        speak       read
            Cantonese              V           nc          nc
            Mandarin               V           nc          nc
            English                TS          nc          nc

scripture:  Bible

rlg chg:    indifferent
att chr:    somewhat favorable

religion:                          adherents
            Roman Catholic           1%
            Protestant               2%
            Traditional Chinese     60%
            Secularism              37%

churches:                          community
            Chinese Oseas. Chr. Msn.  2,000
            Roman Catholic            nc
```

profile: 3% No awareness
            7% Aware of existence
           75% Some knowledge of gospel
            8% Understand the message
            3% Personal challenge
            1% Decision
            2% In a fellowship
            1% Propagators of the gospel

As is true of most of the Chinese in Europe, the Chinese of England are heavily involved in the restaurant business (the heaviest concentration found in the London area). Approximately 95 percent are so employed, with three percent in nursing and two percent in other trades such as export-import, leatherwear, banking, and grocery. Most of the restaurant people speak their own Chinese dialect, but also have learned English in order to run their business.

Their distinctive occupational situation creates a problem in reaching into the some 2,000 restaurants and grills with the gospel. They have long working hours, usually from 10 a.m. until midnight, with a break of three hours in the afternoon. It is tiring and strenous work. Workers normally have a day off, taken in turn from Monday to Thursday, but not on weekends when business is good. It is difficult to find a common time, except in afternoon break hours, when workers can gather as a group for worship or study.

Most of the restaurant workers have lesser degrees of education than the intellectuals and professionals that are also found in England. Salary is high. Social gatherings are normally with other Chinese people. While most of them claim to be Buddhists, the actual "religion" seems to be secularism and a concern for economic advancement. Concern for ancestors remains strong.

Receptivity has been higher among the nurses and professional groups that are the smallest percentage of the Chinese population. If the restaurant workers are to be reached, it will require a new approach. Ideally, persons who are restaurant owners or workers themselves would be the best persons to do the evangelism.

CHINESE REFUGEES IN FRANCE   marc id: 1226

alt names: Indo-China Refugees

pop: 100,000
also in: Netherlands
             German Federal Rep.

EXPANDED DESCRIPTIONS

distinct: ethnicity
             legal status
             significant problems

languages: uses   speak   read
             Mandarin   V   nc   nc
             Tien-Chiu   V   nc   nc
             French   T   nc   nc

scripture: Bible

rate chg: rapid
rlg chg: somewhat open
att chr: somewhat favorable

religion: adherents
             Roman Catholic   1%
             Protestant   1%
             Traditional Chinese   88%
             Secularism   10%

churches: community
             Christian & Msny Alliance   150
             Chinese Oseas. Chr. Msn.   nc
             Roman Catholic   nc

profile: 9% No awareness of Christianity
             15% Aware of existence
             70% Some knowledge of gospel
              2% Understand the message
              2% Personal challenge to receive Christ
              1% Decision to accept Christ
              1% In a fellowship
              0% Propagators of the gospel

   Streaming out of refugee camps in Saigon and Thailand have
come an enormous number of Chinese refugees. The conflict in Vietnam, as well as the subsequent events in Laos and Cambodia, have
been viewed as detrimental to the future of the Chinese merchants
and business. Considered part of the well-to-do oppressors of the
"people," the Chinese fear for their future in communist-dominated
governments. Approximately two hundred fifty new Chinese arrive in
France every month.
   They can be divided into two main groups. Those who have settled
down and have jobs are being spread throughout various cities and
areas of France. Those who are still in the refugee camps and not
certain of their future are concentrated near Paris. Both groups are
receptive to the Gospel, but the latter group is much more so. As long
168

as their situation is still unsettled, their receptivity is high. Once they find jobs and move out of the camp area and begin moving up socially, their receptivity decreases.

The need for reaching them is strategically urgent at the present time. The chief obstacle to gathering in the harvest seems to be the lack of Chinese evangelists and churchmen. There are only two small Chinese churches in the Paris area. One church is made up of recent refugees. The other is made up of the numerically larger Chinese restaurant workers.

```
CHITRALIS                                        marc id:  1234
Pakistan

pop:        120,000
distinct:   language
            ethnicity
            kinship
            sense of unity
            discrimination

languages:                          uses      speak      read
            Khuwar                   VG         100%      nc
            Urdu                     TSW          2%       1%

scripture:  none

rate chg:   moderate
rlg chg:    somewhat closed
att chr:    somewhat opposed

religion:                        adherents      practicing
            Islam                   80%            16%
            Animism                 20%            20%

profile:    85% No awareness of Christianity
            10% Aware of existence
             5% Some knowledge of gospel
             0% Understand the message
             0% Personal challenge to receive Christ
             0% Decision to accept Christ
             0% In a fellowship
             0% Propagators of the gospel
```

These are the people who live in the northern-most district of Pakistan, pressed up against the mountain borders of Afghanistan and Russia. They are somewhat heterogeneous. The majority of them are known as Khos and their language is called Khowar, as well as

EXPANDED DESCRIPTIONS

Chitrali. This former princely state, due to its snow-bound isolation for six months of the year, has seen very little development.

The land is characterized by mountain ranges with not enough arable land to support its population. The majority of the people are shepherds with mixed flocks of goats and sheep. Staple food supplies are flown in when the roads are closed. Recently, the Pakistan Army moved a contingent in for strategic reasons and the government began a drive to promote tourism in the picturesque green river valleys.

Because of its extreme isolation, the people are quite different in customs and language from the other mountain tribes. Some of them are Sunni (orthodox) Muslims, and perhaps half are Ismailis of the Shiah branch of Islam. In neither case is Islam strictly observed. There is still evidence of shamans who are the priests of animistic religious practices that predate the coming of Islam to the area.

Change is coming because of migration and government programs. In the wintertime, thousands of young men move to the plains and hire out as laborers on road-building programs. They bring back to the valley the new ideas they have learned while living among other types of Pathans. Society is roughly divided into the nobility of the ruling family (now on government stipend), the lesser officials and town people, and the shepherd/farmer class.

The only Christians are a handful of government employees from other ethnic backgrounds. Itinerant evangelists have found these people somewhat receptive and among the literate there is a desire for Christian scripture. Because it is a sensitive border area, foreigners are discouraged from residing there, but Pakistani Christians have free access to the region.

COLOUREDS OF SOUTH AFRICA   marc id: 1217

pop:	2,000,000
distinct:	ethnicity
	social class
	discrimination
	legal status
	significant problems

languages:		uses	speak	read
	English	VTWG	50%	50%
	Afrikaanse	SG	75%	70%

| chr lit: | 75% |
| scripture: | Bible |

```
rate chg:   moderate
rlg chg:    somewhat open
att chr:    indifferent
```

religion:

	adherents	practicing
Roman Catholic	5%	2%
Protestant	70%	15%
Islam	20%	nc
Unknown	5%	nc

churches:

	community
Dutch Reformed	400,000
Anglican	260,000
Methodist	120,000

profile:

```
0% No awareness of Christianity
0% Aware of existence
40% Some knowledge of gospel
40% Understand the message
10% Personal challenge to receive Christ
0% Decision to accept Christ
5% In a fellowship
5% Propagators of the gospel
```

The coloureds (those of mixed black and white ancestry) are a people without an identity. Their description in race-conscious South Africa is entirely in terms of what they are not (e.g. not white, not Turk or Asian, not bushmen, etc.), rather than in terms of what they are. Very legitimately, they want to be accepted as white, for to be such would immediately mean better jobs, pay, housing, and opportunities. They are thankful that they are not black since there is greater discrimination against blacks. But they are not "proud" to be coloured in the sense that Zulus or Xhosas are proud to be who they are.

Identity ambiguity for coloureds is also a problem in work and family life. They are never permitted to be in authority over whites and the pay for the same work, if such jobs can be found, will always be less than for whites. Yet the coloured is at a disadvantage in the competition with blacks for unskilled work, since blacks work for even less. Thus to provide for their families, more than half of the women have to work, mostly as domestic servants.

Christianity, especially in the form of the Dutch Reformed church, is perceived as the oppressor's religion. For the religious, the Anglican faith and Islam are becoming more popular. Sensitive, color-blind, English approaches may be most effective in reaching this people of South Africa for Christ.

EXPANDED DESCRIPTIONS

```
COMORIANS
Comoros                                            marc id:  139

pop:        300,000
distinct:   language
            ethnicity

languages:                          uses      speak     read
            Comorian (Shingazidja)   V         85%       25%
            French                   T         15%       nc
            Arabic                             nc        nc
            Swahili                            nc        nc

scripture:  nc

att chr:    indifferent

religion:                           adherents
            Islam                     99%
            Christianity               1%

churches:                           community
            Roman Catholic            3,000
            Africa Inland Mission        40
```

Ruled for 150 years by the French, the Comoro Islands obtained independence in 1975. Virtually all the doctors and teachers left at the time. Emergency medical care was provided by an Africa Inland Mission doctor. The leaders of the country requested further help and for a time there were about 15 missionaries in residence on the islands. Most were to be found on the Grande Comore, site of the capitol and largest population concentration—(150,000). Recently they were expelled.

Grande Comore, Moheli (population 12,000), and Anjouan (population 100,000) are formally independent. The fourth island of Mayotte with its associated former French garrison of Dzaoudzi (combined population of 40,000) is still held under French tutelage. In addition, 60,000 Comorians live an embattled existence on Madagascar and are being repatriated because of hostilities from the Malagasy peoples which have led to serious bloodshed.

French colonialism existed primarily in terms of control and neglect. The legacy of that colonialism places the Comoro Islands among the dozen poorest nations of the world. With but one physician for every 35,000 (the U.S. average is approximately 61 doctors for 35,000), an infant mortality rate of 160 children for each 1,000 born, and a soft drink bottling plant as the only industry, the nation faces tremendous needs for nation development in the future. Bananas and coconuts represent the major factor in the economy.

Though the nation is staunchly Muslim, a new law has been passed permitting freedom of religion. In fact, the Comoros are the southern-most extremity of the Islamic World.

The Comorians are a mixed population that stem from a history of Arab dominance. At one time, small sultanates existed and the Islamic elite ruled over the blacks and poorer Muslims. Until recently, there were distinct Arab, freemen, and slave quarters in all towns.

```
CUNA
Colombia                                      marc id:  9

alt names:   Tule

pop:         600
also in:     Panama
distinct:    language
             ethnicity

languages:                     uses      speak     read
             Cuna               V        100%      nc
             Spanish            T         50%      20%

chr lit:     80%
scripture:   nc

rlg chg:     somewhat closed
att chr:     indifferent

religion:                      adherents
             Animism              93%
             Protestant            2%
             Roman Catholic        5%

churches:                      members
             OMS International      10
             Roman Catholic         nc
             Inter-American Msn. Society   nc
```

The Cuna of Colombia are part of a larger group of some 15,000. The vast majority of this group dwells in the San Blas Islands off the coast of Panama and live by fishing. There is a significant language difference, however, between the Colombian Cuna and those inhabiting the San Blas islands.

EXPANDED DESCRIPTIONS

In the Colombian settlements, the Cuna are settled along a river for a mile or so. All of the households are out of sight of the river but within easy walking distance of each other along broad shady paths. Each household has a number of nearby gardens. Fishing in the river with hook and line, spears, and poison produces much of their food. Sometimes fish are trapped by building dams and using an ingenious wicker tube.

The Cuna live in large families with an elderly patriarch, his daughters and sons-in-law working together. They are excellent craftsmen, known for the weaving of baskets. Other sources of income and food include domesticated animals, selling of coconuts, and the sale of their produce.

They have a strong belief in one supreme god, the source of all goodness who lives in heaven and punishes evil and rewards the good. They see themselves as surrounded by evil spirits which they must placate in a variety of ways. Priests or shamans act as mediators between the Cuna and the spirit world. Healing and setting things straight when affairs go wrong in a village are his specialty.

Small carved figures, *nuchus,* are found in every household. They serve to rescue one's vital force when it has been stolen by an evil spirit and brought about serious illness. Christianity has had little impact in spite of a number who have been baptized.

```
DANI, BALIEM
Indonesia                                    marc id:  1219

pop:        50,000
distinct:   language
            ethnicity
            residence

languages:                       uses      speak      read
            Dani, Grand Valley   VWG       100%       15%
            Indonesian           TG        nc         nc

scripture:  none

rate chg:   moderate
rlg chg:    somewhat closed
att chr:    indifferent

religion:                        adherents
            Protestant           5%
            Animism              95%
```

174

churches: community
              Christian & Msny. Alliance   2,500

profile: 0% No awareness of Christianity
             70% Aware of existence
             10% Some knowledge of gospel
             10% Understand the message
              5% Personal challenge to receive Christ
              0% Decision to accept Christ
              5% In a fellowship
              0% Propagators of the gospel

In March, 1941, *National Geographic* published an article entitled "Unknown New Guinea," which detailed the discovery of a group of people who had "never before seen a white man." The discovery was sensationalized as headlines of papers worldwide called the area in which they lived "cannibal valley, the valley that time forgot," and the "Incredible Shangri-la." The Baliem Dani were the point of further worldwide interest when a U.S. army plane crashed while engaging in the pastime of flying lower over the area to see the "natives," and a rescue operation was again dramatically reported in *National Geographic* (December, 1945) (also see *National Geographic* May, 1962).

The Dani culture, though rapidly changing, is indeed strange to western eyes. Westerners are impressed by such unique features as their classification of over 70 varieties of sweet potatoes. Their ash-blackened bodies, hair smeared with pig grease, and long penis gourds have been fascinating. And the reports of cannibalism, wife stealing, orgiastic feasts and barbaric funeral rites (cutting off the fingers of young girls in mourning), have seemed shocking.

Missionary and government activity among the Baliem Dani have brought these colorful "stone-age" people quickly into the 20th century, and much of their culture has now been better understood and even transformed. Many are now seeking independence such as that achieved by the Papuans. There has been some recent violence and hostage activity. Unlike their kinsmen, the Western Dani, who have come to Christ in large numbers, the Baliem Dani have remained largely resistant to the gospel. Perhaps this is because they are the conservators of traditional Dani ways. While all Danis evidently originated in the Baliem valley, the Baliem Dani are the ones who never left. They were not the pioneers, and they remain much less open to "outside" customs. Even so, evangelists from Western Dani groups have won some converts among the Baliem.

EXPANDED DESCRIPTIONS

```
DOGON
Mali                                              marc id:  150

alt names:   Habbe
             Kaco
             Dagom

pop:         312,000
also in:     Upper Volta

languages:                         uses      speak      read
             Dogon                  V        100%        nc

scripture:   New Testamant

att chr:     indifferent

religion:                          adherents
             Animism                 60%
             Islam                   30%
             Protestant               5%
             Roman Catholic           5%

churches:                          community
             Christian & Msny. Alliance   7,000
             Roman Catholic         15,600
```

Dogon country is located due south of Timbuktu on the borders of Upper Volta and Mali. There, close to the cliffs of colossal sandstone blocks, are the walled-in compound villages of the Dogon. The Dogon are divided into social classes or castes that are engaged in different productive activities. The top class is the cultivators and administrators. Below them are the various trade castes such as the smiths and the cobblers.

Land has a high premium. Often every available plot of land for miles about is cultivated. Millet, rice, and maize are grown as a staple diet. Various garden produce is also grown and sold in the markets on the plains below where the Fulani live.

Every aspect of life is related to their traditional mythology. The most important person in the society is the Hogon, who is both priest and chief of a region. He passes on and interprets the myths and theological beliefs of the Dogon. There is a strong religious awareness of the contradictions and difficulties of human life. Dogon religious art, expressed in carved masks and terracotta ancestor figures is internationally famous.

The four main tribes of Dogon society are believed to be descendants of the original four male ancestors of all humanity. Villages are

176

patrilineal, ruled by the old men. The occupational castes are separated not only by prestige but also by such cultural practices as male and female circumcision (not given to smiths and cobblers). Polygamy is present and divorce relatively easy to obtain.

Christianity is having a significant impact. The Christian and Missionary Alliance began churches in 1931 as a result of answered prayer at the end of a great famine. There are ordained Dogon pastors who are Bible school graduates, as well as catechists and churches throughout the district.

```
DRUZES
Israel                                        marc id:  1230

pop:        33,000
also in:    Lebanon
            Syria
distinct:   religion
            sense of unity

languages:                        uses      speak     read
            Arabic                VGS       100%      40%
            Hebrew                T         nc        nc

scripture:  Bible

rate chg:   moderate
rlg chg:    somewhat closed
att chr:    somewhat opposed

religion:                         adherents
            Folk Religion         100%

profile:     0% No awareness of Christianity
            70% Aware of existence
            20% Some knowledge of gospel
            10% Understand the message
             0% Personal challenge to receive Christ
             0% Decision to accept Christ
             0% In a fellowship
             0% Propagators of the gospel
```

The Druzes are a small Middle Eastern quasi-Islamic sect known for their conservatism and their belligerence. Numbering just over 300,000, about half are in Syria, while another 100,000 are in Lebanon and about 45,000 live in Israel and Jordan. While their monotheistic faith is a historical derivative of Shiah Islam, they do not regard themselves nor are they regarded by others as being a proper Muslim sect. They reject the supreme prophethood of Muhammed,

177

the Koran, and the five pillars of Islam.

The Druzes cloak their religion in secrecy. It would be considered rude to ask a Druze about his religious beliefs since the common people are supposed to be ignorant of them. There are, however, seven fundamental duties for all Druzes: 1) recognition of the divinity of Al-Hakim, the sixth caliph, 2) the negation of all non-Druze tenets, 3) eschewal of the devil, 4) acceptance of all God's acts, 5) submission to God, 6) truthfulness, and 7) mutual help and solidarity with other Druzes. The duty of truthfulness, however, applies only in relations with other Druzes. Toward non-Druzes, strict secrecy is practiced and they may deny their faith at any time if their life is in danger. The Druzes believe there are 200 million of their faith in China, a place they regard as paradise.

Druzes in Arab lands often pass themselves off as Muslims, partially for convenience, but also because of another religious tenet stating that when among Muslims, they should act like Muslims and when among Christians, they should act like Christians. The basic policy of getting along with the majority religious groups with whom they live extends to the political scene as well. In general, their approach is "whoever lets you live, and is in power, should get your support".

The problems facing the Druzes are the standard ones of a poverty stricken and backward people caught up in an industrial world. But, because they have been a reclusive, static, and ultraconservative group for a thousand years, the adjustment to modern, dynamic lifestyles is especially difficult.


```
ELITE PARISIAN
France                                           marc id:  1105

pop:          500,000
distinct:     sense of unity
              education
              social class
              economic status

languages:                              uses      speak     read
              French                    VGW       100%      100%

chr lit:      100%
scripture:    Bible
```

```
rate chg:   moderate
rlg chg:    somewhat open
att chr:    strongly favorable
```

religion:

	adherents	practicing
Roman Catholic	75%	10%
Protestant	1%	1%
Secularism	24%	

profile:
```
 0% No awareness of Christianity
 0% Aware of existence
50% Some knowledge of gospel
45% Understand the message
 3% Personal challenge to receive Christ
 0% Decision to accept Christ
 0% In a fellowship
 2% Propagators of the gospel
```

Paris is the city with the most magnificent cathedrals in the world. Yet only a tiny minority of the populace attend any services, and an even smaller percentage of either Catholics or Protestants are born-again believers. Parisians are extremely class conscious, and the classes keep to themselves.

The "upper crust" of Paris is one of the most unusual Parisian groups. Nearly all would claim to be Catholic, but very few actually know Christ as their Savior. Some are remnants of a former aristocratic elite. Others are *nouveau riche*—those who have made their own fortunes recently in business or entertainment. Some live in the old parts of the city in the huge flats with high ceilings and grand stairways. Others live in the posh suburbs, commuting frantically to the city each day with the blue collar workers. The really rich may still be clinging to a costly chateau in the country.

Few groups are more socially closed than the elite of Paris. They invite one another to their cocktail parties or to banquets, if the maids and butlers are available, but they are inhibited in their traditions of formality and would rather not do it if they can't do it "right." The new rich who work very long and hard, with long lunch hours, long dinners, and long commuting journeys, have little time for outsiders or for religious matters.

As Jesus told us, it is hard for the rich to find a place for him in their lives. But this group certainly knows about the Christian faith and could possibly be very important in influencing others to accept Christ.

EXPANDED DESCRIPTIONS

FALASHA
Ethiopia   marc id: 159

alt names: Black Jews

pop: 30,000
distinct: language
              ethnicity
              religion

languages:		uses	speak	read
	Agau	V	100%	nc

scripture: Bible

rlg chg: somewhat open
att chr: somewhat favorable

religion:		adherents
	Judaism	93%
	Christianity	7%

churches:		community
	Churches Ministry Among Jews	12,000
	Ethiopian Orthodox	nc

The Falasha are farmers who live in widely scattered parts of north central Ethiopia. Dispersed among the larger and more dominant Amhara people, they maintain a strong commitment to an ancient form of the Hebrew religion. The form of Judaism which they practice is older than the Talmud and is based directly upon the Old Testament.

The Falasha are part of a large group of peoples known as the Agau. Normally they are classified as a subgroup within the larger Kemant (Qemant) people. But, traditionally they have been enemies of the Kemant and much more thoroughly Hebraized. Because the Falasha resisted subjugation to the Amhara in the late nineteenth century, they were totally defeated and dispersed, unlike the more pagan Kemant. But the subsequent attempt to enforce Christianization and Amharization failed with the Falasha, whereas the Kemant have almost completely adjusted to becoming a "Christian" people within the Orthodox church.

The Anglican church's Ministry Among the Jews has worked among the Falasha since 1860. Any Falasha converts are referred to the Ethiopian Orthodox Church for membership and training. Many desire to become Christians because of the social and economic pressures of the Orthodox Amhara culture surrounding them. They are without a distinctively Falasha Church, however, and growth is slow. They are essentially being asked to assimilate to the dominant Amhara population. Barrett estimates that possibly 80 percent still have not heard the gospel so that the desire to become Christian is not met with an equal opportunity to do so.

The most successful work by the Ministry Among the Jews has been a residential families school. Two years of training is given to parents as their children attend government school. Then they return to their village with mission support for one year where they are able to witness and lead other Falasha to Jesus Christ.

The once militant Hebraism is declining in force. Some have suggested a strategy similar to that used by the Jews for Jesus Movement might stimulate a people movement among the Falasha, permitting them to retain many of their Hebrew forms as they come to faith in the Messiah Jesus.


```
FULANI
Cameroon                                          marc id:  37

alt names:   Bororo
             Ako

pop:         250,000
also in:     Nigeria
distinct:    language
             ethnicity

languages:                        uses      speak      read
             Fulani                 V        100%        nc
             Pidgin English                   5%

scripture:   New Testament

rlg chg:     somewhat open
att chr:     somewhat opposed

religion:                        adherents
             Christianity            1%
             Islam-Animist          99%
```

There are really no national boundaries for the Fulani. Of obscure and controversial origins, the Fulani have spread over 18 countries in western and central Africa. Possibly having Berber blood, the Fulani are taller, slimmer, and lighter skinned than many of their African

181

EXPANDED DESCRIPTIONS

neighbors. Even though they are a minority in the northeast part of Cameroon, politically and culturally they dominate the groups that surround them. The Fulani language is the lingua franca in Northern Cameroon.

Originally the Fulani were a pastoral people, and even today such pastoral Fulani enjoy greater prestige than their sedentary counterparts in towns, including those in the Cameroon. The nomadic Fulani have no permanent dwellings but move from camp to camp following the sparse grass of the Sub-Sahara. Further south the Fulani have tended to be seminomadic with some permanent dwellings and communities from which herds are followed several months at a time. About 80 percent of the Fulani in Cameroon get their livelihood from stockraising and farming. Others are craftsmen, traders, religious teachers (*marabout*), and government workers.

The devoutly Muslim Fulani have seen themselves as propagators and preservers of the Islamic faith from as early as the fourteenth century. As nomads, they had little time to settle down and practice their Islam and so were not aggressive in spreading their faith. As they became more powerful and affluent, though, they began to take their religion more seriously and often waged "holy" wars to extend and "purify" Islam. There are only ten or so known Christians among the Fulani in Cameroon. In recent years, churches and missions have awakened to the strategic place of the Fulani in the evangelization of Sub-Saharan Africa. Largely as a result of radio ministries, some Fulani have begun to show interest in Christianity. Continued radio broadcasting, effective scripture translations, especially in oral forms such as radio, tape, and easily learned Bible stories oriented to a shepherd culture, may be effective in winning some Fulani to Christ. However, the number of workers actively engaged in evangelism among the Fulani is extremely small in comparison to the vast numbers of peoples to be reached.

GUANANO
Colombia   marc id: 442

alt names: Wanano
             Uanana
             Kotiria

pop: 1,000
also in: Brazil

distinct:	language			
	ethnicity			
	kinship			
languages:		uses	speak	read
	Guanano	V	100%	5%
	Kotira, Tucano		nc	nc
	Spanish		25%	nc
scripture:	New Testament			
rlg chg:	somewhat closed			
att chr:	indifferent			
religion:		adherents		
	Christo-Paganism	99%		
	Christianity	1%		
churches:				
	Roman Catholic			
	Wycliffe Bible Translators			

In a beautiful tropical forest two rivers come together and separate Colombia from Brazil. Here on the Vaupes river live the Guanano, an Amerindian people trembling on the edge of major social and economic change.

Helicopters buzz overhead. The Brazilian government is paying large sums of money to the chief for invading this territory. The Trans-Amazonia highway is reaching into this part of the world and bringing with it that curious mixture of good and evil we call "civilization". The traditional ways of living, farming, hunting, and gathering will undoubtedly be affected as outsiders and money flow into the area at a much higher rate.

Many years of careful study and labor have now resulted in a New Testament. God's Word can now be heard in Guanano. Literacy training is going on as are other skill training courses. Yet for all the love, for all the communication, for all the prayers, the evangelistic breakthrough is yet in the future.

Animism and witchcraft are strong, and locally made alcohol is consumed in large quantities and produces hallucinations that are believed essential to tapping the spiritual powers of their world. The deep awareness of these powers and their ability to harm keeps most from seriously considering Jesus Christ.

A few are outspoken believers in Christ. More embrace Christ only at the point of death. Some believe in their hearts but are fearful of living that belief out before their families and friends. But the major response is stony indifference.

Two things appear crucial for any breakthrough. A significant, God-given encounter with the Holy Spirit by leaders of the people needs to occur. Apart from a Guanano-initiated revival, prospects for real progress in evangelization seem dim. Secondly, an understanding of the relevance of the New Testament to real needs must develop.

```
GUARANI
Bolivia                                                        marc id:  206

alt names:  Chiriquanos
            Chane

pop:        15,000
also in:    Argentina
            Paraguay
distinct:   language
            ethnicity

languages:                              uses        speak        read
            Guarani                      V          100%          45%
            Spanish                      T           50%          nc

chr lit:    45%
scripture:  New Testament

rlg chg:    somewhat open
att chr:    strongly favorable

religion:                               adherents
            Animism                       85%
            Protestant                    12%
            Roman Catholic                 3%

churches:                               community
            Evangelical Christian Union   980
            Roman Catholic                nc
```

The Bolivian Guarani are a small segment of the much larger Guarani group further south in Paraguay and Argentina. The larger group has been largely assimilated into Paraguayan culture. It is only in peripheral areas such as Bolivia that traditional customs survive.

Many Guarani were Christians in the past. The Jesuits established several successful missions during the seventeenth century which constituted a famous "Jesuit Utopia" in Paraguay. However, the Jesuits were expelled, the Guarani Christian Indians were scattered, and further outreach has been minimal since that time.

Most Bolivian Guarani today remain animistic, hoarding religious paraphernalia. Events of life for them require innumerable rituals and specific precautions. For example, after child birth, the husband does no work and goes to bed for about a week on a special religious diet. They believe that the father's behavior at this crucial time determines the child's future well-being. Shamans, dances, trances, dreams, sacred plants, and many other animistic phenomena are of vital importance to the Guarani.

Ritual chants are sometimes said to invade the mind of certain individuals as a gift from God. "Ownership" of these chants gives great spiritual comfort in times of trouble and allows one to be recognized as a religious leader. One so endowed may act as a messenger from God, whose wisdom makes him a permanent advisor to his people. Few would ever think of disobeying such a person. To the Guarani's credit, they are not at all materialistic. No prestige is gained by the accumulation of goods. However, this attitude has been a primary hinderance in their participation in modern markets.

Wycliffe has completed a Guarani New Testament, and Guaranis are now being evangelized by their own trained leaders. Tape ministries, correspondence courses, TEE, and church planting by Guaranis are useful means of evangelization which should be pursued.

GYPSIES IN SPAIN   marc id: 393

pop: 200,000
also in: France
              Yugoslavia
              German Federal Rep.
distinct: discrimination
              language
              ethnicity

languages:		uses	speak	read
	Romany	V	nc	nc
	Spanish	T	nc	nc

scripture: Bible

rlg chg: somewhat open

EXPANDED DESCRIPTIONS

```
att chr:      indifferent

religion:                        adherents
              Christianity            4%
              Folk Religion          96%
```

"You earn money and say 'I'll save it for this!' We earn a thousand pesetas and spend it. We do not worry about tomorrow. We enjoy life in a different way than you do. That's the way we are—different from you. That life satisfies us . . . that's why we are Gypsies."

Gypsies are one of the largest groups in the world without a homeland. A nomadic people, they are found on every continent but mostly in Europe, typically traveling by horse-drawn or motorized caravan. Gypsies call themselves Rom, meaning Man, but are known to others by many names including Bohemians, Tartars, and in Spain, Gitanos. Tradition has it that they came from Egypt (hence the name *Gypsies*), but linguistic and anthropologic evidence points to Indian origin. In Spain, they use either Spanish or the Gypsy language called Romany.

There are three main divisions of Gypsies worldwide: the Kalderash from the Balkans, the Manush from France and Germany, and the Gitanos from Iberia and North Africa. Locally, Gitanos are organized into bands of from ten to a few hundred. Each is led by a chieftain who acts as treasurer for the group, decides on patterns of migration and acts as spokesman to local authorities.

Discrimination and ill-treatment are so common to Gitanos that it is borne like bad weather. Typically they have engaged in seasonal occupations—circuses or fairs—and other pursuits too menial or otherwise distasteful to the majority of the population. Many are engaged as undertakers, executioners, entertainers, horse dealers, and fortune-tellers. They have tended not to become farmers even when settled in rural areas.

While few Gitanos have ideas of submission to any fixed professions of faith, their Gypsy religion has tended to approximate the dominant religion of the areas they have occupied. There is considerable similarity between the traditional monotheism of Gypsies with its mythologies and Roman Catholicism, especially with respect to patron saints and homage to Sara, the legendary Gypsy Black Virgin. Very few Gitanos practice Christianity without various syncretistic elements.

Because of the highly personalized nature of Gitano relationships, which almost entirely exclude the stranger, initial contacts are best made through personal introductions by persons previously known and respected by them. At present, a great hindrance to Gitano evangelism is the lack of a good Bible translation. Music centered ministries and camp meeting style evangelism may be most suited to their life-style and hence be most effective in bringing them to a sound faith in Christ.

```
HEWA
Papua New Guinea                                marc id:  1238

pop:        1,500
distinct:   language
            ethnicity
            religion
            kinship
            residence
            discrimination

languages:                        uses      speak      read
            Hewa                  VGW       100%        nc
            Melanesian Pidgin     T           6%        1%

chr lit:    10%
scripture:  none

rate chg:   moderate
rlg chg:    somewhat open
att chr:    somewhat favorable

religion:                         adherents      practicing
            Protestant               10%             5%
            Animism                  90%            90%

churches:                          members       community
            Wabag Lutheran            40             10

profile:    20% No awareness of Christianity
            30% Aware of existence
            25% Some knowledge of gospel
             7% Understand the message
            10% Personal challenge to receive Christ
             5% Decision to accept Christ
             2% In a fellowship
             1% Propagators of the gospel
```

The Hewa are a nomadic hunting and gathering people of the Enga province of Papua New Guinea. Divided into small clans, they are often at war with one another. When they are not fighting, they also practice slash-and-burn agriculture and build tree houses in their "gardens." Continually moving from one location to another within their clan area, they do not spend much over nine months in any one place. These nomadic habits make it difficult to carry on missions among them with traditional sedentary patterns.

The government of Papua New Guinea has invited the Hewa to leave their very rugged area and settle on new land where they can become gardeners instead of nomads. To date, however, no Hewa group has responded to this invitation to change their life-style.

The Hewa suffer from many illnesses and are interested in receiving medical help. Combined medical/evangelistic teams, sent by the Wabag Lutheran Church, have received a hearing among the Hewa. Attempts are also being made to have Hewa clans choose men who will go to a Christian community in the Duna area to learn about Christ and then return to their own people with the message of Life.

Successful evangelism among the Hewa will require people who are willing and able to travel with them and to aid them with both physical healing and the Word of God. Under such conditions, Christian evangelists from other seminomadic New Guinea people will be more effective than virtually any stationary Western missionary.

HUNZAKUT
Pakistan   marc id: 1236

alt names: Burusho

pop: 10,000
distinct: language
             ethnicity
             religion
             health situation
             legal status
             significant problems

languages:		uses	speak	read
	Burushaski	VG	100%	nc
	Urdu	TSW	20%	20%

scripture: none

rate chg: moderate
rlg chg: somewhat open
att chr: somewhat favorable

religion:		adherents	practicing
	Islam	80%	40%
	Islam-Animist	20%	8%

profile:	
0%	No awareness of Christianity
60%	Aware of existence
30%	Some knowledge of gospel
5%	Understand the message
5%	Personal challenge to receive Christ
0%	Decision to accept Christ
0%	In a fellowship
0%	Propagators of the gospel

The state of Hunza is a mountainous land where Pakistan meets China and Afganistan. Their land is called "the roof of the world" because the joining of three mountain ranges occurs here—the Hindu Kush, the Karakoran, and the Pamirs. Most of the land is uninhabitable. The average altitude is 7,800 feet. Most of the people live in an eight-mile valley. Until this century, these people were the terror of the region, raiding caravans on the trade routes. The British subdued this area and installed a new ruler who reigned for 46 years and was the first Mir to die a natural death.

Land is so precious that the only road in is a mere six feet wide. Travel to out-of-the-way villages is by foot on the borders of irrigated terraces. Apple, peach, pear, and apricot orchards abound. Water is not abundant so the skill of developing irrigation ditches has been highly developed. The job of the women is to maintain these. Incompetence in this duty can lead to divorce.

The Hunzakut are nominally Muslim of the Shiah persuasion. Fairly recently they converted to the Ismaili sect of which the Agha Khan is the religious head. Even though Muslim, the women are neither secluded, nor veiled.

Hunza is considered of strategic importance to the Pakistan government. It has enjoyed telephone links with the outside world for several decades. The sons of the nobility have enjoyed education in the best schools of the land and abroad. There are vernacular schools in several of the villages.

The people have come to know something of Christianity through resident foreigners who have lived there as teachers and advisors. Several of the leading families own Bibles and are kindly disposed toward Christians. As yet, there are no known believers among the Hunzakut. Medical workers and teachers are needed here.

EXPANDED DESCRIPTIONS

INDIANS IN FIJI   marc id: 131

pop: 265,000
also in: India
distinct: language
              ethnicity

languages: uses   speak   read
              Hindustani   V   90%   85%
              English   T   90%   nc
              Hindi   nc   nc

chr lit: 95%
scripture: Bible

rlg chg: somewhat open
att chr: somewhat opposed

religion: adherents
              Hinduism   65%
              Islam   33%
              Protestant   1%
              Roman Catholic   1%

churches: community
              Assemblies of God   nc
              Methodist   3,200
              Roman Catholic   3,200

Most Indians in Fiji have no recollection of India or Pakistan. Ninety-seven percent of the present population was born in Fiji. The vast majority of them are descendants of kidnapped slave labor and indentured slaves, brought to work the plantations of Fiji, an arrangement that ended in 1920.

Since World War II, a voluntary influx of free Indians has led to the development of a commercial and industrial Indian sector. Hindu and Muslim religious leaders also were brought and a strong religious movement developed in opposition to Christianity, the religion held by the native island Fijians (the majority of whom are Methodists).

Indian and Fijian population sizes are almost equally balanced. The occupational distribution indicates that there are both rural and urban communities. Some 22 percent are concentrated in urban and town areas, mostly school age, young adult, and middle-aged Indians. Any strategy for evangelization will have to take into account these two differing settings. While Hindustani is increasingly becoming the lingua franca, there are still seven or eight other Indian languages in use. The most effective evangelists would be those who are bi- or trilingual and Indian in their ethnic background.

Because the country has put fairly tight controls on visas for persons wanting to come into Fiji from the outside, the work of evangelizing the Indians will largely fall to the current Indian evangelical leaders in Fiji. Alternatively, as the opportunity presents itself, the evangelicals in the country of India might see this as a tremendous mission field for their prayer and outreach. The caste system as it is known in India is absent from Fiji. Though elements of family pride and class status are important in social life, caste is not the barrier to evangelism that it is in India.

```
INDIANS, EAST
Trinidad and Tobago                        marc id:  1221

alt names:  Indians

pop:        400,000
distinct:   ethnicity
            religion
            discrimination

languages:                    uses      speak     read
            English           VTGS       90%       70%
            English with Hindi  VW       100%       nc

chr lit:    70%
scripture:  Bible

rate chg:   moderate
rlg chg:    somewhat open
att chr:    somewhat favorable

religion:                    adherents     practicing
            Roman Catholic       2%            1%
            Protestant          10%            4%
            Christian Cultic     1%            1%
            Hinduism            67%           15%
            Islam               20%           10%

churches:                    members       community
            World Team          200            500
            Pentecostal       2,000          5,000
            Presbyterian      2,000          5,000
            Roman Catholic       nc             nc

profile:     0% No awareness of Christianity
            37% Aware of existence
```

EXPANDED DESCRIPTIONS

30% Some knowledge of gospel
10% Understand the message
10% Personal challenge to receive Christ
 1% Decision to accept Christ
10% In a fellowship
 2% Propagators of the gospel

When the Negroes were freed from slavery in the West Indies, East Indians were brought into Trinidad and Tobago as indentured workers for canefield labor. They remained and today make up almost 40 percent of the 1.1 million people of this nation. Today they do most of the farming and have penetrated almost every area of economic and political life.

The East Indians have retained much of their culture along with their Hindu or Muslim religion in the 125 years they have been in Trinidad. Though living in a pluralistic society, intermarriage has been minimal. The Presbyterians reached a number of these East Indians in the late nineteenth century through education programs but this church has been largely ineffective since then. Pentecostal ministries have been most effective in reaching these people in recent years.

There has been some softening in their attitudes toward Christianity through prolonged contact with Christians, and a people movement could possibly be precipitated if the gospel were preached and churches planted that utilized forms more familiar to them. Past evangelism has been foreign or otherwise ineffective, and approximately 230-250,000 Hindus and 70,000 Muslim East Indians have yet to see Christianity as a viable option.

JAPANESE IN BRAZIL   marc id: 1

pop:	750,000			
distinct:	language ethnicity			
languages:		uses	speak	read
	Japanese	V	40%	99%
	Portuguese	T	80%	99%
chr lit:	99%			
scripture:	Bible			
rlg chg:	somewhat closed			
att chr:	somewhat opposed			

religion:		adherents	practicing
	Unknown	5%	
	Buddhism	50%	nc
	Animism	2%	nc
	Other	3%	nc
	Protestant	2%	2%
	Roman Catholic	38%	6%

churches:		community
	Assemblies of God	1,800
	Episcopal	1,160
	Free Methodist	1,653
	Holiness	1,226
	Roman Catholic	280,000
	Sul-America	120

Some 750,000 Japanese immigrants live in Brazil at present, and this number is expected to rise to perhaps 1,000,000 in a decade. Christian groups have been at work among them, but in over 50 years, less than 10 percent have become practicing Christians.

The first Japanese immigrants came to Brazil in 1908. Slaves had been used on the Brazilian coffee plantations until the 1880s and the Japanese were part of the new labor sources sought by the Brazilians. Before World War II, most had come to work, earn, and save enough to go back to Japan. After their loss in the war, they were cut off from the fatherland and consequently began to invest their savings and improve their lot in what was now their permanent home. The Japanese proved to be excellent workers and as they moved up from wage laborers to tenant farmers to land owners, they were exceptionally innovative in farming techniques. They were the first in Brazil to use fertilizers and were in the forefront in agriculture technology.

About 50 percent are still in rural areas, but many have moved to the cities, especially Sao Paulo, and have become active and successful in commerce and industry. Their literacy rate of over 99 percent is far higher than that of the rest of Brazil (60.7 percent) and they participate in education, government, and other white collar professions in far higher propotions than would be expected by their numbers.

Important aspects of strategy for reaching this group will include multilevel training of leaders, the involvement of the laity in church planting, and the creation of missionary agencies from Japanese Christian churches.

EXPANDED DESCRIPTIONS

JAVANESE (RURAL)
Indonesia   marc id: 73

pop: 60,000,000
distinct: language
              ethnicity

languages:		uses	speak	read
	Javanese	V	100%	20%
	Bahasa Indonesia	T	65%	nc

chr lit: 20%
scripture: Bible

rlg chg: somewhat open
att chr: somewhat favorable

religion:		adherents
	Islam-Animist	95%
	Protestant	1%
	Roman Catholic	1%
	Unknown	3%

churches:		community
	Javanese Protestant	nc
	Baptist	nc
	Roman Catholic	15,000

The Javanese live on land that supports one of the densest populations in the world.

Land shortage is an increasingly acute problem that pressurizes the future and is rapidly inflating the ranks of the landless. Normally the Javanese live in a household that includes only parents and children but increasingly an odd relative or two will join the family life. Divorce is extremely common under the Muslim laws. In many rural areas there is one divorce for every two marriages.

The intense belief in Allah is accompanied by lax attitude toward Muslim practices and an accommodation with ancient Hindu and animist beliefs. The average peasant is called *won abangan* to distinguish his lax Islamic outlook from the truly devout Muslim, the *wong putihan* or *santri* (more commonly from the commercial class).

Guidance and help in weathering the ambiguities and storms of life are sought in dreams, numerology, and from the dozen different specialists (*dukun*) who practice various forms of magic and sorcery. The more advanced form of animism, *Kebatinan*, is pervasive and motivates a number of strong movements. The goal of *Kebatinan* is to "know" the ultimate feeling deep within oneself, which is "God."

194

A basic feeling of the relativity of religion leads to a pervasive syncretism. Religion is a means to the subjective inner knowledge of God, or to help in crisis situations. Doctrinal or ritual purity is not considered important. Self-control and emotional equanimity are sought as part of the search for spiritual powers, and they motivate the ethical imperative not to offend or upset others. To show anger in interpersonal relationships is almost an unforgiveable sin.

Twelve Protestant groups are doing rural evangelization. Christianity has impact when Jesus Christ is seen as the great Healer and Helper. Sensitivity to the rich cultural heritage, and more Javanese-speaking laborers are all needed to facilitate effective evangelism in this heartland of Indonesia.

```
KABYLE
Algeria                                              marc id:  145

alt names:  Berbers of Kabylia

pop:        1,000,000
also in:    France
            Belgium
distinct:   language
            ethnicity

languages:                          uses       speak       read
            Kabyle                   V          100%        25%
            Arabic                   T           50%        nc
            French                               15%        nc

chr lit:    50%
scripture:  New Testament

rlg chg:    somewhat closed
att chr:    strongly opposed

religion:                           adherents
            Islam                      99%
            Christianity                1%

churches:                           community
            Assemblee Evangelique (Algiers)  8
            North African Mission           nc
```

Before the French left in 1962, the little Methodist church in remote, mountainous Kabylia used to fill every Sunday, mostly with non-Christians. By 1973, only a family or two attended. Most of the Kabyles who were Christian or sympathetic to Christianity left after

EXPANDED DESCRIPTIONS

Algeria won independence from France. Many had sided with the French during the revolution, while the non-Christian majority had fought fiercely for independence.

The Kabyle are a Berber people who inhabit the most densely populated region of Algeria. Their traditional dress is especially bright with colorful, striped robes, dresses and headscarves, and heavy silver jewelry ornamented in coral. The pressure of the rapidly growing population has forced thousands to migrate each year to the coastal cities and to France where they constitute about two-thirds of the migrant workers from Algeria. Even though they are now widespread, they retain their independence, group solidarity, and well-organized village and social life.

While the Christian church in Algeria is not persecuted, it appears that for national development reasons literature in Kabyle is forbidden. Missionary activity among the Kabyle must be discreet. Response to radio broadcasts and Bible correspondence courses from Marseille, France have been encouraging, but mail irregularities have raised suspicions of interference with the mail. It is certainly true that Christians in Kabylia or anywhere in Algeria must also collaborate in developing the country, not as the ones giving orders, but as members of a team. Ministries such as maternity and other health care, cooking, sewing and other skill classes, youth hostels and *casbahs,* which offer food, counsel, clothes, and employment help to young people, may promote Christianity among the Kabyle. As is true everywhere, Christian lives are just as important as Christian words.

```
KAFIRS
Pakistan                                        marc id:  1233

alt names:   Nuristanis

pop:         3,000
also in:     Afghanistan
distinct:    language
             occupation
             ethnicity
             religion
             sense of unity
             social class
```

languages:		uses	speak	read
	Kafiristani (Bashgali)	VG	100%	nc
	Urdu	TSW	15%	2%

```
scripture:    none

rate chg:     moderate
rlg chg:      very open
att chr:      somewhat favorable

religion:                          adherents      practicing
              Animism                100%           100%

churches:     Assemblies of God
              Worldwide Evangelization Crus.

profile:      75% No awareness of Christianity
              20% Aware of existence
               5% Some knowledge of gospel
               0% Understand the message
               0% Personal challenge to receive Christ
               0% Decision to accept Christ
               0% In a fellowship
               0% Propagators of the gospel
```

Kafir means "blasphemer". Those in Afghanistan are known as Red Kafirs and number about 67,000. They have been renamed Nuristanis (people of light) after their forcible conversion to Islam. The Pakistani branch of the Kafirs numbers only about 3000. They are called Black Kafirs. The Pakistan Kafirs are almost totally animistic, though some have voluntarily become Muslims. Many of their villages have wooden temples to a female goddess thought to protect the family's children and the home. Spring and autumn festivals are built around these ancient religious practices. The people are also known as Kalash Kafirs.

The economic behavior is clearly different for the sexes. Men do the pasturing of the herds and women till the terraced slopes, maintaining the irrigation ditches. The basic economic group is the extended family, with a patriarch and his married sons and their families.

One of the unique features of Kalash Kafir culture is the small hereditary group of skilled craftsmen. Building techniques for timber houses on steep cliffs, cantilever bridges shaping the sharp gorges, and geometric wood-carving decorations on the houses are distinct features of this people.

The women of this group on the Pakistani side are not veiled and have a great deal more freedom than their sisters in Afghanistan, but they, too, are segregated during ceremonies and feasts.

Recently, exploratory teams of evangelists have discovered that

197

these people are very receptive to the gospel. They have invited both missionaries and Pakistani Christians to come in and teach them. They have also requested medical help. Very few of them know Urdu, the lingua franca of Pakistan. The most urgent need is for linguists to master their language and begin ministering to them while they are in this receptive state and before they convert to Islam.

```
KAREN
Thailand                                          marc id:  613

pop:        80,000
also in:    Burma
distinct:   language
            ethnicity

languages:                          uses      speak     read
            Sgaw Karen               V        100%       nc
            Northern Thai            T         80%       nc
            Burmese                             2%       nc

chr lit:    80%
scripture:  Bible

rlg chg:    somewhat open

religion:                                   adherents
            Animism                            99%
            Christianity                        1%

churches:                                   community
            Baptist                            2,500
            Roman Catholic                     2,000
            Worldwide Evangelization Crus.      nc
```

The fires are awesome. Huge clouds of smoke and flame billow hundreds of feet into the air. As the fires roar the exploding bamboo stems sound like bursts of cannon fire. In less than an hour over 100 acres can be reduced to bare hillside in preparation for rice planting.

As with most of the hill tribes in Southeast Asia, life flows in the rhythm of the rice crop: burning the fields in January, planting in April, tedious weeding through the rainy season, and harvest in October and November. Throughout the year the gods of the hills, of the rains, and of the rice will be implored with sacrifices of chickens and rice wine to produce a good crop:

Rice O! Come back good again. Return white again. Come back green and swaying. Come back with grain as big as melons. Come back and eat chicken blood, O Rice Lord!

The Sgaw Karen are one of several closely related Karen sub-groups which together number close to two million persons. The Karen church of Burma, begun in 1880, is one of the largest and healthiest in Asia. Karen missionaries from Burma ministered to the Sgaw in Thailand sporatically for many years carried by other missionaries but it was not until the 1950s that significant beginnings were made by the Baptists and OWF. In the meantime, the Sgaw were emerging out of animism but unlike many other hill tribes who were turning to Christ, most of the Sgaw were lost in the darkness of Buddhism. And, unfortunate experiences with English teakwood companies working in the area turned many away from the good news.

"Mission compound" approaches among the Sgaw Karen have been largely ineffective. Recently, interesting audio visual approaches have been favorably received and these and other creative approaches utilized with sound anthropological principles may result in strong, growing churches among the Sgaw Karen.

```
KASHMIRI MUSLIMS                              marc id: 1231
India

pop:        3,060,000
distinct:   political loyalty
            religion
            sense of unity
            discrimination
            legal status
            significant problems

languages:                      uses      speak     read
            Kashmiri            VG        80%       5%
            Urdu                TSW       90%       5%
            Hindi               S         nc        nc

chr lit:    40%
scripture:  Bible

rate chg:   moderate
rlg chg:    somewhat open
att chr:    somewhat favorable

religion:                       adherents    practicing
            Protestant          1%           1%
            Islam               99%          49%
```

EXPANDED DESCRIPTIONS

churches: members
            Church of North India   300
            Independent Indian Assemblies 600

profile: 30% No awareness of Christianity
            59% Aware of existence
            10% Some knowledge of gospel
             1% Understand the message
             0% Personal challenge to receive Christ
             0% Decision to accept Christ
             0% In a fellowship
             0% Propagators of the gospel

Found in the former princely state of Jummu-Kashmir, the Muslims make up 68 percent of the total population. Hindus are concentrated in the Jummu part of the foothills. The Vale of Kashmir is itself 95 percent Muslim.

Kashmiri Muslims are a heterogeneous group. Some are descendants of three major waves of immigration, the Arabs, Mughals, and Pathans. Others are descendants of Hindu converts whose caste or trade subcaste names are still recognizable. Most recently, Gujar and Bakarwak pastoral Muslims, who speak a different dialect, have entered the area. What has produced unity and an unusual degree of intermixing of these diverse peoples has been the need for a united front against the Hindus.

Kashmiri civilization has been strongly influenced by the Muslim mystics and Persian culture. Poetry, music, cuisine, and craftmanship in woodcarving and weaving are all highly developed.

Kashmir has been a battleground since the partition of the Indian subcontinent in 1947. Ironically, the Kashmiris themselves wanted independence and autonomy. Now they find themselves alternately wooed and abused by both neighboring countries seeking to exercise hegemony over them.

All of the above factors have worked together to make this people more open to the gospel than perhaps any other Muslim group on the subcontinent. Hundreds of conversions have been reported, many of them refugees from Pakistan. Here is a responsive group, an opportune time. Perhaps commonwealth citizens who do not need visas should see them as a beckoning Macedonia.

KOALIB   marc id: 580
Sudan

alt names: Kawalib
200

pop:	320,000			
distinct:	language			
	ethnicity			

languages:		uses	speak	read
	Koalib (Nuba)	V	100%	nc
	Arabic	T	nc	nc

scripture: New Testament portions

religion:		adherents
	Animism	70%
	Islam	20%
	Protestant	10%

The Kaolib are a subgroup of the Nuba who live in the Nuba mountains, an interruption of Sudan's otherwise featureless horizon, on the eastern fringe of the Sahara Desert. Some of these mountains are over 3000 feet above the surrounding plain, but most are mere humps rising oddly out of the surrounding flatness of the central Kadofan Province of the Sudan. The hills attract the rain and the rain is gathered at the base of the wadis carved in their sides. Thus, the "hill people" (as they call themselves) can live year around in permenent villages, distinguishing their life-style from the peoples of the plains.

The Koalib are themselves made up of several subgroups that are distinct from other Nuba groups by language and by the fact that they alone practice extensive polygamy. This is quite rare among the other Nuba peoples. Their life-style is essentially that of the sedentary agriculturalists. They keep animals, including cattle, sheep, donkeys, guinea fowl, and pigs. Their keeping of pigs is interesting since they are considered unclean by the Arabs and the practice of raising pigs has been virtually eliminated throughout North Africa. They are thus almost alone in the continuation of a pig-raising culture and this has been a hindrance to their being Islamized. "Allah forbids me to eat pork, but it is delicious," they explain.

The Koalib still practice their traditional religion. Many follow fertility cults with much stress on masculinity. Wrestling and fighting have religious significance and are engaged in fiercely but fairly. The wrestlers coat themselves in ash, which is sacred to the Nuba groups. In their land where trees are scarce, ash represents endurance and virility. A man coated in ash is in a holy state. The most successful wrestlers are the most desirable to the women, while the losers must manfully conceal their pain and humiliation.

201

EXPANDED DESCRIPTIONS

While the Koalib have tended to resist Islam, the dominant religion of the Sudan, a few have come to Christ, formerly under the ministry of the Sudan United Mission. Presently, the Muslim brotherhood, an Egyptian Christian group, is working among them. Like other groups in Southern Sudan, the Koalib suffered in the 17 years of war between the north and south, but the changes and exposure to outside forces may have created a receptivity that should not be ignored.

```
KURDS                                          marc id:   180
Turkey

pop:          4,000,000
also in:      Iraq
              Iran
              Syria
distinct:     language
              ethnicity

languages:                          uses      speak      read
              Kurdish (Zaza)         V         nc         nc
              Kurdish (Kirmancho)    V         nc         nc
              Turkish                T         55%        nc

scripture:    nc

rlg chg:      somewhat closed
att chr:      indifferent

religion:                           adherents
              Islam                 95%
              Secularism            5%

churches:     Syriac Evangelical
```

The Kurds are the third most numerous people in the Middle East and number about four million in Turkey. They have occupied the same area for 3000 years, an area that is now part of five different countries: Turkey, Iraq, Iran, Syria, and the USSR. The migration of the people in this area, disregarding established national boundaries, has kept them from assimilating with other nationalities and often contributed to their conflict with those national governments.

The Kurds are varied people. Many are nomadic herdsmen; some are farmers; some engage in a variety of occupations in the cities. They have a tribal, kin-based sociopolitical structure, characterized by a distinction between nobles and commoners. The Kurdish language is closely related to Persian and is very important in Kurdish unity. "Kurdistan" is a beautiful mountainous land which includes the biblical city of Nineveh in the south and Mount Ararat in the north.

Turkish authorities have tended to deny that the Kurds have a separate ethnic identity. They are not called Kurds but "Mountain Turks," for the government accepts no other "nation" as living in Turkey except Turks. The Kurdish areas of Turkey are far less developed economically than the western provinces. There are far fewer vehicles and roads and almost no industrialization. Schools are poor and most Kurds do not speak Turkish.

Religion has a very important influence among the Kurdish tribes. About two-thirds of Turkey's Kurds are thought to be Sunni Muslims. The remainder are Alevi Muslims. There are also small numbers of Kurdish Yazabis who are adherants of a secretive faith combining elements of paganism, Islam, Christianity, Judiasm, and Zoroastrianism.

The Syriac Evangelical Church is one of the few groups known to be working among the Kurdish people. Literacy training, effective translation, and distribution of the Bible are needed for the spread of Christianity. Marxism and the rugged and secluded area in which they live are the primary hindrances to Kurdish evangelism.

LAO   marc id: 121
Laos

pop: 1,908,600
also in: Thailand
distinct: language
            ethnicity

languages:		uses	speak	read
	Lao	V	100%	20%
	French		15%	nc
	English		10%	nc

chr lit: 50%
scripture: Bible

rlg chg: somewhat closed
att chr: indifferent

religion:		adherents
	Buddhism	95%
	Animism	4%
	Christianity	1%

EXPANDED DESCRIPTIONS

churches:		community
	Christian Church	3,000
	Gospel Church of Laos	6,845
	Roman Catholic	47,715
	Southern Baptist	

It is the end of the rainy season and the end of the Buddhist "Lent." Carefully, reverently, a small wooden raft laden with candles is slipped into the Mekong river. It hesitates, then catches the current and joins many similar rafts bobbing in the murky water. It is a "scapegoat" raft and along with it floats the year's guilt and trouble. It symbolizes a new spiritual start at the beginning of a new season.

The Lao constitute about half of the 3,500,000 people of Laos. They are Theravada Buddhists, but superstition, evil spirits, and sorcery characterize much of their life-style. As Buddhists, they seek by good behavior and by ritual sacrifices to achieve the blissful extinction of desire—Nirvana. Honor and respect of temples and images of the Buddha will give them merit toward Nirvana. Giving to the red-robed monks will also earn merit, and gongs each morning remind the people to do so. Praying and self-prostration are likewise important. For every Laotian the year is full of religious observances, and religious practices account for a large proportion of a village household's expenditure.

It is evident that innovative, culturally sensitive evangelistic means are needed to reach the Lao for Christ. The Bible has been translated into Lao but actual circulation of Bibles is quite small. No Christian broadcasting has been allowed within the country but programs are being aired into Laos from the Philippines. The political situation is still unstable and missionaries must be discreet. There are many Laotians abroad and in neighboring countries now and these people need to be trained and dedicated to bringing their own to Christ. Redemptive analogies, such as that of the "guilt raft" mentioned here, may be found which can point the people to the one true Sacrifice.

LAPPS   marc id: 1215
Norway

pop: 20,000
also in: Finland
            Soviet Russia
            Sweden

distinct: language
             occupation
             ethnicity
             kinship
             sense of unity
             discrimination
             legal status

languages:		uses	speak	read
	Lappish	VTWG	66%	55%
	Scandinavian languages	SG	90%	nc
	Russian	SG	nc	nc

chr lit: 95%
scripture: nc

rate chg: moderate
rlg chg: somewhat open
att chr: somewhat favorable

religion:		adherents	practicing
	Protestant	90%	15%
	Unknown	10%	

churches: Lutheran

profile: 8% No awareness of Christianity
            20% Aware of existence
            50% Some knowledge of gospel
            10% Understand the message
             5% Personal challenge to receive Christ
             0% Decision to accept Christ
             5% In a fellowship
             2% Propagators of the gospel

   Winter in vast, snow-covered Lapland is long and silent. The
Lapps must live on the frozen cache of fish, reindeer, and seal meat
in small villages with others of their clan. Since relatives tend to
cluster in the same areas, people are identified by their clan names.
The summers are short, but the long days afford ample time for the
main pursuit—preparing for winter.
   There are three main types of Lapp culture. The Coast Lapps were
formerly nomadic, living on hunting and fishing. Now they have settled into an agricultural life-style or engage in commercial fishing or
stock breeding. The Forest Lapps have relatively permanent seasonal dwellings and live by fishing, trapping, and hunting wild reindeer.
   The Mountain Lapps are fully nomadic reindeer herders, who fol-

EXPANDED DESCRIPTIONS

low the regular migration of the animals to the mountain pastures in the summer and the frozen lowlands in the winter. The reindeer provide the food, clothing, implements, and transportation. These Mountain Lapps must be ready to move on short notice as the thaws begin and to live in tents for long periods as they follow the reindeer.

Many Lapps are being assimilated into the southern Scandanavian cultures and are adopting the Lutheran state church. Many of those resistant to such assimilation are also nominal Lutherans, but the number of committed Christians is small. Other missions have some outreach to the Lapps, but it is important to develop new evangelical churches in the communities which will draw whole families to Christ.

```
MADURESE                                              marc id:  78
Indonesia

alt names:    Orang Madura
              Suku Madura

pop:          7,000,000
distinct:     language
              ethnicity

languages:                           uses      speak      read
              Madurese               V         100%       nc
              Bahasa Indonesia       T         40%        40%

chr lit:      90%
scripture:    New Testament

rlg chg:      somewhat closed
att chr:      strongly opposed

religion:                            adherents
              Christianity           1%
              Islam                  99%

churches:                            community
              Chinese Prot. & Pentecostals   25
              Javanese Protestant            100
              Sidang Persekutuan Injil         6
              Roman Catholic                  nc
```

The Javanese, Sundanese, and Madurese are the three large ethnic groups that make up the majority of the population of the core islands of Java and Madura in Indonesia. A bit less than half of the

Madurese, the third largest of these groups, are located on the island of Madura, the remaining being found in eastern Java. Madura is a rather arid, infertile land. While most are peasants like the Javanese, the principal crop is maize rather than rice. Also, animal husbandry, especially cattle, is very important. On the coast, fishing is the predominate source of food.

The Madurese live in compact villages, normally 300-1000 in size, surrounded by the agricultural land owned by various families. The household is normally made up of husband-wife-children, though population pressures are forcing more to live with relatives.

The Madurese were isolated from the Hindu and animist influences that affected Java. They retain a stronger sense of Muslim identity than the majority of rural Javanese. In other words, they have a higher degree of commitment to the *santri* (devout) form of Islam than the *abangan* (nominal Muslim) form that is influential among Javanese peasantry.

In a group of such size, there are a number of important subgroups that make up more manageable and homogeneous subjects for evangelistic strategy. Distinctions of livelihood (coastal fishing, merchants, farmers), dialect (Pamekasan or western, and Sumenep or eastern Madurese), and residence (Madura, Java) are potentially important in forming subcultural groupings to be evangelized within the larger people.

There is no Madurese church. The Madurese are viewed as strongly resistant and many Indonesian churches hesitate to attempt evangelization. The few converts who have embraced Christ have often had to seek refuge from angered family members. While some attempts at evangelization are taking place, the results thus far are minimal. The best prospect for reaching the Madurese at present seems to be to concentrate on those living in Java. Ministry in their vernacular and the use of such methods as cassettes with carefully constructed, culturally relevant content promise the best results.

```
MAGUZAWA                                    marc id:  202
Nigeria

alt names:   Pagan Hausa
             Bamaguje

pop:         100,000
distinct:    language
             ethnicity
```

EXPANDED DESCRIPTIONS

languages:		uses	speak	read
	Hausa	V	100%	18%

chr lit: 50%
scripture: Bible

att chr: strongly favorable

religion:		adherents
	Animism	99%
	Christianity	1%

churches:		members
	Church Missionary Society	100
	Roman Catholic	nc
	Evangelical Church W. Africa	800
	Baptist	nc

The Maguzawa are being forced to become either Christians or Muslims. The rapid development of Nigeria will no longer allow them simply to offer sacrifices to their ancestors. When their children register for school, they have to indicate their religious commitment. And in increasing numbers young Maguzawa are choosing to become responsible Christians.

Generations ago they rejected the customs of Islam at the very time that 90 percent of their fellow tribesmen became Muslims. That was why they were despised and called Maguzawa, a name that means "those who fled from the Sala" (Muslim daily prayers). Their way of life was felt to be incompatible with Islam—for instance, their beer drinking, which to the Maguzawa is consuming a substance rich in spiritual force.

They are scattered throughout the areas occupied by the Hausa people in some 100 or more single family villages. They live as a single unit with the household head whose word is law. They are known for their industrious farming, their scrupulous honesty and their strong family loyalty. Most of them raise maize, guinea corn, ground nuts, and cotton.

Their worship includes an ancestor cult. It is centered about a shrine of stone to which offerings from the farm are brought. The first major response to the gospel was the result of Anglican work in 1965. The Evangelical Churches of West Africa have a thriving work in Kano State. At present, the Maguzawa are responding in significant numbers. ECWA sent out 19 new evangelists in 1976-77 and saw an influx into their church of some 500 new Christians. Most were between the ages of 18 and 25.

No one knows for sure the total population size of the Maguzawa which may range as high as 500,000. If household conversion is sought by approaching the family head, the father and his brothers and sons, an enormous harvest in the next decade will come to pass. Already, ECWA's missionary arm, the Evangelical Missionary Society, is strengthening itself to reap that harvest by sending out additional Nigerian missionaries.

```
MALAYS OF SINGAPORE                              marc id:   120

pop:          300,000
also in:      Malaysia
              Thailand
distinct:     language
              ethnicity

languages:                        uses      speak      read
              Malay                V         100%       85%
              English              T          70%       nc
              Mandarin                         2%       nc
              Hokkien                          nc       nc

scripture:    New Testament

rlg chg:      somewhat open
att chr:      somewhat opposed

religion:                         adherents
              Islam                 99%
              Christianity           1%

churches:     Christian Church (Batak)
```

The economy of the island city state of Singapore is developing as rapidly as any other country in Asia. Singapore is extremely diverse, with three official languages and many distinct people groups. The Malays are second largest of these groups, but lag far behind most of the others in their participation in the economic success syndrome that pervades Singapore.

The present Malay community centers in maze-like Kampong Melayu, an exclusive Malay reservation on the edge of Paya Lebar Airport. A few Malays live in other *kampongs* scattered about the island or on the coast, and a few more live in the offlying islets which are mainly Malay in population. Malays are associated with the police (one-half of the force) and military, and many others work as

EXPANDED DESCRIPTIONS

drivers, clerks, machine operators, and servants.

The Malays in Singapore are Muslims and the separate Muslim educational system has in the past provided only three to four years of inferior education for a minority of the children. The government has made efforts to improve the school system and include Malays more equitably in job placements and social life but the Malays have not tended to work in the new factories, to mix well with the Chinese, or least of all, to live a competitive life. Most, however, have now agreed to live in new housing developments built by the government.

The Malays have been hostile to open propagation of the gospel. They face the unique hindrance of losing their ethnic identity as well as their Muslim faith if they accept Christianity, since non-Muslims are not accepted as Malays. Ethnic and religious identity are not linked for any of Singapore's other groups.

Evangelization by Batak Javanese Christians and by Muslim converts is most likely to be successful. High rise "house church" concepts and ministries which provide for social welfare and skill training may also be productive.

```
MANDINGO                                        marc id:  622
Liberia

alt names:   Malinke

pop:         36,000
also in:     Guinea
             Mali
distinct:    language
             ethnicity

languages:                        uses      speak     read
             Mandingo             V         100%      nc
             English              T         30%       nc
             Arabic                         20%       nc

scripture:   portions

att chr:     strongly opposed

religion:                         adherents
             Islam                99%
             Christianity         1%

churches:    Lutheran Bible Translators
```

210

History gives an important role to the Mandingo. Formerly successful Muslims conquerors, they are now widely scattered in West Africa (perhaps as many as a million). Concentrations are found especially in Guinea, Mali, and Ivory Coast.

Liberian Mandingo are peaceful traders and merchants. They are concentrated in West Liberia but are also found in the Mekka Chiefdoms (lower Lofa country where they are Kpelle speaking) and in northern Lofa country. In neighboring Guinea, Mandingo are agriculturalists.

Traditionally, there have been tensions with the Americo-Liberians who broke the monopoly on trade formerly held by the Mandingo when they settled the coastal lands. Liberian Mandingo travel far and wide across the Sahara and throughout West Africa seeking commercial opportunities.

Education is limited to schools to learn the Koran in Arabic. Only boys attend. The word of Allah is considered the most important thing to know. The Mandingo are Sunnis, following the Malakite school of interpretation of Islam. Knowledge and skills essential as merchants are learned on the job.

Because of their proud and prestigious history, their language is respected and they are effective missionaries for Islam. Living among other tribes, they normally establish a compound or several compounds in larger villages and towns of northwestern Liberia.

Little evangelism has focused on the Mandingo. The Lutheran Bible Translators are currently at work on a translation of the Bible. Christianity is finding encouragement among those who are changing their location and who have a desire to learn English. But there are still prejudice barriers toward the "Christian" Americo-Liberians as well as toward the traditional methods of evangelization.

Education, other than Arabic Islamic study, is not valued. Only a minority of young people are curious and dissatisfied with their traditional Muslim culture. Opportunity to learn about Christianity or to understand anything about Jesus Christ outside of what the Koran teaches is virtually absent for the vast bulk of the Mandingo. Neglect and indifference is the basic treatment they have received from the church.

MARANAO   marc id: 638
Philippines

alt names: Moro

EXPANDED DESCRIPTIONS

pop: 500,000
distinct: language
           ethnicity

languages:		uses	speak	read
	Maranao	V	100%	20%
	Visayan		80%	nc

scripture: New Testament

att chr: strongly opposed

religion:		adherents
	Islam	98%
	Christianity	2%

churches: United Church of Christ
           Lutheran
           International Missions Baptist
           Summer Institute Linguistics

Before World War II, much of the island of Mindinao in the Philippines was sparsely populated by tribes who had turned to Islam in the twelfth century. New land policies after the war encouraged hundreds of thousands of Christian homesteaders into the area. Constant conflict, fear, and mistrust between the Christian settlers and Muslims (called Moros) have been the results.

The Maranao are the largest Moro group and the largest cultural minority in the Philippines. They are found in almost every major population center in western Mindanao. They engage in a wide variety of occupational pursuits including agriculture, fishing, buffalo raising, industrial arts, and trade.

Moros as a whole are racially and linguistically similar to other Filipinos. The term *Moro* refers to at least ten recognized ethnolinguistic groups including the Maranao, the Magindanao, the Samal, and the Tausug. Islamic faith and intermarriage for political reasons have instilled a feeling of unity among them.

Though the degree of orthodoxy varies, Islam is an all-encompassing institution that embraces the whole range of their activities. The Maranao were the last major Philippine group to accept Islam, but like all Moros, they have a very real sense of being part of the Dar-ul-Islam—the household of Islam worldwide. They picture themselves as courageous, explosive, and loving of their own people, their own place, and their own God. Indeed, the strife between the Moros and Christians is often seen as *jihad* or holy war.

212

They feel no Muslim should be ruled by anyone but a fellow Muslim.

Everyone in the disputed areas has suffered immensely from the long standing strife. It is possible that Filipino Christians may have largely spoiled their witness to the Muslims of the Philippines by their bloody wars and their broken promises. Whoever would try to reach the Maranao with the gospel should know the history of the area well. The situation may require new kinds of workers who do not identify with the government, but who can take independent approaches in working with them. Muslim converts might be excellent missionaries to the Maranao. It will take much love to overcome the years of hatred and warfare.

```
MASAI
Kenya                                            marc id:  489

alt names:  Maasai

pop:        100,00
also in:    Tanzania
distinct:   language
            ethnicity
            occupation

languages:                          uses      speak      read
            Masai                     V         100%       nc

scripture:  New Testament

att chr:    somewhat favorable

religion:                           adherents
            Animism                    95%
            Protestant                  3%
            Roman Catholic              2%

churches:
            Roman Catholic
            Elim Pentcostal
            Evangelical Lutheran
            Africa Inland
```

"God gave us cattle and grass. Cattle are in our hearts. Their smell is in our nostrils." The life of the tall, graceful Masai revolves around their cattle. They have over 700 words in their language to describe a cow, and their wealth is counted in the number of cows they have. It

213

is the number, not the quality that matters. They are not raised to be sold at a meat market.

The Masai were once the dominant tribe in East Africa because of their effective military organization. A tribal system of age grades enabled them to have a standing army of young warriors, similar to the Zulu regiments. Military service was compulsory for all youths of the tribe from ages 17-30, but the peace imposed by the British deprived these warriors of their reason for existence. They remain proud and independent. The beauty and stateliness of the Masai with their finely plated and ochered hair styles and distinctive red dress is legendary. Equally well known is their aloofness and resistance to outside influences.

Modern problems have put limitations on their nomadic way of life. Overcrowding and drought have forced them to take up a "degraded" agricultural way of life. Venereal disease and other health problems have plagued them. Rinderpest has taken its toll among their cattle. With depleted herds and government encouragement to become sedentary, the Masai are experiencing rather dramatic changes.

The primary manifestation of the goodness of the Masai god, Ngai, is the water he gives, but in recent years their prayers to Ngai have been unanswered. Ngai has been powerless and the Masai are beginning to soften in their resistance to the "living water." Still, fewer than 10 percent of the Masai know him who said, "whoever drinks of the water that I shall give him, shall never thirst." In certain regions of Kenya, "tree congregations" are springing into existence. Masai evangelists of older age and from a social section identical with that of their listeners are being given ready and favorable response. A school to train evangelists is in session at Kajiado.

MEGHWAR
Pakistan   marc id: 262

alt names: Chamar
             Maraecha

pop: 100,000
also in: India
distinct: caste
             language
             ethnicity

languages:		uses	speak	read
	Marwari	V	100%	2%
	Gujarati		nc	nc
	Sindhi	T	90%	nc
	Punjabi		10%	nc

chr lit:	2%
scripture:	none

rlg chg:	somewhat open
att chr:	somewhat favorable

religion:		adherents
	Hinduism	99%
	Christianity	1%

churches:		community
	Church of Pakistan	nc
	Conservative Baptist	6
	Pentecostal	nc
	Roman Catholic	nc
	Seventh-day Adventist	nc

The Meghwar are a subcaste of the Chamars, one of 30 groups who make up nearly a million people classified as Hindu Scheduled Caste. The Scheduled Castes traditionally were known as untouchables and considered to be despicable by the caste Hindus. At the partition of Pakistan and India, caste Hindus left in large numbers but most of the Scheduled Caste Hindus chose to remain in Pakistan.

People Movements in the Punjab by Fred and Margaret Stock argues that these Scheduled Caste peoples are a strategic concern for the church for three reasons. In Pakistan, more than 90 percent of the present church is made up of converts and their descendants from Scheduled Castes, especially the Chuhras. The churches and mission agencies of Pakistan are working with only six or seven of the 30 Scheduled Castes at present. Their contention is that this tiny Hindu minority in Pakistan is reachable and accessible by Christian evangelization.

The Meghwars live principally in rural areas. The few who live in urban areas are book and cloth makers. They are found scattered throughout the Sindh and Punjab regions as well as India.

The earliest evidence of successful evangelization is found in 1925 in the Sindh. But little was done to foster and preserve the response begun, and at present there are only a handful of Meghwar Christians. Recent interest in learning about Christ has been shown

EXPANDED DESCRIPTIONS

in the Bahawalpur area. The most effective agents of evangelization would be older men, Kutchi Kohlis, and western missionaries.

```
MEITEI
India                                        marc id:   293

alt names:  Manipuris

pop:        700,000
also in:    Burma
distinct:   language
            ethnicity

languages:                        uses      speak      read
            Manipuri              V         100%       nc
            Meitei-Pao                      nc         nc
            English                         32%        nc
            Hindi                           20%        nc

chr lit:    60%
scripture:  New Testament

rlg chg:    somewhat open
att chr:    indifferent

religion:                         adherents
            Hinduism              90%
            Christianity          1%
            Animism               7%
            Islam                 2%

churches:                         members    community
            Baptist               270        300
            N.E.I.G. Mission      nc         nc
            Presbyterian          nc         nc
            Roman Catholic        nc         nc
```

While there are peoples in northeast India that have become Christian in large measure, those in the Manipur Valley have not. The majority of Meiteis who live in the valley are surrounded by hill tribes in the mountains who have largely converted to Christianity. The Meiteis are of a different culture and see themselves as a higher class than the tribespeople. Because a prejudice barrier exists between the Meitei and the hill people "who stink," evangelization cannot be effectively carried on by these hill Christians.

Furthermore, Indian Christians from other parts of India are rejected because the Meitei feel oppressed by the government.

Foreign missionaries are currently prohibited. So, a dilemma exists when considering *who* might be most effective in reaching this people.

Heavily influenced by Hinduism, they have nonetheless retained much of their own traditional way of life. Famous as the practitioners of one of the four classical traditions of Indian dance, they are restless with Hinduism and are beginning to cast it off. Drama, storytelling and dance are high favorites among these largely illiterate people. Some 5000 have adopted a mixture of Christianity and Hinduism called "Samamahi".

About 90 percent of the people live in rural areas. Because of the strong nationalistic and ethnic feelings, they will want their own, unified church. Drama, storytelling, visuals, films and dances would all be effective methods for communicating Christianity. But that gospel-message will have to be carried by Christian groups they respect and to which they will give a hearing.

```
MOKEN
Burma                                              marc id:  157

alt names:   Selong
             Mawken

pop:         5,000
distinct:    language
             ethnicity
             occupation

languages:                        uses     speak     read
             Moken                  V        100%      nc
             Burmese                T         nc       nc

scripture:   none

rlg chg:     somewhat closed
att chr:     somewhat opposed

religion:                         adherents
             Animism                99%
             Christianity            1%

churches:
             Karen Baptist Convention
```

The Moken are a boat dwelling people who live among the islands of the Mergui Archipelago off the Burmese coast. Their name roughly

EXPANDED DESCRIPTIONS

translated means "immersed in the sea".

The Moken stay together in mobile floating villages (known as *kabang*) of from 10-40 boats. Each village is highly protective and suspicious of other floating villages. People generally marry within their own village. If two *kabang* visit the same bay, they will stay at opposite sides and avoid contact.

Without chiefs or other formally constituted leadership, stability and protection comes through a system of alliance with opium traders and peddlers from the land. Shellfish and oysters, snails and seaworms are exchanged with Chinese and Malay traders for necessities like rice, salt, and clothing. Each floating village has one trader with whom it forms a stable alliance. Normally this single tradesman will make them dependent upon him over the years by gradually turning his village partners into opium addicts. While the Moken know they are exploited by their trading partner, they feel without him they would be at the mercy of all the world.

Because of the isolation of the floating villages, language diversity is a reality, each *kabang* having its own dialect. Each also has its own shamans who help placate the spirits who control both good and bad forces of nature. Most illness is attributed to evil spirits and shamans in trances will suck the illness out and spit it into the wind.

While most of their life is spent wresting subsistance from the sea, they do hunt animals on land and gather fruit, roots, and honey. Here also they hollow out the trunks of trees that serve as their boats. Since they last only about two years, much of their time on land is spent boat-building.

Because of their nomadic sea life, their language diversity, their extreme suspicion of outsiders, and the jealousy of their trading partners, evangelization is difficult. The only known Christian contact at present is through missionaries of Burma's Karen Baptist Church.

MOOR & MALAYS
Sri Lanka   marc id: 309

pop: 895,322

distinct: language
              ethnicity
              religion
              sense of unity

218

languages:		uses	speak	read
	Tamil	V	100%	60%
	Sinhala		50%	nc
	Arabic		50%	nc

scripture: Bible

rlg chg: somewhat closed
att chr: strongly opposed

religion:		adherents	practicing
	Islam	100%	nc

churches:
Church of Ceylon (Anglican)
Methodist
Roman Catholic

There was a time when the Arabs of the Arabian Peninsula were among the world's leading sailors. They were well acquainted with South India and what is today Sri Lanka, and many began to settle as early as 900 years ago. The descendants of these early Arab traders are today called the Moors.

In the early 1700s, the Dutch, seeking to protect their spice interests, imported many Javanese, Indonesians, and Malaysians to act as soldiers. This group, numbering today around 42,000, have remained largely apart, concentrated in Colombo, and speaking their own language. They are known collectively as Malays, and continue to occupy senior positions at different levels in the police and armed forces. In matters of food, dress, and life-style they have retained their ethnic identity.

The Moors and Malays today, though quite diverse, are usually thought of as one group because they share a common minority religion—Islam. Because of their common faith, they share a bloody history of persecution first by the Portuguese, then to a lesser extent by the Dutch and British. This persecution is an extension of the Arab-European struggle for the trade of Southeast Asia which the Arabs largely lost. The Muslims of South India and Sri Lanka lost their trade to the Europeans, but did not lose their faith.

Some Moors today are rice cultivators. Most Moors, however, and almost all Malays are traders and bureaucrats. Even in the rural areas, the villages in the daytime are peopled by women and children, the men having gone to work in towns large and small throughout the country.

In spite of the teachings of Islam, Moors and Malays, like the

EXPANDED DESCRIPTIONS

Hindus, recognize various caste distinctions among themselves. This is slowly breaking down but its demise is due to the breakup of the Muslim society rather than any egalitarian motives. There are no Christian churches reported among them and the history of persecution has made them highly resistant to the gospel.

```
MUSLIMS IN UNITED ARAB EMIRATES                    marc id:   365

pop:          202,000
distinct:     religion

languages:                          uses       speak       read
              Arabic                  V         100%         nc
              Urdu                                5%         nc
              Farasi                              5%         nc

scripture:    Bible

rlg chg:      somewhat open
att chr:      strongly opposed

religion:                               adherents
              Islam                         99%
              Christianity                   1%

churches:
              Independent
```

Work starts about 4 a.m. under flood lights and stops around noon. There is plenty of work to do but it is simply too hot. Everywhere one looks, there are clean new buildings, roads, and other projects. Everyone who wants to can work and those who do not are cared for. Thousands of foreign workers, Indians, Pakistanis, Egyptians, and others, legal and illegal, seek even the lowest paying job. It pays better than they could possibly make at home. There is probably no place in the world developing faster than the United Arab Emirates.

The UAE is made up of seven tiny shiekdoms on the Persian gulf. Oil has been discovered in two of the seven Emirates, and one, Abu Dhabi, now has the highest per capita income in the world. Despite public assistance efforts, however, the wealth remains unevenly distributed. Most of the population, including the large number of immigrants, now live in the towns. Everywhere, stunning contrasts may be seen in the people's tendency to combine the traditional devout Muslim culture with a new and sophisticated life-style. Veils

220

and turbans are readily mixed with jewels and Mercedes.

Outside the urban areas, the life of the bedouin nomad is much the same as it always has been. Their environment is one of extreme heat and vast expanses of desert sands. They live on goat and camel milk, meat, dates and unleavened bread. They live in goat hair tents, moving from place to place, following the shifting pastures that spring up from dews or local rainfalls. Disease is uncommon in the sterile, sunbathed climate.

Oil has brought wealth but with it enormous problems. Still, virtually everyone lives better than their forefathers did. Most Christians are non-Arab immigrants or temporary workers. Freedom of worship is ostensibly protected for everyone. Rapid change and increasing exposure to western ideas are making the peoples of the emirates more receptive to the gospel and some converts are being won. Eastern Orthodox Christians, especially Arabs, may be the most effective witnesses to the peoples of the UAE. Oral communication of the gospel in tape, radio, or memorized form will probably best facilitate evangelization of the nomads. And, expressive, poetic translations of scripture that can be chanted are needed to fully communicate to Koran-steeped Arab hearts.

```
NAFAARA
Ghana                                        marc id:  654

alt names:  Banda
            Nafana

pop:        40,000
also in:    Ivory Coast
distinct:   language
            ethnicity

languages:                      uses      speak     read
            Nafaara             V         100%      nc
            Twi                 T         nc        nc
            English                       nc        nc

scripture:  portions

rlg chg:    somewhat open
att chr:    somewhat favorable

religion:                       adherents
            Animism             93%
            Islam               5%
            Christianity        2%
```

EXPANDED DESCRIPTIONS

churches:
> African Faith Congregation
> Presbyterian
> Roman Catholic
> Wycliffe Bible Translators

The Nafaara inhabit the grasslands in the northwest corner of the Brong-Ahafo region of Ghana. Most live in villages of 100-500 people, maintaining small farms on which they grow yams, cotton, and tobacco for cash, and guinea corn, millet, and beans for their own use. Some also raise cattle, goats, and sheep. They consider themselves poor compared to their neighbors, and when the rains fail they are poor indeed.

There is a Christian witness among the Nafaara—Wycliffe is doing Bible translation and has literacy programs in progress. Several missionaries are at work there. The church is small and they have about the same proportion of *committed* Christians as exists in most western churches. The people are fairly mobile and like to travel so they have had a good deal of contact with other customs and other faiths. But most of the people are still ancestor and fetish worshipers. Each home has a family fetish which is passed down from generation to generation. When trouble comes, when sickness attacks, when the rains fail, sacrifices are made by the head of the house. In the towns, there are bigger fetishes—a certain rock, a certain tree—where the whole town gathers to worship. The counsel of fetish priests is sought in times of trouble.

Medical attention and other assistance have been influential among those who have become Christians. Scripture portions and literacy programs should begin to have an effect in the near future. The Gospel of Mark has been translated and recorded on tape and has been favorably received. Further cassette ministries should no doubt be pursued. The churches and missionaries should definitely try to work in Nafaara instead of the Twi language that has been used in the past. But Christian lives of selfless people who will work *with* them as well as witness will continue to be the most visible and understandable manifestation of God's love for the Nafaara.

NDEBELE
Rhodesia   marc id: 1235

alt names: Matabele

pop: 1,000,000
222

distinct:	language ethnicity			

languages:		uses	speak	read
	Sindebele	VGSW	100%	40%
	English	TSW	nc	40%

chr lit: 75%
scripture: New Testament

rate chg: rapid
rlg chg: somewhat open
att chr: somewhat favorable

religion:		adherents	practicing
	Roman Catholic	5%	2%
	Protestant	15%	5%
	Animism	80%	50%

churches:		members	community
	Brethren in Christ	3,400	5,000
	Lutheran Mission Society	nc	nc

profile:
- 0% No awareness of Christianity
- 50% Aware of existence
- 20% Some knowledge of gospel
- 10% Understand the message
- 10% Personal challenge to receive Christ
- 0% Decision to accept Christ
- 9% In a fellowship
- 1% Propagators of the gospel

The Ndebele people live in the hilly bush country of southwestern Rhodesia (Matabeleland). They speak a Khoisan (click) language (Sindebele) related to Zulu. In the country, the Ndebele live in clusters of brown mud and dung huts. In the city, they live in townships outside incorporated white European areas. From there, they stream into the cities on foot and bicycles and on incredibly crowded buses for each day's labor.

The Ndebele emerged as a distinct nation in 1823 when the famous Mzilikazi led his people in rebellion against the Zulus. Mzilikazi and his warriors were defeated and forced to flee from Natal to southwestern Rhodesia. As they fled, they plundered weaker groups and incorporated them into a new, powerful nation in the western half of Rhodesia. Today, the military organization is gone, but the old pride remains and the people remember that they are conquerors of ancient African kingdoms.

Underlying the Ndebele view of life is a conviction of a complete

EXPANDED DESCRIPTIONS

continuity of life. With this view, the ancestral spirits are the dominant factor in interpreting life. Because of this, it is said that "there are not five Ndebele in Rhodesia, even among Christians, who don't also worship their forefathers".

By the end of 1978, if settlement agreements are carried out, Rhodesia will be known as Zimbabwe and the Ndebele will be participating in the management of a new state with great potential. It is vitally important for all of southern Africa that the Ndebele and other groups know the true God who can "hear them from heaven and forgives their sins, and make their land prosperous again."

```
NUER
Sudan                                            marc id:  576

pop:        844,000
also in:    Ethiopia
distinct:   language
            ethnicity

languages:                          uses    speak    read
            Nuer                     V       100%      nc
            Arabic                   T        nc       nc

scripture:  New Testament

att chr:    indifferent

religion:                        adherents
            Animism                 99%
            Christianity             1%

churches:
            Church of Christ
```

Like many of his pastoral neighbors, a Nuer's dearest possession is his cattle. Life depends on cattle and a Nuer will risk his life to defend them or to raid his neighbor's cattle. His world view is that of a herdsman and his prestige is measured by the quantity and quality of the cattle he owns. Men and women take the names of their favorite oxen or cows and prefer to be greeted by their cattle names. While they do engage in agricultural pursuits, the care of cattle is the only labor they enjoy. It is said that conversation on virtually any subject will inevitably involve a discussion of cattle.

It is easy to understand why cattle play an important part in the Nuer's religion and ritual. Cows are dedicated to the ghosts of the

224

lineages of the owner and any personal spirits that may have possessed them at any time. The Nuer establish contact with these ghosts and spirits by rubbing ashes along the backs of oxen or cows dedicated to them, through the sacrifice of cattle. No important Nuer ceremony of any kind is complete without such a sacrifice.

Those who would minister effectively to the Nuer must obviously learn well the language and life-style pertinent to cattle herding. It has been shown, too, that a great many aspects of the Nuer culture are similar to cultural distinctives of Old Testament peoples (McFall, *Approaching the Nuer of Africa Through the Old Testament*, Pasadena: William Carey Library, 1970). These similarities include features of their social structure, the kinship reckoning and extended family systems, aspects of marriage and divorce, rites of passage, and even religious concepts of God, man, spirits, sin, and sacrifices. Clear presentations of God's working among the Hebrews, first when they were a nomadic pastoral group and then when they became sedentary will provide many parallels which will be meaningful to the Nuer.

The southern Sudan has been a troubled and restless area for many years and the largely Muslim government has placed some restrictions on Christian activity there. But in the midst of turmoil and unsettled conditions, people are turning to Christ as rapidly as anywhere in Africa. The Nuer are among these receptive people and it is extremely important to begin in earnest to reap this field which is white unto harvest.

PALAUNG
Burma   marc id: 156

alt names: Palong
             Ta-Ang

pop: 150,000
distinct: language
             ethnicity

languages:		uses	speak	read
	Palaung	V	100%	nc
	Shan	T	nc	nc

scripture: none

rlg chg: somewhat closed
att chr: somewhat opposed

225

EXPANDED DESCRIPTIONS

religion:	adherents
Buddhism	99%
Christianity	1%

The Palaung are located principally in the northwestern corner of the Shan state, although some are to be found in southern Kachin state and China. They live in compact villages on hilltops and ridges from which they practice a slash-and-burn dry rice agriculture. Beans, maize, peas, tea, tobacco also are grown. Wet rice is present only in a small part of their economy. Tea, both dry and pickled, is the major trade item. Opium and betel are present but not widespread.

The Buddhism that is present is wedded to practices and beliefs in many traditional spirits. Almost all villages have a monastery compound. It acts as the residence for the monks as well as the village school where boys receive the little education available. Two schools of Buddhism are followed, the Burmese and the Yuan or Shan forms. Monks from the central Palaung area take advanced training at Mandalay or Rangoon.

Daily life is thought to be face to face with the actions of spirits. Ordinary people make a variety of offerings to placate them. Illness is attributed to the actions of evil spirits and the services of a diviner/medical practitioner serves to identify and counteract the proper spirit. This magical specialist also serves as a source for amulets and incantations to provide success in a number of the important activities of life.

The Palaung are organized under the authority of village headman and elders. The people as a whole are subject to a Prince, a state system with a petty court, similar to the Shan people. In addition to the calendrical ceremonies of Buddhism, the Prince, elders, and people gather annually for a great festival. Buddhist monks recite their scripture and a senior member of the Prince summons all the spirits to receive a special offering.

Most cultural influence has come from the Shan. What written literature is found is in the Shan script. Very little evangelization has taken place. There are only one or two churches. The most effective evangelists would be Shan Christians. While the Bible is available in Shan and many Palaung are bilingual, the vernacular is an influential tool to be used.

Creative approaches to the existential concerns of the Palaung will be crucial in stimulating any major movement. Christian faith and practitioners must be able to connect God's power to everyday anx-

226

iety about evil spirits, to the healing of sickness when medicine is not available, and to the counteracting of the curses of witches.

```
PYGMY (MBUTI)                                        marc id:   396
Zaire

pop:         40,000
also in:     Central African Empire
             Gabon
distinct:    language
             ethnicity
```

languages:		uses	speak	read
	Swahili	T	nc	nc
	local language	V	100%	2%

```
chr lit:     1%
scripture:   none

rlg chg:     somewhat closed
att chr:     indifferent
```

religion:		adherents
	Animism	99%
	Christianity	1%

```
churches:    Africa Inland
             Emmanuel Mission Nyankundi
```

Known since the time of the Egyptian Pharaohs, the Pygmies have maintained their forest way of life for over 4,500 years. Roving about in bands of from six to thirty families, they are fed by a generous forest with abundant game and plant life.

The Pygmies are extraordinarily well suited to their equatorial forest life. While many Africans find the forest not only oppressive and harsh but positively fearsome because of the spirits that live there, the Pygmies actually flourish and celebrate their habitat. For them, the forest is a provider, protector, and deity.

They enjoy an intermittent relationship with their farmer-neighbors. From them they receive various cultivated food goods and metal tools. The farmer-neighbors also lead the rituals for marriage, funerals, and initiation for the Pygmies. In exchange the Pygmies provide temporary labor as well as meat from the numerous animals which they kill in the forest. But the Pygmies reject a settled way of life and live a completely distinctive culture. Each pygmy family is associated with a specific village family in a traditional reciprocal trade relationship. There is no single, shared Pygmy language. Whatever it was, all that remains is the remnants of an intonation pattern that is superimposed on the local African dialect spoken by the villagers with whom they trade.

The Methodists of Zaire, as well as the Africa Inland Church, have contacts with Pygmies. But if they are to be successfully reached, it will necessitate people living and traveling with them in the forest. Only during the honey seasons do large groups of Pygmies gather in communal activity. The rest of the year they are divided into hundreds and thousands of small hunting bands. A nomadic and non-literate form of Christianity will be necessary if this group is to receive a valid opportunity to understand and know Jesus Christ.

Government policy for sometime has been to attempt to induce Pygmies to adopt a settled mode of life, to leave the forest for settlements along the roads being built. A great deal of intermarriage with villagers has occurred among those who have done so.

```
QUICHE                                          marc id:  152
Guatamala
```

pop:	500,000
distinct:	language
	ethnicity

languages:		uses	speak	read
	Quiche	V	100%	5%
	Spanish	T	50%	nc

chr lit:	65%
scripture:	New Testament

rlg chg:	somewhat open
att chr:	somewhat favorable

religion:		adherents
	Christo-Paganism	93%
	Protestant	7%

churches:	Principe De Paz (Pentecostal)
	Presbyterian
	Central American Mission
	Roman Catholic

The Quiches live in the midwestern highlands of Guatemala. Volcanos ulcerate their beautiful land of "eternal spring." When the earth shakes it is said that the gods who hold up the four corners of the world have grown tired and are shifting the burden on their shoulders.

Life revolves around subsistence farming and the production of colorful handwoven fabrics for the tourist market. Most Quiche have two houses, one in the farming areas and one in town. Only on market days and during festivals are the homes in the towns occupied. Thus, their villages are often called "vacant towns", the primary permanent residents being the Ladinos (westernized, spanish-speaking people). The Quiche are surrounded by Christian symbols, but Christ is little more than a statue who is carried about in the Easter festival. He is simply an important member of a religious collection of saints, spirits, gods, devils, and good luck charms.

Conquered in the sixteenth century, they were "Christianized." But the ideas and meanings behind Christian involvements are derived from traditional Indian folk religion. Domestic rituals associated with the beliefs concerning witchcraft, illness, and curing are handled by shamans. Communities are organized by a civil-religious hierarchy that cares for the local saints in the churches as well as organizing the community festivals. Each community also has a number of religious brotherhoods (*cofradias*) who care for the saints. Prestige and respect are given to those who serve these offices well.

The foundations of their syncretistic religious world are being shaken by a mighty movement of the Spirit. After decades of careful church planting, they are now beginning to respond much more rapidly to the gospel. When led by lay leaders and involved in church councils and synods that speak their vernacular language, their congregations tend to grow most rapidly. Dependence upon Ladino pastors and structures is a major hindrance to the spread of the gospel. Theological education by extension finds its origins in the attempt to train the lay pastors and leaders of this part of Guatemala.

RACETRACK RESIDENTS marc id: 476
United States of America

pop: 50,000
distinct: occupation
residence

languages:		uses	speak	read
	English	TV	nc	nc
	Spanish		40%	nc

EXPANDED DESCRIPTIONS

scripture: Bible

rlg chg: somewhat open
att chr: somewhat favorable

religion: adherents
      Unknown   10%
      Secularism   80%
      Christianity   10%

churches: Racetrack Chaplaincy America

Literally "behind" the glamour, silks, and excitement of the horse racing tracks of America, some 50,000 persons live and work. It's called the "backside," and for the people living here, out of the horseracing limelight, the work is hard, monotonous, and lonely.

The job of caring for the celebrities of horse racing—the horses—employs many kinds of workers. "Hot walkers" walk the horses after races to cool them off. It's the lowest prestige position on the backside job scale. Exercise boys and girls have much higher prestige and often even a future as jockeys in the racing circuit. Other workers, many of them older persons, do such jobs as grooming, feeding, "cold walking," and other stable labor.

There are six racetrack chaplains nationwide, and they say the biggest problems are that the workers consider themselves unimportant—going nowhere, or "has beens" from the glamorous life out front. Most of the workers have families but unless they too are racetrackers, they lose contact with them as they migrate from track to track with the racing seasons.

Some racetrack dwellers actually have little contact with the "outside" world, even though they are situated in suburban America. Alcoholism and gambling are major problems. Many, living in poverty caused by gambling, exist under the illusion that the next horse will finally "make it" for them. A large number, too, are illegal Mexican aliens who, because of their status, find it impossible to move about in search of other work. Sixty to 85 percent of the backside workers are Spanish speaking.

Racetrack chaplains presently conduct chapel services in the recreation halls and have an open office door there for counsel. In 1976, the chaplain of the Santa Anita racetrack in the Southern California area reported that 20 workers gave their hearts to Christ and 14 more recommitted their lives to him. More flexible, bilingual, and open-minded Christians, both men and women, able to move with races are needed to evangelize these people. The workers need to have a sense of worth communicated to them and many need legal aid, employment, or other assistance to help them out of a life they feel is unproductive.

```
SAMA-BADJAW                                    marc id:   389
Philippines

alt names:  Orang Laut
            Samal
            Sea Gypsy

pop:        120,000
also in:    Malaysia
            Indonesia
distinct:   occupation
            ethnicity

languages:                          uses     speak     read
            Samal dialects           V       100%       nc
            Samal Moro                        nc         nc

chr lit:    10%
scripture:  portions

rlg chg:    somewhat open
att chr:    somewhat opposed

religion:                        adherents
            Islam-Animist           99%
            Christianity             1%

churches:   Christian & Msny. Alliance
```

The Sea Gypsies live in, by, and with the sea. Traditionally, they lived in floating boat villages, but very few boat communities continue. Most have tended to coalesce into larger settlements made up of houses on stilts in calm lagoons close to market centers. As in the past, they spend most of their time harvesting the teeming life of the submerged terraces and coral reefs.

The Sea Gypsies are suspicious and wary of land dwellers who have often exploited them in the past. They eat only fish and vegetables, regarding the meat of land animals as unclean. Trading relationships (for things such as vegetables, knives, matting, pans) with land people are now relatively peaceful. In the past, they were raided

EXPANDED DESCRIPTIONS

and sold as slaves. Their land neighbors continue to despise them and consider them inferiors who can be exploited. For this reason, Western missionaries who are not associated with the land dwellers are often more effective than national Christians from the island peoples of this area.

No one knows how many they currently number. Estimates range from 20,000 to 200,000. Their area of habitation includes Mindanao, Kalimantan, Sulawesi, the islands of the Muluccan Straits, and south to Flores and Sambawa of Indonesia. They are fragmented into hundreds of lagoon villages with no single unifying factor other than their common focus on livelihood derived from the sea. They speak a number of different Samal dialects.

The religious serenity of the Sea Gypsies is maintained by both the Muslim *imam* and the animistic shaman who join hands in a variety of ceremonies and practices while they worship Allah. Their greatest fear is the surrounding world of spirits that hover about them. They believe that these spirits, when angered, burden people with illness and misfortune. It is the task of the numerous shamans (nearly one for each two or three households) to cure the sick and to help the living avoid offending the spirits.

```
SERERE                                              marc id:  215
Senegal

alt names:   Serer

pop:         700,000
distinct:    language
             ethnicity

languages:                        uses      speak     read
             Serere               V         100%      nc

religion:                         adherents
             Animism              44%
             Islam                40%
             Protestant           1%
             Roman Catholic       15%

churches:    Roman Catholic
             Assemblies of God
```

In sprawling villages in the southern coastal regions of Senegal and northern Gambia live a people remarkable for their skill in grow-

ing peanuts—a group known as the Serere. Independent and proud
of their traditions, the present day Serere are descendants of earlier
Serere who refused to accept Islam, and who, in spite of adversity
and conquest, refused to be assimilated into any other group. Today
they are distinguished by an extraordinarily complex social hierar-
chical system which recognizes at least 11 different social statuses
and an organization of political states under paramount chiefs or
kings.

In addition to peanut farming and other types of agriculture, the
Serere also engage in fishing and shell fishing. Their remarkable
farming and other skills have until recently made very dense settlements possible—up to 250 persons per square mile—the highest
in Senegal. Now, however, the population has outstripped productivity and the Serere have begun to move into new areas and to take
temporary work in the towns. Comparatively few have stayed to live
permanently in the city as yet. Those who do have often designated
themselves as Wolof, the dominant group in Senegal, who are more
often associated with city life.

The Serere have been slower than other groups to accept moder-
nizing trends or new religions. Most still adhere to traditional beliefs
and practices though some have recently become Muslims and
about 15 percent are Roman Catholics. Most educated Serere are
professing Christians, including President and foremost statesman
Leopold Senghor, who is a Roman Catholic. Protestant work to date
has largely emphasized literacy and the production of Bible story
booklets. There are no reports, however, of significant church growth
or of people turning to Christ in any significant fashion.

```
SOMALI                                          marc id:  403
Somalia

pop:       2,500,000
also in:   Ethiopia
           Kenya
distinct:  language
           ethnicity

languages:                        uses      speak     read
           Somali                  V         100%       5%
           Arabic                             nc        nc
           Italian                            nc        nc

chr lit:   95%
scripture: New Testament
```

EXPANDED DESCRIPTIONS

att chr: strongly opposed

religion: adherents
              Islam   99%
              Christianity   1%

churches: community
              Roman Catholic   3,300
              Mennonite   nc

Christians have "no face" in Somalia. That is, said a Somali Bible translator working in Kenya, "they are despised". This translator's life would be in danger were he to do his work in his Islamic homeland. In 1974, there were only 200 known believers in Somalia and any kind of Christian testimony brought immediate opposition.

Somalis are a proud, beautiful people who live a hard nomadic life in a land where annual rainfall is often less than four inches. Camels are their wealth, prestige, and power. Somali life is essentially a pursuit of water and grazing land for the camels. Fierce feuds stemming from water rights are distressingly common, especially in the dry seasons.

The Somalis believe that women should be charming but docile. Traditionally, they have been regarded as inferior to men and even as uneducable. Despite this, their wisdom and experience have always been respected. An old proverb says "he who will refuse to accept the knowledge of an old woman will lose his children." Today, Somali women are treated more or less equally according to the sentiments of the families, and they may become very influential if trends continue.

The Somali language has never had an official means of writing. It has a rich oral literature of poetry and folk tales. Precise, skillful elocution is important for Somali speakers. Spoken or chanted poetry is especially important as a means of communicating folk traditions, ideas, and propaganda. It is used in recording historical events, teaching children, speech making, and entertainment on long night journeys. Somalis use their memories in communication. Often messengers memorize a message and it is a point of honor for them to deliver it exactly as given.

It is clear that evangelism of the Somalis can be facilitated by developing means of oral communication of the gospel. Perhaps Somali Christian poets can be enlisted to develop extensive biblical poetry sagas. Tape and radio ministries may also be useful, and many other means by which the Somalis can "hide God's word in their hearts." At present, foreign Christian evangelists are not welcome in the country. Evangelization of the Somalis will be done strategically in Kenya.

```
SPIRITISTS                                    marc id:  28
Brazil

pop:       9,000,000
distinct:  religion

languages:                        uses      speak      read
           Portuguese              V         100%        nc

scripture: Bible

rlg chg:   somewhat closed
att chr:   strongly opposed

religion:                       adherents
           Animism                 99%
           Christianity            1%
```

The ceremony may last all night. The air is heavy with incense. A "mother of father" of the saints, dressed in white with turbans and beads, leads the dance to the feverish pounding of drums. The people continue until they are possessed by the spirits and consciousness lapses into trance, or until their legs refuse to hold them and they drop in a stupor of exhaustion.

There are many spiritist and cult groups in Brazil, mostly in the urban centers of Rio de Janeiro and Sao Paulo. Some center on fetishes, some on particular saints, others on particular practices. Some have Angolan or Yoruban roots. Most today are a mixture of African cultic, Amerindian, Protestant Pentecostal, and folk Catholic beliefs. Many of the participants are women, for it seems cult participation gives them a temporary dominance over the privileged males. All participants are poor—when a member rises in social standing, he or she may be given a going away feast, for they are expected to leave the group. Every cult follower belongs to a cult "house" where he meets with other followers under the leadership of a particular priest or priestess.

Most people involved in these cults have been drawn by the need to "consult a saint" over personal problems—love, job, health. Sometimes healings take place, sometimes obligations are incurred. As in folk Catholicism, the aid sought is for *this* world rather than for eternal salvation, and often promises are made to do something in exchange if the saints fulfill their desires. The influence and outlook of Spiritism goes far beyond those who actually participate in cultic or ritual acts.

Spiritist cults thrive because they reassert the value of poor, hurting people in the anonymity and misery of the slums. The priests or priestesses act as neighbors, doctors, parents, and pastors all rolled into one. The cult members are comforted and strengthened by the practitioners as well as by other cult members. The cults give them confidence, happiness, freedom, and community. Participation in the Spiritist and cultic movements are efforts at coping with the problems and sufferings of this world as it is experienced in the large urban centers of Brazil. But it is not the spirit of evil, fear, and possession these people need but God's Spirit who gives hope and peace, and a church that also displays concrete, immediate concern for the daily trials and stresses of the urban poor.

SWATIS   marc id: 1232
Pakistan

alt names: Yusafzai Pathans

pop: 600,000
distinct: language
            ethnicity
            religion
            residence
            significant problems

languages:		uses	speak	read
	Swati	VG	100%	nc
	Urdu	TSW	10%	5%

scripture: none

rate chg;   moderate
rlg chg: indifferent
att chr: somewhat opposed

religion:		adherents	practicing
	Islam	60%	30%
	Islam-Animist	40%	36%

churches: Assemblies of God
            Evangelical Alliance Mission

profile: 74% No awareness of Christianity
           20% Aware of existence
            5% Some knowledge of gospel
            1% Understand the message
            0% Personal challenge to receive Christ
            0% Decision to accept Christ
            0% In a fellowship
            0% Propagators of the gospel

The Swatis are a branch of the Yusufzai Pathans of the northwest frontier province of Pakistan. Up until 1969, they were a semiautonomous state ruled by a tribal chieftan, and somewhat isolated from the rest of the country. In 1969, the government of Pakistan "retired" the tribal chief, opened up an all-weather road into the Swat Valley, and introduced civil servants, police, and government-managed schools and hospitals.

Traditionally, all Pathans are a fiercely independent, honor-touchy, warlike mountain people who keep to themselves. But the Swatis, because some have settled on agricultural land and some have gone into business, have mellowed somewhat and are more tolerant than the frontier branch of Yusufzais.

By religion, this group is nominally Muslim. About 30 percent practice the prescribed obligations of Islam. There is evidence of some animistic practices. Because of the exaggerated sense of honor, tempers are short, and blood feuds are common.

This people is undergoing a change in their life-style due to the change of administration internally, outside Pakistanis coming in, and establishing contact with the rest of country. Up until recently, it was forbidden to preach or distribute Christian literature in the state, but since the full incorporation of Swat into Pakistan, it comes under constitutional law which allows the free propagation of religion.

Currently no resident missionaries are working with the Swatis. Gospel teams visit during the summer, and citizens who can read will occasionally enroll in Bible correspondence courses. Pakistani citizens and missionaries from commonwealth countries can come and go easily.

TAMILS (INDIAN)   marc id: 313
Sri Lanka

pop: 1,195,368
distinct: language
            ethnicity

EXPANDED DESCRIPTIONS

languages:		uses	speak	read
	Tamil	V	100%	50%
	Sinhala		10%	nc

chr lit: 60%
scripture: Bible

rlg chg: somewhat open
att chr: somewhat favorable

religion:		adherents
	Hinduism	93%
	Protestant	1%
	Roman Catholic	6%

churches:		community
	Ceylon Pentecostal Mission	2,500
	Church of Ceylon (Anglican)	2,500
	Dutch Reformed	nc
	Methodist	1,000
	Roman Catholic	100,000

There are two distinct Tamil people groups in Sri Lanka. The 1.4 million "Ceylon" Tamils have been in Sri Lanka for nearly 1000 years. They are well-established Sri Lankans and prominent in professions in civil service.

Another 1.2 Tamils are "Indian," brought to Sri Lanka in the nineteenth and twentieth centuries to work on tea plantations in the Kandyan highland region. These people were drawn from the poorest groups of south India and badly exploited by the British. They have remained largely illiterate. No significant interaction has developed between them and the Ceylon Tamils. The Indian Tamils have retained their language and Hindu religion. They have been isolated from the main stream of life and are considered foreign by the other ethnic groups. Various legislative acts have had the effects of rendering many of them stateless, while offers by India to repatriate them have either been unacceptable or agonizingly slow.

The Indian Tamils, most of whom live on the communal tea planta tions, have suffered most when there have been critical food shortages on the island. The food shortage problems have eased in recent years but often at the expense of the tea industry and consequently of the jobs of the Indian Tamils.

Contact with the Indian Tamils by Christian missions has been restricted by the Sri Lankan government, which has taken several reactionary steps to rid themselves of the "taint" of past western rule and influences. These measures include 1) elimination of Sunday as a holiday, replaced by Buddhist holy days that fall on various days, 2) provision for compulsory religious education in the religion of parents (since most parents are Buddhists, the effect is to extend Buddhism), 3) strict limitation of Christian broadcasting, 4) taxation of all religious bodies except Buddhism, and 5) restriction on the entrance of Christian missionaries.

```
TONGA, GWEMBE VALLEY                            marc id:  188
Zambia

pop:        86,000
also in:    Rhodesia
distinct:   language
            ethnicity

languages:                          uses      speak      read
            Chitonga                  V        100%        nc
            English                              5%        nc

chr lit:    90%
scripture:  Bible

att chr:    somewhat opposed

religion:                           adherents
            Animism                    98%
            Protestant                  1%
            Roman Catholic              1%

churches:                           community
            Chabu-Boma Msn. (Holiness)     500
            Church of Christ                71
            Kancindu Mission (Methodist) 1,000
            Roman Catholic                 500
```

"I have never known even one missionary to take 30 minutes to sit down and, without being in a hurry, talk man to man about Christ. It must always be in a group way." This tragic critique by a Tonga man (quoted in Shewmaker's *Tonga Christianity,* William Carey Library, 1970) says volumes about the status of Christianity among the Tonga. Many Tonga feel that missionaries have never really spoken to them *in particular* but have always preached *at* rather than communicated *with* them.

Missions to the Tonga have relied almost exclusively on the school approach—building schools and conducting Sunday services in them. Christianity has become identified as a classroom religion, largely participated in by women and children. The men, often un-consciously humiliated by Christianity's association with children and education, have felt left out with nothing to contribute. The missionaries too, going to the field with great spiritual fervor and then thrust into a school as their primary or only task, have become frustrated and lost their cutting edge.

The Tonga might be considered your "typical" African tribe—considerable contact with "white" Christianity, concerned with the spirits and ancestor veneration, prone to drinking home-brewed beer, desirous of polygamous households, and committed to the extended family. They have been asked though to pull themselves up by their own bootstraps as they have been told, "Put away your wives, stop drinking, and stop worshiping evil spirits *before* you become Christians."

In spite of past mistakes, the Tonga can and should be reached for Christ. Such things as *personal* house to house evangelism, aimed at bringing whole families into the church; meetings exclusively for the influential men to encourage decisions by them first; identification with their life-style, joys, sorrows, and aspirations; teaching stewardship and responsibility; and an emphasis on house churches will very likely stimulate rapid church growth among the Tonga.

```
TUAREG
Niger                                          marc id:   46

pop:        200,000
distinct:   language
            ethnicity
            kinship
            sense of unity

languages:                              uses      speak     read
            Tamachek                     V        100%       nc

att chr:    strongly opposed

religion:                             adherents    practicing
            Islam                       100%           nc
```

Their home is on the margin of an uninhabitable world encompassing an area equivalent to all of West Europe and the United Kingdom. The rainfall is highly uncertain and in recent years, they have sustained massive losses of their herds of camels, goats, sheep, and cattle. The Sahara can be as cruel as it is hot.

Descendants of the early Berber inhabitants of North Africa, the Tuareg are a proud and beautiful people. They retain vestiges of ancient contact with early Christianity, including monogamy and the sign of the cross. Though they are Islamic, it is the men who are veiled. The women have greater freedom than most Muslim women.

Famine has driven many of them from their original campgrounds. They have flocked south into the villages and towns where they could receive food and try to start over again after their camels died one by one. Even their traditional trade in the annual salt caravan across the Sahara Desert is threatened.

Fewer than 5 percent have heard the gospel in any way. Through years of persistent effort, several tracts have been written in Shafina, the indigenous script which is non-Roman, non-Arabic. The Gospel of Mark is translated but not available in this script. Literature distribution takes place in market places to those who can read. Christian songs written to be sung in the Tuareg traditional style have been big hits. Great chiefs have had them sung at their royal courts.

They are curious about Christianity. Yet Islam is still very strong. To become a Christian has often meant to face death. Their name originally came from the Arabs who called them *Tawarek,* which means "God-forsaken." This generous, courageous, and intelligent people need to know that God has not forsaken them, but given his son on the cross which they already use as a sign of their identity.

Basic contact with the Tuareg is to be found in the market stalls or on trek at their shifting campsites. To minimize animosity or suspicion, the Tuareg nobles and religious leaders need to know about the activities and movements of Christian missionaries. The government is aware of Christian missions and open to missionaries. At present so few are seeking to learn the Tuareg language and ways that the degree of evangelization is likely to remain very low.

```
TURKANA FISHING COMMUNITY
Kenya                                          marc id:  475

alt names:  Turkana Tribe

pop:        20,000
distinct:   occupation

languages:                        uses     speak     read
            Turkana                V        100%       2%
            Swahili                T         20%       nc
            English                          nc        nc
```

EXPANDED DESCRIPTIONS

chr lit:	75%	
scripture:	portions	
rlg chg:	somewhat open	
att chr:	somewhat favorable	

religion:		adherents
	Animism	95%
	Secularism	1%
	Protestant	3%
	Roman Catholic	1%

churches:		community
	Africa Inland Church	250
	Roman Catholic	nc

For generations the Turkana have been a widely scattered tribe of nomadic families. Roaming an area of over 30,000 square miles in north-western Kenya, they have driven their cattle, goats, camels, and donkeys in search of vegetation and water. Survival has been made difficult by the widespread overgrazing of the vast windswept desert plain on which they exist.

As a result of a drought in 1960-61, thousands of nomadic Turkana sought relief in famine camps. As the years went by, the relief economy was slowly replaced by an economy based on the catch of fish in the huge neighboring lake—Lake Turkana.

Now located in semisettled villages stretching up and down about 160 miles of the lakeshore, they eat and sell the abundance their nets are able to take. The largest center is at Kalokol with a permanent community of nearly 5000.

The various boarding schools, medical clinics, government agencies and churches are ministering to the variety of needs. Tremendous responsiveness to the gospel is present among this 10 percent of the larger Turkana tribe. Many are abandoning adherence to the old traditional Turkana religion, identified mainly by its reliance upon the ministrations of diviners, independent prophets, and witch doctors.

Hard times are ahead for the traditionally nomadic Turkana. As more and more of them find it necessary to settle in agricultural or fishing communities, they will be open to a new way of life. The reaching of the fishing Turkana is strategic since many of them continue to maintain their family connections with their herding relatives. When they become Christian, they are able to share Christ with their nomadic relatives. The Christian faith will spread among the nomadic Turkana only if there are other Turkana Christians to be with them and to care for them. Western missionaries and the dedicated Kenyan school teachers and evangelists who have gone to evangelize the Turkana are effective largely among the settled groups. The nomadic way of life is too difficult for most of them.

```
TURKISH IMMIGRANT WORKERS
German Federal Republic                        marc id:  134

alt names:  Turkish Guest Workers

pop:        1,000,000
also in:    Netherlands
            Austria
            France
distinct:   language
            ethnicity

languages:                      uses      speak     read
            Turkish              V         100%       60%
            German               T          nc        nc

chr lit:    30%
scripture:  Bible

att chr:    somewhat opposed

religion:                        adherents
            Islam                   99%
            Christianity             1%

churches:
            Assyrian Orthodox
            Roman Catholic
            Protestant
```

    Found in both rural and urban areas of Germany, the Turkish "guest" workers are immigrants who work predominantly in German factories, such as automobile factories or steel mills. They are called guest workers because the Germans do not consider them permanent. The label implies that they come only at the behest of Germany and that Germany is doing them a service. In the initial years after World War II, their labor was seriously in need. Now the spectre of German unemployment makes them less welcome. They fill an important need in Germany for unskilled labor and often take jobs that Germans consider too menial to perform. Economically, they are wanted; psychologically, they are not.

EXPANDED DESCRIPTIONS

The temporary concept is misleading since many workers stay for many years with only a few days or weeks per year back at home. Some are able to bring families but the difficulties are such that most cannot. Because of prejudice, many Germans are unwilling to have Turkish families as tenets. Formerly, workers lived in long barracks with three men to a small twelve-by-six-foot room with the rule always the same—no women. Immorality was encouraged and the divorce rate is four times that of the Turkish population at home. Now most live in city ghettos.

Most Turkish guest workers have tended to remain isolated— defensively preserving their own language and customs. Islam influences their entire way of life, though this is largely cultural and most are quite secularized. For some, Allah has become equated with fate, others are departing from spiritual values and are using materialism to fill the void.

Christians are having some success in winning them through weekend home social gatherings. Typically, they show slides of Turkey and encourage the workers to talk about their families at home. Christians then visit them when they are sick and, as is needed, when they are in jail. These personal ministries are augmented by radio programs and tape ministries.

```
UNIVERSITY STUDENTS
France                                          marc id:  702

pop:        800,000
distinct:   residence
            education

languages:                        uses      speak      read
            French                  V        100%       100%

chr lit:    100%
scripture:  Bible

rlg chg:    somewhat closed
att chr:    indifferent

religion:                        adherents      practicing
            Secularism              26%
            Islam                    2%             nc
            Judaism                  1%             nc
            Protestant               1%             1%
            Roman Catholic          70%             1%
```

churches:

> Campus Crusade for Christ
> Evangelical Alliance Mission
> Navigators
> Operation Mobilization
> Inter-Varsity Christian Fellowship
> Roman Catholic

The fundamental evangelistic problem in relating to French university students is their bitter or skeptical attitude towards the traditional Catholic Church. They fail to understand how or where God could fit into their lives.

Though they have little or no basic Christian doctrinal understanding, except for some confused Catholic theology, they have strong stereotypes of the invalidity and irrelevance of traditional Christianity. The Catholic Church built a beautiful student center at Orleans. When students did not come and would not come, it eventually had to be closed.

Existential philosophy is pervasive. Many are extremely lonely, purposeless and disillusioned with society in general and the education system in particular. There is a strong felt need for deep meaningful human relationships. There also is a strong awareness of injustice and evil in the world and a deep questioning of how God can allow it.

Their openness to change is not matched by opportunity to come to understand what it means to be a real Christian. The most effective communicators to this group are other college students as well as any cultural heroes such as sports stars, entertainers, and even professors. For evangelism to be effective it must appear to be nontraditional, to relate to real felt needs and to be intellectually defensible.

French students, found in some 60 universities, 15 prestigious specialized schools, and numerous technical schools, are tremendously affected by popular culture from the United States. Much of the music and media that find popularity are produced in the States. Nevertheless, there is a strong barrier when the students feel they are being offered a Jesus "imported from America."

Basic techniques to establish contact with students include book tables, casual encounters in cafeterias, door-to-door surveys in dormitories, and special events. Recent reports indicate significant evangelization occuring at Lyons and responsiveness in the Alsace-Lorraine area.

EXPANDED DESCRIPTIONS

UNIVERSITY STUDENTS
German Federal Republic   marc id: 1106

pop: 850,000
distinct: language
              ethnicity
              education
              residence
              economic status
              age

languages:		uses	speak	read
	German	VGW	100%	100%

chr lit: 100%
scripture: Bible

rate chg: moderate
rlg chg: somewhat closed
att chr: indifferent

religion:		adherents
	Roman Catholic	35%
	Protestant	35%
	Unknown	30%

churches:		members	community
	Campus Crusade for Christ	350	350
	Inter-Varsity Chr. Fell.	2,000	1,000
	Navigators	300	300
	Christliche-Tech. Bund	200	200

profile: 0% No awareness of Christianity
              0% Aware of existence
             96% Some knowledge of gospel
              1% Understand the message
              1% Personal challenge to receive Christ
              1% Decision to accept Christ
              1% In a fellowship
              0% Propagators of gospel

Despite Germany's economic progress, only 8 percent of German youth go to colleges and universities (over 40 percent attend in the United States). University students thus tend to be serious, thorough, and well informed. Many are politically involved and leftists of all sorts are quite prevalent among them. Even though Germany has startling material prosperity, many students have a feeling of confusion, anxiety, and impatience—the nagging feeling that all the hard work may really get them nowhere.

Germany's university students are generally quite liberal and few have any Christian outlook on life. Having had religious education in lower-level schools, some might call themselves Christians, but few see any need for life-changing commitments. Unless their fathers happen to be ministers, confirmation or a friend's wedding may have been their last contact with the church.

German university students are much less likely than U.S. students to engage in "frivolous" extracurricular activities such as television watching or attendance at athletic contests. They do, however, sit down for hours over coffee or beer with a few friends and discuss current issues. Some live in dormitory-like student housing, but most live with a family in the university town, sharing the bathroom and eating meals with the family.

Protestant Christianity sprang up on German soil, but in the heat of technology and secularism, it has withered away. Personal, friendship evangelism, Christian music groups, and discussions in coffee houses or other informal locations are the most useful in bringing them to Christ.

UZBEKS
Afghanistan   marc id: 1229

pop: 1,000,000
distinct: language
            ethnicity
            religion
            discrimination
            significant problems

languages:		uses	speak	read
	Uzbeki, Turkic	VG	100%	15%
	Dari, Turkic	TSW	20%	5%

scripture: portions

rate chg: moderate
rlg chg: indifferent
att chr: somewhat favorable

religion:		adherents	practicing
	Islam	40%	30%
	Islam-Animist	60%	60%

profile: 87% No awareness of Christianity
            10% Aware of existence
             2% Some knowledge of gospel

247

EXPANDED DESCRIPTIONS

```
1% Understand the message
0% Personal challenge to receive Christ
0% Decision to accept Christ
0% In a fellowship
0% Propagators of the gospel
```

The one million Uzbeks in Afghanistan along with their six million fellow Uzbeks in Russia constitute the proud progeny of Ghengis Khan, who once ruled all of central Asia. The present group in Afghanistan are displaced people who fled Russia's efforts to collectivize them. They have become goldsmiths, tinsmiths, potters, jewelers, leather workers, and operators of hostel inns for caravaners in northern Afghanistan. Where Tajik are in the ascendancy, the Uzbeks have the more menial jobs such as butchers and ironmongers. Some are shepherds and farmers. None are fully nomadic any longer.

The Uzbeks are Sunni Muslims of the Hanafi sect. Commonly, however, they follow animistic beliefs. Shamans seek communion with the spirit world and receive "guidance" in trance-like states. Black magic is practiced, usually by female witches. The Uzbek *mullah* (Muslim religious leader) is often one who teaches Islam *and* white magic *and* shamanistic divination.

The Uzbeks are strongly independent. Though a minority, they are the largest group of Turkic speakers in Afghanistan and have been agitating to get Turkic accepted as an official language.

Much of history is reflected in Uzbek customs. Being the exchange point for East-West caravan routes, they boast of dishes resembling Italian ravioli and Chinese noodle soups, as well as others borrowed from nearby Tibet. The national sport is Buzkashi. It is a game of consummate skill on horseback in which teams seek to pick up on the run the body of a slain goat. The goat is to be carried to a goal two or three miles away and back. Success depends on close cooperation within the framework of fierce, individual competition.

Recently some Uzbeks in Afghanistan have shown interest in Christianity. Since missionary work, per se, is forbidden in Afghanistan, the need is for "tent-makers" to go in to work in government projects, where Christians known for their integrity are being called for! Such workers interested in the Uzbek people should be prepared to learn Turkic.

YANOMAMO IN BRAZIL   marc id: 1059

alt names: Xirixana
             Uaica

```
pop:          3,000
also in:      Venezuela
distinct:     language
              ethnicity
              kinship
```

languages:		uses	speak	read
	Yanomam (Waica)	V	100%	1%

```
chr lit:      20%
scripture:    portions

rate chg:     slow
rlg chg:      very open
att chr:      indifferent
```

religion:		adherents
	Animism	99%
	Christianity	1%

```
churches:
              Unevangelized Fields Mission
              Roman Catholic
              New Tribes Mission
```

The Yanomamo are an exceptionally fierce and warlike people. Fundamental goals in life include capturing women as wives and killing enemy men. So violent and aggressive are they that head-splitting duels between relatives and friends increase along with the village size. Seldom does the village grow beyond 200 people without splitting into two factions who then become mortal enemies. Villages, obviously, are widely scattered.

Their way of life is sustained by the cultivation of food crops using the slash-and-burn technique. Small patches of tropical forests are cleared, burned and then planted with root cuttings or seeds. The agriculture is prosperous and game in the surrounding forests is plentiful so that subsistance is not a major problem. Some 12,000 additional Yanomamo live in Venezuela in areas surrounding the Orinoco River.

The Yanomamo are accessible by air and radio, and several missions are seeking to introduce them to Christianity. Infant mortality and the death rate from Western diseases is high. Tremendous cultural problems exist in preparing them for their eventual assimilation into modern Venezuelan and Brazilian life. Missions competing with one another as well as tourism are factors gradually shattering their traditional cultural patterns.

249

EXPANDED DESCRIPTIONS

Anthropologists have made this one of the best known Amerindian groups in the United States. Because some missions have been culturally insensitive, the Yanomamo are cited as evidence for banning missionary contact with the Amerindians.

The traditional religious system makes heavy use of an hallucinogenic snuff powder, *ebene*. Shamans blow quantities of this into their nostrils and then call upon spirits to inhabit them as they practice witchcraft against enemy villages. This is a daily practice since the war with the spirits sent by enemy shamans, with the potential of illness and death, is never ending.

The evangelization of the Yanomamo has only just begun. Until and unless Christianity is able to divest itself of its Western cultural outlooks and let Christ live in Yanomamo cultural terms, that task will fail.


```
YAO
Thailand                                              marc id:  611

pop:          19,867
also in:      Laos
              Viet Nam
distinct:     language
              ethnicity

languages:                            uses      speak      read
              Yao (Mien Wa)             V        100%        20%
              Northern Thai            T         80%        nc
              Yunnanese                           60%        nc

chr lit:      40%
scripture:    New Testament

rlg chg:      somewhat open
att chr:      somewhat favorable

religion:                                     adherents
              Animism                            98%
              Protestant                          2%

churches:                                     community
              American Baptist                    nc
              Churches of Christ                 100
              Overseas Missionary Fellowship     500
              Seventh-day Adventist               nc
              Worldwide Evangelization Crusade    nc
```

The Yao myth says that around 2440 B.C. the emperor Kao Hsin promised to give his daughter to anyone who could rid him of his enemy, General Wou. A five colored dog named P'an Hou succeeded in tricking and killing General Wou. With reluctance the emperor kept his promise, the dog married the princess, and their children became the forefathers of the Yao tribe.

Even apart from their myths, the Yao are an exceptionally colorful people. The women often wear beautifully embroidered red and black clothes garnished with silver chains and beads. The Yao practice a careful slash-and-burn agriculture in their mountain villages rotating their fields to allow the forest to regenerate. Traditional ways are still followed and crime is virtually unknown.

The Yao have the highest earning ability of any of the hill tribes of Northern Thailand. They are industrious and friendly, and are adept businessmen, eager to trade and improve their lot. Living at a lower altitude than their neighbors, they are more easily reached by traders and missionaries. While they have considerable contact with outsiders, they rarely intermarry, and the unity and togetherness of the family is one of their highest values.

But life is not really idyllic among the Yao. Opium is their major cash crop and smoking it often becomes a debilitating habit, especially among the old. Their lives are darkened too by the complex beliefs of Taoism. The Yao believe in a variety of gods and demons, such as the gods of the doors, the lord of creation, the lord of longevity, etc. Ghosts and spirits are greatly feared, especially the ghosts of persons who have died violent deaths. Temples and shrines contain the figures of both real and imagined ancestors. Dogs are considered sacred. Sacrifices, exorcism, sorcery, and demonic ceremonies further characterize the Yao's life. These people need the light of Christ to illumine the darkness of superstition.

```
YEMENIS
Yemen, Arab Republic                        marc id:  1061

pop:        5,600,000
distinct:   language
            political loyalty
            ethnicity
            religion
            kinship

languages:                        uses     speak     read
            Arabic (Eastern)      VTSG      100%      10%
```

EXPANDED DESCRIPTIONS

```
chr lit:      10%
scripture:    New Testament

rate chg:     very slow
rlg chg:      very closed
att chr:      strongly opposed
```

religion:		adherents	practicing
	Islam	100%	nc

```
churches:
              Southern Baptist Convention

profile:      0% No awareness of Christianity
             90% Aware of existence
             10% Some knowledge of gospel
              0% Understand the message
              0% Personal challenge to receive Christ
              0% Decision to accept Christ
              0% In a fellowship
              0% Propagators of the gospel
```

The Arab Republic of Yemen is classed by the United Nations as one of the least developed countries in the world, with a per capita GNP estimated at about $210 per year. For 11 centuries before the 1962 revolution, Yemen was ruled by autocratic *Imams*. Under their rule there was no national budget since the revenue of the state was considered part of the Imam's personal income. Thus, public services were nonexistent.

The costumes worn even today reflect the traditions of the country and the present unsettled conditions. The men wear bright scarves and turbans and a kilt-like skirt. Over this most carry a short curved dagger called a *jambia* as a symbol of manhood. Women in the cities are generally kept isolated in their homes and wear veils in public.

Yemenis are about equally split between Zeidi-Shiites and Shafi-Sunni Muslims. This split is reinforced by a corresponding rural-urban dichotomy. The Zeidis live in the mountains and valleys either as nomads or settled agriculturalists. The Shafis live in the cities and control the commerce and craftsmen sectors. The major crafts are weaving, indigo dyeing, boat building, and leather working.

Perhaps because life is so harsh, Yemenis developed the habit of chewing a mildly narcotic plant called *qat* (or kat). Most men and many women and children spend entire afternoons "at the qat." The habit has become a hazard to both mental and physical health, and a social evil because of the large sums spent on it by the poor.

252

Zinacantecos

The Southern Baptists began a clinic in 1964 and established a hospital at Jibla in 1968. The gospel has been presented to patients, but as a whole, Yemenis remain very resistant to the good news.

```
ZINACANTECOS
Mexico                                           marc id:  95

pop:         10,000
distinct:    language
             ethnicity
             religion

languages:                          uses      speak      read
             Tzotzil, Chenalho        V        100%        nc
             Spanish                  T         40%         5%

chr lit:     5%
scripture:   New Testament

rlg chg:     somewhat closed
att chr:     strongly opposed

religion:                        adherents
             Christo-Paganism       99%
             Roman Catholic          1%

churches:                         members      community
             Roman Catholic          nc           100
             Reformed Church in America  15          nc
```

Casual visitors to the 15 hamlets and one large ceremonial center might think they were visiting one of the most Christian peoples in the world. Hundreds of wooden crosses dot the land like flowers in the desert after a rain. They are found atop the three Catholic churches, in house patios, beside all waterholes, at the foot and on the top of mountains and in caves. But the meaning of these "Calvarys," as they are called by the Zinacantecos, is far removed from God's sacrifice of his son. They are doorways for communication with the ancestral gods who inhabit the mountains and the earth god who lives under the ground. They are places for humans to offer sacrifices of black chickens, white candles, and incense, to pray and hope for help from the gods.

The Zinacantecos were converted to Catholicism in the 1500s, but they hold to only the thinnest veneer of Christianity. Underneath what appear to be Christian symbols and practices, flows the ancient

253

EXPANDED DESCRIPTIONS

Zinacantan religion. a composite of beliefs in various gods, spirits, saints, and forces. Shamans are commonly called upon for a variety of religious services, especially in healing the sick.

The Zinacantecos are maize farmers. They live in the highlands, farming small plots as well as working rented land in the lowlands. All surplus money is saved for the expenses of the civil-religious offices which give a man and his family prestige and provide the major unifying element holding the Zinacantecos together. Enormous resources, planning, and years of waiting go for preparing and serving at one's own expense the religious and civil offices in the ceremonial center. If a Zinacanteco stops participating in this civil-religious system, it is a clear sign that he is passing into the dominant Ladino (westernized, Spanish-speaking) culture.

Change is coming as the Spanish culture works its way into their lives. But so far they have been so satisfied and involved in their own distinctive way of life that Protestant Christianity and Latin culture has been firmly and completely resisted. An approach that would enable whole hamlets or communities to become Christian together would be the most viable strategy. Those who have become Protestants as individuals have been harrassed by jail sentences and actual violence.

PART 4
Registry of the Unreached

The information on the 666 unreached peoples in the registry is presented in five different lists. Each list organizes the information differently. Only the first list, which indexes the peoples alphabetically by group name, includes the percentage that profess Christianity. Groups are also listed by receptivity, principal professed religion, language, and country. All five lists indicate those groups reported to be very receptive (**) or receptive (*). We have also attached another code (1) to the group name if it is described in greater detail in Part 3 of this book. All groups with a (1) by their name have an expanded description of their situation in this book.

INDEX BY GROUP NAME

This is the basic listing of groups in this registry. Peoples are listed by their primary name, as reported on survey questionnariesm Effort has been made to standardize names and use the most commonly accepted English spelling. This listing includes the country for which the information was provided, principal vernacular language used by the group, latest population estimate of the group in the country listed, principal *professed* religion (which in some cases is less than 50 percent of the total group membership), and the percentage of the group that *professes* Christianity in any recognized tradition, whether or not they practice their faith. Included in this percentage are Roman Catholic, Protestant, Orthodox, African Independent, and other Christian groups. Excluded in this percentage were Christo-pagans and Christian cultic groups such as Mormons and Jehovah's Witnesses.

INDEX BY RECEPTIVITY

This index lists groups by their reported attitude toward the gospel. The judgment of receptivity or resistance to the gospel is a subjective and difficult question. Often times what appears to be resistance to the gospel turns out to be a rejection of the Western or foreign cultural trappings with which the gospel is offered. Or perhaps it is a resistance to the agents who bear witness because they come from a country or people not respected by those who are being asked to hear the gospel. Nonetheless, this index gives the considered judgment of those who have reported these unreached peoples. Within each category, very receptive, receptive, indifferent, reluctant, very reluctant, and unknown, peoples are listed alphabetically by group name. Their country of location is also listed.

INDEX BY PRINCIPAL PROFESSED RELIGION

This list indicates predominant *professed* religion, whether or not a majority of those who profess the religion are active practitioners. Many of the groups have more than one professed religion present but only the one with the largest percentage of followers is indicated in this section.

INDEX BY LANGUAGE

Groups are listed according to their primary *vernacular* language. In many cases, groups are bilingual or trilingual, speaking several languages including a more commonly known trade language.

INDEX BY COUNTRY

Groups are listed by the countries for which information has been reported by questionnaires. In most cases, this means they are listed in the country where they are primarily located. Many peoples are found in several countries. This listing is limited to the country for which the MARC files have information. Groups are listed alphabetically under each country listed. Please note that not all countries will be found in this index. Peoples have not been reported from every country. Cambodia is listed under its new name, Kampuchea. The Republic of China is listed as Taiwan. Dahomey is listed under its current name, Benin. The population estimate given is an indication of the size of that people in that one country. In some cases, it is only a part of a large people to be found in several other countries as well.

INDEX
by
Group
Name

Name	Country	Language	Pop.	Religion	%
Archehnese	Indonesia	Achehnese	2,200,000	Islam	1
Adamawa	Cameroon	Fulani	380,000	Animism	0
Adi**	India	Adi	80,300	Animism	2
Adja*	Benin	Ge	250,000	Animism	5
Afar (1)	Ethiopia	Afar	300,000	Islam	1
Afawa	Nigeria	Afanci	10,000	Animism	1
Afo*	Nigeria	Afo	25,000	Animism	1
Ahl-i-Haggin Iran* (1)	Iran	Kurdish dialects	500,000	Islam	0
Ajuran (1)	Kenya	Somali (Ajuran)	17,098	Islam	1
Aka	India	Aka	2,257	Animism	0
Akha* (1)	Thailand	Akha	9,916	Ancestor Worship	1
Alaba	Ethiopia	Alaban	50,000	Islam	3
Alago	Nigeria	Alago	35,000	Animism	2
Alak	Laos	Alak	8,000	Animism	1
Alas	Indonesia	Alas	30,000	Islam	0
Alawites (1)	Syria	Arabic	600,000	Islam	0
Algerian (Arabs)	Algeria	Arabic	8,000,000	Islam	1
Algerian Arabs in France	France	Arabic	804,000	Islam	0
Ambonese	Netherlands	Ambonese	30,000	Animism	2
Ampeeli*	Papua New Guinea	Ampale	1,000	Christo-Paganism	1
Ankwe	Nigeria	Ankwai	10,000	Animism	1
Anuak	Ethiopia	Anuak	52,000	Animism	0
Anuak	Sudan	Anuak	30,000	Animism	4
Apartment Residents—Seoul*	Korea, Republic of	Korean	87,000	Folk Religion	15

Apatani*	India	Apartani	11,000	Animism	1
Apayao*	Philippines	Isneg	12,000	Christo-Paganism	15
Arawa	Nigeria	Hausa	200,000	Islam	1
Arusha	Tanzania	Arusha	10,000	Animism	12
Asmat (1)	Indonesia	Asmat	30,000	Animism	10
Ata of Davao	Philippines	Manobo	10,000	Animism	5
Atta	Philippines	Atta	1,000	Animism	1
Ayao*	Malawi	Chiyao	600,000	Islam	4
Aymara*	Bolivia	Aymara	850,000	Animism	12
Azteca** (1)	Mexico	Nahuatl, Hidalgo	250,000	Christo-Paganism	2
Babur Thali*	Nigeria	Bura (Babur)	75,000	Animism	5
Bagri	Pakistan	Bagri	20,000	Hinduism	1
Bajania (1)	Pakistan	Gujarati Dialect	20,000	Hinduism	1
Bakuba*	Zaire	Tshiluba	75,000	Animism	21
Balangao*	Philippines	Balangao	4,500	Christo-Paganism	4
Balanta	Senegal	Balanta	49,200	Unknown	nc
Balante	Guinea-Bissau	Balanta	100,000	Animism	11
Balinese	Indonesia	Balinese	2,000,000	Hinduism	1
Balmiki	Pakistan	Hindustani	20,000	Hinduism	1
Bambara	Mali	Bambara	1,660,000	Islam	2
Banai*	Bangladesh	Bengali	2,000	Buddhism	1
Banaro**	Papua New Guinea	Banaro	2,500	Animism	8
Bandi	Liberia	Bandi	32,000	Animism	10
Banyun	Guinea-Bissau	Banyun	15,000	Animism	8
Baoule**	Ivory Coast	Baule	1,200,000	Animism	12

263

Name	Country	Language	Pop.	Religion	%
Barabaig (1)	Tanzania	Tatoga	49,000	Animism	2
Barasano, Northern	Colombia	Barasano, Northern	450	Animism	3
Barasano, Southern	Colombia	Janena	400	Animism	2
Bariba	Benin	Bariba	200,000	Animism	1
Basakomo	Nigeria	nc	60,000	Animism	20
Basari	Togo	Basari	100,000	Animism	15
Basari	Senegal	Gasari	8,000	Unknown	nc
Basotho, Mountain** (1)	Lesotho	Southern Sesotho	70,000	Animism	15
Bassa	Liberia	Bassa	200,000	Animism	15
Bassa*	Nigeria	Bassa	100,000	Animism	12
Bhil*	Pakistan	Marwari	200,000	Hinduism	1
Bhils* (1)	India	Dangi	800,000	Animism	1
Bhojpuri	Nepal	Bhojpuri	806,480	Hinduism	1
Biafada	Guinea-Bissau	Biafada	15,000	Animism	7
Bijogo*	Guinea-Bissau	Bidyogo	25,000	Animism	12
Bilan*	Philippines	Bilaan	75,000	Animism	0
Bimanese	Indonesia	Bima	300,000	Islam	1
Bipim**	Indonesia	Bipim	450	Christo-Paganism	25
Birifor	Ghana	Birifor	40,000	Animism	3
Black Caribs, Belize* (1)	Belize	Moreno	10,000	Christo-Paganism	1
Black Caribs, Guatemala*	Guatemala	Moreno	1,500	Christo-Paganism	1
Black Caribs, Honduras*	Honduras	Moreno	20,000	Christo-Paganism	1
Bobo	Mali	Bobowule	100,000	Animism	0
Boko*	Benin	Boko (Busa)	30,000	Animism	2

Name	Alternative	Country	Population	Religion	%
Bontoc, Central	Bontoc, Central	Philippines	20,000	Animism	1
Bontoc, Southern *	Southern Bontoc	Philippines	12,000	Christo-Paganism	4
Boran	Boran	Ethiopia	37,500	Islam	5
Bororo	Bororo	Brazil	500	Animism	1
Boya	Boya	Sudan	15,000	Animism	0
Brao (1)	Brao	Laos	18,000	Animism	1
Bua	Bua	Chad	20,000	Animism	0
Budugum	Masa	Cameroon	10,000	Animism	0
Bugis	Bugis	Indonesia	2,500,000	Islam	1
Builsa	Buli	Ghana	97,000	Animism	0
Bukidnon*	Manobo, Binukid	Philippines	100,000	Animism	25
Bunu	Bunu	Nigeria	150,000	Animism	0
Burungi	Burungi	Tanzania	20,000	Animism	10
Bus Drivers, South Korea*	Korean	Korea, Republic of	26,000	Unknown	25
Busa	Busa (Bokobarn Akiba)	Nigeria	50,000	Islam	1
Busanse*	Bisa (Busanga)	Ghana	50,000	Animism	5
Bushmen (Heikum)	Heikum	Namibia	16,000	Animism	10
Bushmen (Hiechware)	Kwe-Etshari	Rhodesia	1,600	Animism	10
Bushmen (Kung) (1)	Ku	Namibia	10,000	Animism	10
Bushmen in Botswana	Buka-khwe	Botswana	30,000	Animism	10
Businessmen, Brazil*	Portuguese	Brazil	100,000	Christianity	100
Butawa	Buta	Nigeria	20,000	Islam	0
Calena*	Spanish	Colombia	1,200,000	Christianity	92
Cambodians	Northern Cambodian	Thailand	1,000,000	Buddhism	1
Caste Hindus (Andra Prd)	Telugu	India	44,000,000	Hinduism	3

Name	Country	Language	Pop.	Religion	%
Cebu, Middle-Class**	Philippines	Cebuano	500,000	Christo-Paganism	25
Ch'ol Sabanilla**	Mexico	Ch'ol	20,000	Christo-Paganism	5
Ch'ol Tila	Mexico	Tila Chol	38,000	Animism	1
Chakossi*	Ghana	Chakossi	22,000	Animism	0
Chakossi	Togo	Chakossi	29,000	Animism	3
Cham	Viet Nam	Cham	45,000	Islam	1
Cham (Western)	Kampuchea, Democratic	Cham	90,000	Islam	0
Chamorro	Turks and Caicos Islands	Chamorro	15,000	Christo-Paganism	15
Chamula (1)	Mexico	Tzotzil (Chamula)	50,000	Christo-Paganism	1
Chawai	Nigeria	Chawai	30,000	Animism	0
Chayahuita*	Peru	Chayawita	6,000	Christo-Paganism	20
Chinese (Hoklo) in Taiwan	Taiwan	Taiwanese (Minnan)	11,470,00	Trad. Chinese	2
Chinese Factory Workers	Hong Kong	Cantonese	500,000	Trad. Chinese	2
Chinese Hakka of Taiwan* (1)	Taiwan	Hakka	1,750,000	Trad. Chinese	1
Chinese ifin Amsterdam	Netherlands	Cantonese	15,000	Unknown	1
Chinese in Australia*	Australia	Cantonese	30,000	Trad. Chinese	12
Chinese in Austria	Austria	Mandarin	1,000	Trad. Chinese	5
Chinese in Bangladesh**	Bangladesh	Bengali	75	Christianity	85
Chinese in Brazil*	Brazil	Hakka	45,000	Trad. Chinese	11
Chinese in Burma	Burma	Mandarin	600,000	Trad. Chinese	2
Chinese in Costa Rica	Costa Rica	Cantonese	5,000	Unknown	1
Chinese in Holland	Netherlands	Mandarin	35,000	Unknown	1
Chinese in Hong Kong*	Hong Kong	Cantonese	4,135,000	Trad. Chinese	12
Chinese in Indonesia*	Indonesia	Indonesian	3,600,000	Trad. Chinese	10

Chinese in Japan	Japan	Mandarin	50,000	Trad. Chinese	3
Chinese in Korea	Korea, Republic of	Chinese	35,000	Secularism	5
Chinese in Laos	Laos	Mandarin	25,000	Trad. Chinese	1
Chinese in Malaysia	Malaysia	Chinese dialects	3,555,879	Trad. Chinese	10
Chinese in New Zealand	New Zealand	Cantonese	9,500	Trad. Chinese	5
Chinese in Osaka, Japan	Japan	Japanese	9,000	Unknown	1
Chinese in Puerto Rico	Puerto Rico	Hakka	200	Unknown	nc
Chinese in Sabah*	Malaysia	Hakka	180,000	Trad. Chinese	20
Chinese in Sarawak*	Malaysia	Mandarin	330,000	Trad. Chinese	11
Chinese in South Africa	South Africa	Cantonese	10,000	Trad. Chinese	25
Chinese in Thailand	Thailand	Hakka	3,600,000	Buddhism	2
Chinese in United Kingdom* (1)	United Kingdom	Mandarin	105,000	Trad. Chinese	3
Chinese in United States*	United States of America	Mandarin	550,000	Trad. Chinese	11
Chinese in Vancouver B.C.*	Canada	Cantonese	80,000	Trad. Chinese	8
Chinese in West Germany	German Federal Rep.	Mandarin	5,200	Secularism	2
Chinese Mainlanders	Taiwan	Mandarin	2,010,000	Secularism	10
Chinese Merchants	Ghana	Chinese dialects	40	Unknown	nc
Chinese of W. Malaysia	Malaysia	Cantonese	3,500,000	Trad. Chinese	4
Chinese Refugees in Macau	Macau	Burmese	10,000	Trad. Chinese	1
Chinese Refugees, France* (1)	France	Tien-Chiu	100,000	Trad. Chinese	2
Chinese Restaurant Wrkrs.	France	Won Chow	50,000	Trad. Chinese	2
Chinese Villagers	Hong Kong	Cantonese	500,000	Trad. Chinese	1
Chiriguano*	Argentina	Guarani (Bolivian)	15,000	Animism	15
Chitralis (1)	Pakistan	Khuwar	120,000	Islam	0
Chokwe Lunda	Angola	Chokwe	400,000	Animism	12

Name	Country	Language	Pop.	Religion	%
Chola Naickans	India	Canarese	100	Animism	0
Chrau*	Viet Nam	Jro	15,000	Animism	20
Chuabo	Mozambique	Chwabo	250,000	Animism	14
Chuj of San Mateo Ixtatan	Guatemala	Chuj	17,000	Animism	20
Cirebon	Indonesia	Javanese, Tjirebon	2,500,000	Islam	1
Citak**	Indonesia	Citak (Asmat)	6,500	Animism	0
College Students in Japan	Japan	Japanese	350,000	Secularism	2
Coloureds of South Africa (1)	South Africa	English	2,000,000	Christianity	75
Comorians (1)	Comoros	Comorian (Shingazidja)	300,000	Islam	1
Coreguaje*	Colombia	Coreguaje	500	Animism	1
Cubeo	Colombia	Cubeo	1,900	Animism	30
Cuna (1)	Colombia	Cuna	600	Animism	7
Dagari	Ghana	Dagari	200,000	Animism	0
Dagomba*	Ghana	Dagbanli	350,000	Islam	1
Daka	Nigeria	Dakanci	10,000	Animism	3
Dani, Baliem (1)	Indonesia	Dani, Grand Valley	50,000	Animism	
Degodia	Kenya	Somali	68,667	Islam	1
Dendi	Benin	Dendi	15,000	Islam	0
Dewein	Liberia	De	5,000	Islam	1
Dghwede	Nigeria	Zighvana (Dghwede)	13,000	Animism	1
Dhodias*	India	Dhodia Dialects	300,000	Hinduism	1
Didinga	Sudan	Didinga	30,000	Animism	0
Dinka	Sudan	Dinka	1,940,000	Animism	4
Diola	Senegal	Diola	216,000	Animism	1

Group	Country	Language	Population	Religion	
Diola	Guinea-Bissau	Diola	15,000	Islam	5
Dogon (1)	Mali	Dogon	312,000	Animism	10
Dompago	Benin	Dompago	19,000	Animism	10
Doohwaayo*	Cameroon	Doohyaayo	15,000	Animism	20
Dorobo	Kenya	Nandi	22,000	Animism	1
Dorobo	Tanzania	Hadza	3,000	Animism	1
Druzes (1)	Israel	Arabic	33,000	Folk Religion	0
Dubla*	India	Gujarati	202,218	Hinduism	4
Duka*	Nigeria	Dukanci	10,000	Animism	1
Dumagat	Philippines	Dumagat	1,000	Animism	3
Duru	Cameroon	Duru	20,000	Animism	0
Eggon	Nigeria	Eggon	80,000	Animism	20
El Molo	Kenya	Samburu	1,000	Animism	3
Elite Parisian** (1)	France	French	500,000	Christianity	76
Factory Workers, Young	Hong Kong	Cantonese	40,000	Unknown	8
Fakai*	Nigeria	Faka	15,000	Animism	1
Falasha* (1)	Ethiopia	Agau	30,000	Judaism	7
Fali*	Nigeria	Fali	25,000	Animism	2
Farmers of Japan	Japan	Japanese	24,988,740	Trad. Japanese	1
Fra-Fra	Ghana	Fra-Fra	230,000	Animism	0
Fula	Guinea	Fula	1,500,000	Islam	1
Fulah	Upper Volta	Fulani	300,000	Islam	1
Fulani (1)	Cameroon	Fulani	250,000	Islam	1
Fulani	Benin	Fulani	70,000	Islam	1
Fulbe	Ghana	Fulani	5,500	Islam	0

Name	Country	Language	Pop.	Religion	%
Ga-Dang	Philippines	Ga-Dang	5,500	Animism	1
Gabra	Kenya	Galla	12,000	Islam	1
Gade	Nigeria	Gade	25,000	Animism	1
Gagre*	Pakistan	Punjabi	40,000	Animism	1
Gagu	Ivory Coast	Gagou	25,000	Animism	1
Galla (Bale)	Ethiopia	Galla	750,000	Islam	10
Galla of Bucho	Ethiopia	Gallinya (Oromo)	1,500	Christo-Paganism	0
Galla, Harar	Ethiopia	Gallinya	1,305,400	Islam	1
Galler	Laos	Galler	50,000	Animism	1
Gayo	Indonesia	Gayo	200,000	Islam	0
Gbande	Guinea	Bandi	66,000	Animism	5
Gbari	Nigeria	Gbari	500,000	Animism	2
Gbazantche	Benin	Gbazantche	9,000	Islam	0
Ghimeera*	Ethiopia	Gimira	50,000	Animism	5
Gio	Liberia	Dan (Vacouba)	92,000	Animism	5
Giryama	Kenya	Giryama	335,900	Animism	14
Gisei	Cameroon	Masa	10,000	Animism	0
Gisiga	Cameroon	Gisiga	30,000	Animism	1
Glavda*	Nigeria	Glavda	9,000	Animism	6
Godie**	Ivory Coast	Godie	15,000	Animism	15
Gonds	India	Gondi	4,000,000	Animism	1
Gonja	Ghana	Gonja	108,000	Islam	2
Gourency	Upper Volta	Gourendi	300,000	Animism	5
Gouro*	Ivory Coast	Gouro	200,000	Animism	4

Government officials				
Grebo*	Thailand	Thai	Buddhism	0
Grunshi	Liberia	Grebo Dialects	Animism	10
Guajiro	Ghana	nc	Animism	0
Guanano (1)	Colombia	Guajiro	Animism	20
Guarani** (1)	Colombia	Guanano	Christo-Paganism	1
Guarayu	Bolivia	Guarani	Animism	15
Guayabero	Bolivia	Guarayu	Christo-Paganism	1
Gude	Colombia	Guayabero	Animism	20
Gugu-Yalanji	Cameroon	Gude	Animism	1
Gujarati	Australia	Gugu-Yalanji	Animism	1
Gurage	United Kingdom	Gujarati	Hinduism	1
Gurensi	Ethiopia	Gurage Dialects	Islam	3
Gurreh-	Ghana	Gurenne	Animism	1
Gurung	Kenya	Somali	Islam	1
Gwendora	Nepal	Gurung	Unknown	nc
Gypsies in Spain (1)	Nigeria	Gwandara	Animism	0
Hajong*	Spain	Rom	Folk Religion	4
Hewa*	Bangladesh	Bengali	Hinduism	1
Hewa* (1)	Papua New Guinea	Hewa	Animism	1
Higi**	Papua New Guinea	Hewa	Animism	10
Hopi	Nigeria	Higi	Animism	7
Huave*	United States of America	Hopi	Animism	4
Huila*	Mexico	Hauve	Christo-Paganism	5
Hukwe	Angola	Huila	Animism	1
	Angola	Hukwe	Animism	5

271

Name	Country	Language	Pop.	Religion	%
Hunzakut* (1)	Pakistan	Burushaski	10,000	Islam	0
Ibaji	Nigeria	Ibaji	20,000	Animism	0
Ica	Colombia	Ica	3,000	Animism	18
Ifugao Antipolo	Philippines	Keley-i	5,000	Animism	10
Ifugao	Philippines	Ifugao	95,000	Animism	10
Ifugao (Kalangoya)*	Philippines	Kalangoya	35,000	Animism	10
Igbira	Nigeria	Igbirra	400,000	Islam	20
Indians in Fiji (1)	Fiji	Hindustani	265,000	Hinduism	2
Indians in Rhodesia	Rhodesia	Gujarati	9,600	Hinduism	11
Indians, East* (1)	Trinidad and Tobago	English with Hindi	400,000	Hinduism	12
Indust. Workers Yongdungpo	Korea, Republic of	Korean	140,000	Folk Religion	6
Industry Laborers-Japan	Japan	Japanese	nc	Trad. Japanese	1
Ingassana	Sudan	Tabi	35,000	Animism	0
Inland Sea Island Peoples	Japan	Japanese	1,000,000	Trad. Japanese	1
Iragw	Tanzania	Iragw	218,000	Animism	16
Iwaidja	Austria	Iwaidja	150	Animism	1
Ixil	Guatemala	Cuyolbal	45,000	Christo-Paganism	1
Izi*	Nigeria	Izi	200,000	Animism	15
Jaba	Nigeria	Jaba	60,000	Animism	nc
Jama Mapun	Philippines	Cagayan	15,000	Islam	nc
Japanese in Brazil (1)	Brazil	Japanese	750,000	Buddhism	40
Japanese in Korea	Korea, Republic of	Japanese	5,000	Trad. Japanese	1
Japanese Students In USA*	United States of America	Japanese	nc	Secularism	1
Jarawa*	Nigeria	Jaranchi	150,000	Animism	10

Name	Country	Language	Religion	Population	
Javanese (rural)* (1)	Indonesia	Javanese	Islam	60,000,000	2
Javanese of Central Java*	Indonesia	Javanese	Islam	20,000,000	5
Javanese of Pejompongan*	Indonesia	Bahasa Jawa	Islam	5,000	10
Jemez Pueblo	United States of America	Towa(Jemez)	Christo-Paganism	1,800	5
Jeng	Laos	Jeng	Animism	500	0
Jerawa	Nigeria	nc	Animism	70,000	0
Jewish Imgrnts.—American	Israel	Hebrew	Judaism	25,797	0
Jewish Imgrnts.—Argentine	Israel	Hebrew	Judaism	17,686	0
Jewish Imgrnts.—Australia	Israel	Hebrew	Judaism	1,257	0
Jewish Imgrnts.—Brazilian	Israel	Hebrew	Judaism	4,005	0
Jewish Imgrnts.—Mexican	Israel	Hebrew	Judaism	1,065	0
Jewish Imgrnts.—Uruguayan	Israel	Hebrew	Judaism	2,720	0
Jewish Immigrants, Other	Israel	Hebrew	Judaism	5,520	0
Jews of Montreal	Canada	English	Judaism	120,000	1
Jews, Sephardic	Canada	French	Judaism	26,000	1
Jibu	Nigeria	Jibu, Jibanci	Animism	20,000	1
Jivaro (Achuara)*	Venezuela	Jivaro	Christo-Paganism	20,000	9
Jiye	Uganda	Jiye	Animism	34,000	0
Jiye	Sudan	Jiye (Karamojong)	Animism	7,000	0
Jikun	Nigeria	nc	Animism	20,000	0
K'anjobal of San Miguel*	Guatemala	K'anjobal	Ancestor Worship	18,000	20
Ka'mis	Papua New Guinea	Waffa Dialect	Christo-Paganism	50	2
Kabre	Togo	Kabre	Animism	273,000	14
Kabyle (1)	Algeria	Kabyle.	Islam	1,000,000	1
Kadara	Nigeria	Kadara	Animism	40,000	15

Name	Country	Language	Pop.	Religion	%
Kaffa	Ethiopia	Kaffenya (Kefa)	170,000	Christo-Paganism*	1
Kafirs* (1)	Pakistan	Kafiristani (Bashgali)	3,000	Animism	0
Kagoro	Mali	Logoro (Bambara)	30,000	Animism	0
Kaipeng-Koloi*	India	Kaipeng	30,000	Animism	1
Kalagan*	Philippines	Kalagan	19,000	Animism	1
Kalanga	Botswana	ChiKalanga	150,000	Animism	20
Kalinga, Southern	Philippines	Kalinga, Sumadel-Tinglayan	11,000	Animism	5
Kalinga, Northern*	Philippines	Kalinga	20,000	Christo-Paganism	5
Kamantan	Nigeria	Kadara	5,000	Animism	nc
Kambari	Nigeria	Kambarci	100,000	Animism	10
Kamuku	Nigeria	Kamuku	20,000	Animism	5
Kanarese	India	Kannada	21,707,000	Hinduism	12
Kankanay, Central*	Philippines	Kankanay	40,000	Animism	4
Karamojong	Uganda	Karamojong	24,000	Animism	45
Karen (1)	Thailand	Sgaw Karen	80,000	Animism	1
Kasena*	Ghana	Kasem	70,000	Animism	15
Kashmiri Muslims* (1)	India	Kashmiri	3,060,000	Islam	1
Kasseng	Kaos	Kasseng	15,000	Animism	0
Kayagar	Indonesia	Kayagar	9,000	Animism	10
Kayapo	Brazil	Kayapo	600	Animism	0
Kepas	Papua New Guinea	Kewa	5,000	Animism	1
Kerewe	Tanzania	Kikerewe	35,000	Animism	1
Khana	Nigeria	Khana	90,000	Unknown	2
Kichepo	Sudan	Kichepo	16,000	Animism	0

Kimyal	Indonesia	7,000	Animism
Kissi	Sierra Leone	43,000	Animism
Kissi	Guinea	266,000	Animism
Kissi	Liberia	35,000	Animism
Kita	Mali	150,000	Islam
Koalib (1)	Sudan	320,000	Animism
Koch*	Bangladesh	35,000	Hinduism
Kolam*	India	60,000	Hinduism
Kolbila	Cameroon	1,000	Islam
Koma	Ghana	1,000	Animism
Komo	Ethiopia	20,000	Animism
Kond**	India	900,000	Animism
Konkomba	Togo	25,000	Animism
Konkomba	Ghana	175,000	Animism
Kono*	Sierra Leone	133,000	Animism
Konso	Ethiopia	30,000	Animism
Koranko*	Sierra Leone	103,000	Islam
Korean Prisoners*	Korea, Republic of	45,000	Secularism
Koreans in Germany**	German Federal Rep.	10,000	Unknown
Koreans of Japan	Japan	600,000	Secularism
Korku	India	250,000	Animism
Koro	Nigeria	35,000	Animism
Koroma	Sudan	30,000	Animism
Kotokoli	Benin	1,000	Islam
Kotopo	Cameroon	10,000	Animism

275

Name	Country	Population	Religion
Kimyal	Kimyal	Indonesia	7,000	Animism

Name	Country	Language	Pop.	Religion	%
Kotta	India	Kota	1,200	Animism	0
Kowaao*	Liberia	Kowaao	7,000	Animism	5
Kpelle	Liberia	Kpelle	200,000	Animism	10
Krahn**	Liberia	Krahn	55,000	Animism	9
Krahn	Ivory Coast	Krahn	250,000	Animism	4
Krongo	Sudan	Krongo	121,000	Animism	1
Kuatinema	Brazil	Asurini	70	Animism	0
Kubu	Indonesia	local dialects	6,000	Animism	1
Kudisai Vagh Makkal	India	Tamil	1,000,000	Hinduism	15
Kui	Thailand	Kui	160,000	Buddhism	1
Kuknas	India	Kukni	125,000	Hinduism	1
Kulango	Ivory Coast	Kulango	50,000	Animism	4
Kunimaipa*	Papua New Guinea	Kunimaipa	9,000	Christo-Paganism	10
Kurds (1)	Turkey	Kurdish (Kirmancho)	4,000,000	Islam	0
Kurfei	Niger	Hausa	50,000	Animism	0
Kusaasi*	Ghana	Kusaal	150,000	Animism	3
Kutchi Kohli*	Pakistan	Gujarati	50,000	Hinduism	4
Kwere	Tanzania	Kwere	63,000	Animism	17
Labans	India	Labaani	nc	Hinduism	0
Laka	Cameroon	Laka	10,000	Animism	0
Lamba	Togo	Lamba	29,000	Animism	3
Lampung	Indonesia	Komering	1,500,000	Islam	0
Lango	Ethiopia	Lango	8,000	Animism	0
Lao (1)	Laos	Lao	1,908,600	Buddhism	1

276

Lapps* (1)	Norway	Lappish	20,000	Christianity	90
Lawa	Thailand	Lawa	10,000	Buddhism	4
Lebong	Indonesia	Redjang-Lebong	nc	Islam	0
Lepers of N.E. Thailand*	Thailand	Northeast Thai	390,000	Buddhism	1
Libyans	Libya	Arabic	2,300,000	Islam	0
Ligbi	Ivory Coast	Ligbi	20,000	Animism	0
Ligbi	Ghana	Ligbi	6,000	Islam	0
Limba	Sierra Leone	Limba	233,000	Animism	5
Lobi	Ivory Coast	Lobi	40,000	Animism	1
Lohar	Pakistan	Gujarati Dialect	nc	Hinduism	1
Loho Loho*	Indonesia	Kolaka	10,000	Animism	0
Loko	Sierra Leone	Loko	80,000	Animism	1
Lokoro	Sudan	Lokoro	22,000	Christo-Paganism	5
Loma	Guinea	Loma	66,000	Animism	3
Loma	Liberia	Loma	60,000	Animism	20
Lomwe	Mozambique	nc	1,000,000	Animism	14
Lotuka*	Sudan	Latuka	150,000	Other	6
Loven	Laos	Loven	25,000	Buddhism	1
Lugbara	Uganda	Lugbara	260,000	Unknown	20
Luhya**	Kenya	Oluluyia	1,800,000	Animism	20
Lungu	Nigeria	Lungu	10,000	Animism	0
Macu	Colombia	Macu	1,000	Animism	0
Macuxi*	Brazil	Macuxi	6,000	Animism	10
Madurese (1)	Indonesia	Madurese	7,000,000	Islam	1
Magar*	Nepal	Magar	300,000	Hinduism	1

Name	Country	Language	Pop.	Religion	%
Maguindano	Philippines	Maguindano	450,000	Islam	1
Maguzawa** (1)	Nigeria	Hausa	100,000	Animism	1
Maharashtrians	India	Marathi	50,412,235	Hinduism	1
Maiongong	Brazil	Maiongong	86	Animism	1
Maithili	Nepal	Maithili	1,000,000	Hinduism	0
Maji	Ethiopia	Maji	15,000	Animism	0
Makonde	Tanzania	nc	550,000	Islam	8
Makua	Mozambique	Makua	1,200,000	Animism	16
Malayo	Colombia	Malayo	1,000	Animism	10
Malays of Singapore (1)	Singapore	Malay	300,000	Islam	1
Mam Indian*	Guatemala	Mam	470,000	Christo-Paganism	15
Mamanwa (Mamanua)*	Philippines	Minamanwa	1,000	Christo-Paganism	3
Mambila	Cameroon	Mambila	40,000	Animism	0
Mamprusi	Ghana	nc	80,000	Animism	0
Mancang	Senegal	Mankanya	35,200	Unknown	nc
Manding	Senegal	Malinke, Senegalese	208,400	Unknown	nc
Mandingo (1)	Liberia	Mandingo	36,000	Islam	1
Mangs	India	Marathi	nc	Hinduism	0
Mangyan*	Philippines	Mangyan	60,000	Animism	10
Manikion*	Indonesia	Sough	8,000	Animism	33
Manjack	Senegal	Mandyale	44,200	Unknown	0
Manjaco*	Guinea-Bissau	Mandyako	80,000	Animism	11
Mano	Liberia	Mano	65,000	Animism	5
Manobo, Cotabato*	Philippines	Cotabato Manobo	10,000	Animism	1

Manobo, Ilianen	Philippines	Ilianen Manobo	5,000	Animism	4
Manobo, Salug*	Philippines	Manobo, Tigwa	4,000	Animism	5
Manobo, Tigwa*	Philippines	Manobo, Tigwa	4,000	Animism	3
Manobo, Western Bukidnon*	Philippines	Manobo, Binokid	12,000	Animism	10
Manobos, Pulangi	Philippines	Manobo, Pulangi	5,000	Animism	3
Mansaka*	Philippines	Mansaka	25,000	Christo-Paganism	20
Mapuche	Chile	Mapuche	300,000	Christo-Paganism	1
Maranao (1)	Philippines	Maranao	500,000	Islam	2
Masa	Chad	Masa	80,000	Animism	10
Masai* (1)	Kenya	Masai	100,000	Animism	5
Masengo	Ethiopia	Majangiir	7,000	Animism	1
Matakam	Cameroon	Matakam	140,000	Animism	2
Matumbi	Tanzania	Matumbi	72,000	Islam	15
Maures	Senegal	Arabic	57,000	Islam	0
Mauri	Niger	Hausa	100,000	Animism	0
Mazahua*	Mexico	Mazahua	150,000	Christo-Paganism	6
Mbukushu	Angola	Kusso	6,000	Animism	10
Meban	Sudan	Maban-Jumjum	130,000	Animism	1
Meghwar* (1)	Pakistan	Marwari	100,000	Hinduism	1
Meitei (1)	India	Manipuri	700,000	Hinduism	1
Mejah*	India	Mejah	5,500	Animism	1
Mende	Sierra Leone	Mende	600,000	Animism	20
Meo*	Thailand	Meo	29,173	Animism	15
Middle-East Businessmen	Brazil	Arabic	nc	Christianity	71
Migrants of Cuiaba	Brazil	Portuguese	30,000	Christianity	100

279

Name	Country	Language	Pop.	Religion	%
Mimika	Indonesia	Mimika	10,000	Christo-Paganism	5
Minangkabau	Indonesia	Minangkabau	2,000,000	Islam	0
Miniaka	Mali	Suppire	300,000	Animism	0
Mirung	Bangladesh	Mirung	12,000	Animism	1
Mishmi	India	Mismi	22,350	Animism	0
Mixes*	Mexico	Mixe	60,000	Christo-Paganism	2
Mixteco, San Juan Mixtepic	Mexico	Mixteco	15,000	Christo-Paganism	1
Miya	Nigeria	Miya	5,200	Animism	1
Mo	Ghana	Mo (Degha)	13,000	Animism	1
Moba	Ghana	Bimoba	80,000	Animism	0
Moba	Togo	Bimoba	70,000	Animism	12
Mocha**	Ethiopia	Mocha	45,000	Animism	5
Moken (1)	Burma	Moken	5,000	Animism	1
Mokole	Benin	Mokole	7,000	Animism	0
Molbog	Philippines	Molbog	5,000	Islam	0
Monpa	India	Monpa	22,000	Buddhism	0
Moor & Malays (1)	Sir Lanka	Tamil	895,322	Islam	0
Mopan Maya*	Guatemala	Mopan Maya	2,000	Christo-Paganism	15
Mopan Maya*	Belize	Mopan Maya	4,000	Christo-Paganism	15
Mru	Bangladesh	Murung	50,000	Animism	1
Mualthuam	India	Mualthuam	2,000	Animism	7
Mumuye	Nigeria	Mumuye	200,000	Animism	1
Murle	Sudan	Murle	40,000	Animism	1
Murngin (Wulamba)	Australia	Dhuwal	3,500	Animism	1

Muslim Community of Bawku	Ghana	Hausa, Ghana	Islam	20,000	0
Muslim Immigrants in U.K.*	United Kingdom	nc	Islam	500,000	0
Muslim Malays	Malaysia	Bahasa Malaysia	Islam	5,500,000	0
Muslims (West Nile Dist.)	Uganda	Lugbara	Islam	45,000	1
Muslims in U.A.E. (1)	United Arab Emirates	Arabic	Islam	202,000	1
Muslims in Yugoslavia	Yugoslavia	Albanian	Islam	2,500,000	0
Muslims of Jordan	Jordan	Arabic	Islam	1,000,000	0
Muslims of Thailand	Thailand	Malay	Islam	600,000	1
Nafaara* (1)	Ghana	Nafaara	Animism	40,000	2
Nahua, North Pueblo	Mexico	Nahua	Christo-Paganism	55,000	13
Nambikuara	Brazil	Nambikuara	Animism	400	3
Nambya*	Rhodesia	Nambya	Animism	40,000	15
Namshi	Cameroon	Namshi	Animism	30,000	1
Nawuri	Ghana	Nawuri	Animism	10,000	1
Nchimburu	Ghana	Nchumburu	Animism	7,000	9
Ndebele* (1)	Rhodesia	SiNdebele	Animism	1,000,000	20
Ndoro*	Nigeria	Ndoro	Animism	10,000	10
Ndunpa Duupa	Cameroon	Ndunpa Duupa	Islam	1,000	1
Nepali	Nepal	Nepali	Hinduism	6,060,758	0
Newari	Nepal	Newari	Hinduism	500,000	0
Neyo	Ivory Coast	Nevo	Unknown	5,000	nc
Ngamo*	Nigeria	Ngamo	Animism	18,000	8
Ngen	Ivory Coast	Ngen	Animism	20,000	3
Ngeg	Laos	Negeg	Animism	50,000	5
Ngere	Ivory Coast	nc	Animism	150,000	0

281

Name	Country	Language	Pop.	Religion	%
Nigerians of Kano	Nigeria	Hausa	10,000	Islam	1
Ningerum	Papua New Guinea	Ningerum	3,000	Animism	0
Nkoya	Zambia	Shinkoya	nc	Animism	30
Nocte**	India	Nocte	19,400	Animism	0
Ntrubs	Ghana	Ntrubo	5,000	Animism	1
Nuer	Ethiopia	Nuer	70,000	Animism	0
Nuer (1)	Sudan	Nuer	844,000	Animism	0
Nupe*	Nigeria	Nupe	600,000	Islam	2
Nyaheun	Laos	Nyaheun	15,000	Animism	2
Nyamwezi	Tanzania	Nyamwezi	590,000	Animism	15
Nyantruku	Benin	Aldejo	4,000	Animism	0
Nyzatom	Sudan	Toposa, Donyiro	80,000	Animism	0
Od	Pakistan	Odki	40,000	Hinduism	1
Oeang Asli*	Malaysia	Native Senoi	337,395	Animism	2
Ogadenya	Kenya	Somali	99,129	Islam	1
Oi	Laos	Oi	10,000	Animism	1
Ouaddai	Chad	Maba	320,000	Islam	1
Paez**	Colombia	Paez	40,000	Christo-Paganism	12
Paiute, Northern	United States of America	Paiute, Northern	5,000	Peyote Religion	4
Pakabeti of Equator**	Zaire	Pakabeti	3,000	Christianity	51
Palaung (1)	Burma	Palaung	150,000	Buddhism	1
Parkari Kohlis*	Pakistan	Gujarati	100,000	Hinduism	5
Phu Thai	Laos	Phu Tai	100,000	Buddhism	1
Pila*	Benin	Pila-Pila	50,000	Animism	1

Podokwo	Cameroon	Podokwo	Animism	0
Portuguese in France*	France	Portuguese	Christianity	90
Pular	Senegal	Fouta Toro	Unknonw	0
Pwo Karen	Thailand	Pwo Karen	Animism	1
Pygmy (Binga)	Burundi	local dialects	Animism	10
Pygmy (Binga)	Central African Empire	local dialects	Animism	0
Pygmy (Mbuti) (1)	Zaire	local languages	Animism	1
Quechua*	Peru	Quechua	Christo-Paganism	2
Quechua*	Bolivia	Quechua	Christo-Paganism	13
Quechua, Huanco*	Peru	Quechua, Huancayo	Animism	6
Quiche* (1)	Guatemala	Quiche	Christo-Paganism	7
Rabha	India	Rabha	Hinduism	5
Rabinal-Achi	Guatemala	Rabinal Achi	Christo-Paganism	5
Racetrack Residents* (1)	United States of America	English	Secularism	10
Rai	Nepal	Rai	Hinduism	0
Rai, Danuwar	Nepal	Danuwar Rai	Hinduism	0
Rajbansi	Nepal	Rajbansi	Hinduism	0
Rava	India	Rava	Hinduism	1
Red Bobo*	Upper Volta	Buamu (Bobo Wule)	Animism	13
Redjang	Indonesia	Rejang	Islam	0
Reshiat	Ethiopia	nc	Animism	0
Rural Ranch Workers	Brazil	Portuguese	Christianity	85
Ryukyuan	Japan	Ryukyuan	Trad. Japanese	4
Safwa	Tanzania	Safwa	Animism	3
Saguye*	Kenya	Galla	Islam	1

Name	Country	Language	Pop.	Religion	%
Sama Bangingi	Philippines	Sinama Bangini	70,000	Islam	0
Sama Pangutaran	Philippines	Sama Pangutaran	15,000	Islam	0
Sama-Badjaw (1)	Philippines	Samal dialects	120,000	Islam	2
Samburu	Kenya	Masai, Samburu	60,500	Animism	3
Samo-Kubo	Papua New Guinea	Samo	1,200	Animism	1
Sangil	Philippines	Sangil	7,500	Islam	1
Santhali*	Nepal	Santhali	nc	Animism	3
Sanuma	Brazil	Sanuma	326	Animism	1
Sapo	Liberia	nc	30,000	Animism	20
Sarakole	Senegal	Soninke	67,600	Islam	0
Sasak	Indonesia	Sasak	100,000	Islam	1
Save*	Benin	Save (Yoruba)	15,000	Animism	1
Senufo	Ivory Coast	Senari	300,000	Animism	2
Serawai	Indonesia	Serawai (Pasemah)	60,000	Islam	2
Serere (1)	Senegal	Serere	700,000	Animism	16
Seychellois	Seychelles	Creole	51,000	Christianity	99
Shanga	Nigeria	Shanga	5,000	Animism	0
Shankilla (Kazza)**	Ethiopia	Shankilla (Kazza)	20,000	Christo-Paganism	1
Sherpa	Nepal	Sherpa	20,000	Buddhism	0
Shirishana*	Brazil	Shirishana	240	Animism	20
Sindhis of India	India	Sindhi	3,000,000	Hinduism	1
Sindhis of Pakistan*	Pakistan	Sindhi	4,000,000	Islam	1
Sinhalese	Sri Lanka	Sinhala	9,146,679	Buddhism	7
Sisaala*	Ghana	Isaalin	60,000	Animism	1

So	Laos	So	15,000	Animism	1
Sochi	Pakistan	Sindhi	nc	Hinduism	1
Soka Gakkai Believers	Japan	Japanese	6,500,000	Buddhism	0
Somagai	Indonesia	Somagai	nc	Animism	0
Somali	Ethiopia	Somali	1,000,000	Islam	1
Somali (1)	Somalia	Somali	2,500,000	Islam	1
Somba*	Benin	Somba (Detammari)	60,000	Animism	1
Sonjo	Tanzania	Sonjo	7,400	Animism	5
Soruba	Benin	Soruba	5,000	Animism	0
Spiritists (1)	Brazil	Portuguese	9,000,000	Animism	1
Students in Cuiaba	Brazil	Portuguese	20,000	Christianity	55
Subanen (Tuboy)*	Philippines	Subanen, Tuboy	20,000	Animism	2
Subanen. Sindangan*	Philippines	Subanun	80,000	Animism	0
Suena*	Papua New Guinea	Suena	2,000	Christo-Paganism	5
Suk	Kenya	nc	133,200	Animism	10
Sumba	Indonesia	Sumba	400,000	Unknown	nc
Sundanese*	Indonesia	Sundanese	25,000,000	Islam	1
Suri*	Ethiopia	Suri	30,000	Animism	1
Suriguenos*	Philippines	Surigueno	23,000	Christianity	100
Swatis (1)	Pakistan	Swati	600,000	Islam	0
Ta-Oi	Laos	Ta-Oi	15,000	Animism	1
Tagbanwa, Aborlan*	Philippines	Tagbanwa	10,000	Animism	1
Tagbanwa, Kalamian	Philippines	Tagbanwa, Kalamian	4,500	Christo-Paganism	1
Tagin**	India	Tagin	25,000	Animism	0
Tamang	Nepal	Tamang	nc	Hinduism	0

Name	Country	Language	Pop.	Religion	%
Tamil (Ceylonese)	Sri Lanka	Tamil	1,415,567	Hinduism	7
Tamil Brahmins	India	Tamil	98,112,000	Hinduism	0
Tamil Plantation Workers**	Malaysia	Tamil	137,150	Hinduism	1
Tamils (Indian)	Malaysia	Tamil	600,000	Hinduism	7
Tamils (Indian)* (1)	Sri Lanka	Tamil	1,195,368	Hinduism	7
Tampulma	Ghana	Tampulensi	8,000	Animism	2
Tandanke	Senegal	Tandanke	1,000	Unknown	0
Tangsa*	India	Tangsa	10,700	Animism	0
Tatuyo*	Colombia	Tatuyo	300	Animism	1
Taucouleur	Senegal	nc	464,700	Islam	0
Tausug	Philippines	Tausug	300,000	Islam	1
Tboli*	Philippines	Tboli	67,500	Animism	3
Teenbu	Ivory Coast	Lorhon	4,000	Animism	1
Tem	Togo	Kotokoli	100,000	Islam	7
Temne*	Sierra Leone	Temne	750,000	Animism	6
Tengger	Indonesia	Tenggerese	400,000	Hinduism	1
Teribe*	Panama	Teribe	1,000	Christo-Paganism	15
Thailand Farmers (Ctl)	Thailand	Thai	5,000,000	Buddhism	1
Tharadari Kohlf*	Pakistan	Gujarati	40,000	Hinduism	1
Tharu	Nepal	Bhojpuri	495,000	Hinduism	0
Tigon	Cameroon	Tigon	25,000	Animism	0
Tin	Thailand	Tin	25,000	Animism	0
Tofi	Benin	Tofi	33,000	Animism	3
Tonga	Rhodesia	ChiTonga	90,000	Animism	3

Tonga, Gwembe Valley (1)	Zambia	ChiTonga	86,000	Animism	2
Topotha	Sudan	Toposa	60,000	Animism	2
Totis	India	Gondi	nc	Hinduism	0
Tripuri*	India	Tripuri	400,000	Animism	1
Tsachila*	Ecuador	Colorado	1,100	Christo-Paganism	10
Tuareg (1)	Niger	Tamachek	200,000	Islam	0
Turkana	Kenya	Turkana	224,000	Animism	4
Turkana Fishing Comm.* (1)	Kenya	Turkana	20,000	Animism	4
Turkish Immig. Workers (1)	German Federal Rep.	Turkish	1,000,000	Islam	1
Turu	Tanzania	Nyaturu	316,000	Animism	13
Uduk	Sudan	Uduk	7,000	Animism	15
Ulithi-Mall	Turks and Caicos Islands	Ulithi	2,000	Christo-Paganism	0
University Students (1)	France	French	800,000	Christianity	71
University Students (1)	German Federal Rep.	German	850,000	Christianity	70
Urban Workers in Taiwan	Taiwan	Taiwanese	nc	Trad. Chinese	1
Uzbeks* (1)	Afghanistan	Uzbeki, Turkic	1,000,000	Islam	0
Vagala	Ghana	Vagala	3,000	Animism	0
Vagari	Pakistan	Gujarati Dialect	30,000	Hinduism	1
Vai	Liberia	Vai	30,000	Islam	1
Vere**	Nigeria	Vere	20,000	Animism	15
Vietnamese	Laos	Vietnamese	20,000	Buddhism	1
Vietnamese in the USA*	United States of America	Vietnamese	130,000	Buddhism	13
Voko	Cameroon	Woko	1,000	Islam	1
Wadiara Kohli*	Pakistan	Gujarati	40,000	Hinduism	1
Wajita*	Tanzania	Kijita	65,000	Animism	1

Name	Country	Language	Pop.	Religion	%
Wala	Ghana	Wali	60,000	Animism	2
Wanchoo*	India	Wanchoo	nc	Animism	0
Warjawa	Nigeria	Warji	70,000	Animism	1
Watchi	Togo	Ge	400,000	Animism	5
Wazinza	Tanzania	Kizinza	2,000	Animism	12
Wimbum*	Cameroon	Limbum	50,000	Animism	1
Winji-Winji	Benin	Winji-Winji	5,000	Islam	0
Wobe	Ivory Coast	Wobe	40,000	Animism	20
Woleat	Turks and Caicos Islands	Woleat	1,000	Christo-Paganism	0
Wolof	Senegal	Wolof	1,500,000	Islam	1
Yakan	Philippines	Yakan	50,000	Islam	1
Yala*	Nigeria	Yala	60,000	Animism	9
Yalunka	Sierra Leone	Yalunka	25,000	Islam	1
Yanguis	Mexico	Yangui	14,000	Christo-Paganism	0
Yanomamo in Brazil (1)	Brazil	Yanomam (Waica)	3,000	Animism	1
Yanyula	Australia	Yanyula (Yanjula)	150	Other	15
Yao	Mozambigue	Yao	220,000	Islam	19
Yao* (1)	Thailand	Yao (Mien Wa)	19,867	Animism	2
Yei*	Botswana	Yei	10,000	Animism	10
Yemenis (1)	Yemen, Arab Republic	Arabic (Eastern)	5,600,000	Islam	0
Yinga	Cameroon	Yinga	300	Animism	1
Yucuna	Colombia	Yucuna	500	Christo-Paganism	1
Zapoteco, S. de Juarez	Mexico	Zapoteco, S. de Juarez	12,000	Christianity	100
Zaramo	Tanzania	Zaramo	296,000	Islam	2

Zaranda Hill Peoples*	Nigeria	local languages	10,000	Animism	2
Zinacantecos (1)	Mexico	Tzotzil, Chenalho	10,000	Christo-Paganism	1
Zoliang	India	Naga, Zoliang	50,000	Animism	0
Zowla	Ghana	Ewe	800,000	Animism	2
Zuni	United States of America	Zuni	6,000	Animism	1

INDEX
by
Receptivity

VERY RECEPTIVE
Adi, India
Azteca (1), Mexico
Banaro, Papua New Guinea
Baoule, Ivory Coast
Basotho, Mountain (1), Lesotho
Bipim, Indonesia
Cebu, Middle-Class, Philippines
Ch'ol Sabanilla, Mexico
Chinese, Bangladesh
Citak, Indonesia
Elite Parisian (1), France
Godie, Ivory Coast
Guarani (1), Bolivia
Higi, Nigeria
Kond, India
Koreans in Germany, German
    Federal Rep.
Krahn, Liberia
Luhya, Kenya
Maguzawa (1), Nigeria
Mocha, Ethiopia
Nocte, India
Paez, Colombia
Pakabeti of Equator, Zaire

Shankilla (Kazza), Ethiopia
Tagin, India
Tamil Plantation Workers,
    Malaysia
Vere, Nigeria

RECEPTIVE
Adja, Benin
Afo, Nigeria
Ahl-i-Haqq (1), Iran
Akha (1), Thailand
Ampeeli, Papua New Guinea
Apartment Residents—Seoul,
    Korea, Republic of
Apantani, India
Apayao, Philippines
Ayao, Malawi
Aymara, Bolivia
Babur Thali, Nigeria
Bakuba, Zaire
Balangao, Philippines
Banai, Bangladesh
Bassa, Nigeria
Bhil, Pakistan
Bhils (1), India

Bijogo, Guinea-Bissau
Bilan, Philippines
Black Caribs, (1), Belize
Black Caribs, Guatemala
Black Caribs, Honduras
Boko, Benin
Bontoc, Southern, Philippines
Bukidnon, Philippines
Bus Drivers, South Korea
Busanse, Ghana
Businessmen, Brazil
Calena, Colombia
Chakossi, Ghana
Chayahuita, Peru
Chinese Hakka (1), Taiwan
Chinese, Australia
Chinese, Brazil
Chinese, Hong Kong
Chinese, Indonesia
Chinese in Sabah, Malaysia
Chinese in Sarawak, Malaysia
Chinese, United Kingdom (1)
Chinese, USA
Chinese, Vancouver B.C.
Chinese Refugees, France (1)
Chiriguano, Argentina
Chrau, Vietnam
Coreguaje, Colombia
Dagomba, Ghana
Dhodias, India
Doohwaayo, Cameroon
Dubla, India
Duka, Nigeria
Fakai, Nigeria
Falasha (1), Ethiopia
Fali, Nigeria
Gagre, Pakistan
Ghimeera, Ethiopia
Glavda, Nigeria
Gouro, Ivory Coast

Grebo, Liberia
Hajong, Bangladesh
Hewa, Papua New Guinea
Hewa (1), Papua New Guinea
Huave, Mexico
Huila, Angola
Hunzakut (1), Pakistan
Ifugao (Kalangoya), Philippines
Indians, East (1), Trinidad and
    Tobago
Izi, Nigeria
Japanese Students, USA
Jarawa, Nigeria
Javanese (rural) (1), Indonesia
Javanese of Central Java,
    Indonesia
Javanese of Pejompongan,
    Indonesia
Jivaro (Archuara), Venezuela
K'anjobal of San Miguel,
    Guatemala
Kafirs (1), Pakistan
Kaipeng-Koloi, India
Kalagan, Philippines
Kalinga, Northern, Philippines
Kankanay, Central, Philippines
Kasena, Ghana
Kashmiri Muslims (1), India
Koch, Bangladesh
Kolam, India
Kono, Sierra Leone
Koranko, Sierra Leone
Korean Prisoners, Korea,
    Republic of
Kowaao, Liberia
Kunimaipa, Papua New Guinea
Kusaasi, Ghana
Kutchi Kohli, Pakistan
Lapps (1), Norway
Lepers of N.E. Thailand, Thailand

REGISTRY OF THE UNREACHED

Loho Loho, Indonesia
Lotuka, Sudan
Macuxi, Brazil
Magar, Nepal
Mam Indian, Guatemala
Mamanwa (Mamauna),
   Philippines
Mangyan, Philippines
Manikion, Indonesia
Manjaco, Guinea-Bissau
Manobo, Cotabato, Philippines
Manobo, Salug, Philippines
Manobo, Tigwa, Philippines
Manobo, Western Bukidnon,
   Philippines
Mansaka, Philippines
Masai (1), Kenya
Mazahua, Mexico
Meghwar (1), Pakistan
Mejah, India
Meo, Thailand
Mixes, Mexico
Mopan Maya, Guatemala
Mopan Maya, Belize
Muslim Immigrants, United
   Kingdom
Nafaara (1), Ghana
Nambya, Rhodesia
Ndebele (1), Rhodesia
Ndoro, Nigeria
Ngamo, Nigeria
Nupe, Nigeria
Oeang Asli, Malaysia
Parkari Kohlis, Pakistan
Pila, Benin
Portuguese, France
Quechua, Peru
Quechua, Bolivia
Quechua, Huanco, Peru
Quiche (1), Guatemala

Racetrack Residents (1), USA
Red Bobo, Upper Volta
Saguye, Kenya
Santhali, Nepal
Save, Benin
Shirishana, Brazil
Sindhis, Pakistan
Sisaala, Ghana
Somba, Benin
Subanen (Tuboy), Philippines
Subanen, Sindangan, Philippine
Suena, Papua New Guinea
Sundanese, Indonesia
Suri, Ethiopia
Suriguenos, Philippines
Tagbanwa, Aborlan, Philippines
Tamils (Indian) (1), Sri Lanka
Tangsa, India
Tatuyo, Colombia
Tboli, Philippines
Temne, Sierra Leone
Teribe, Panama
Tharadari Kohli, Pakistan
Tripuri, India
Tsachila, Ecuador
Turkana Fishing Community (1),
   Kenya
Uzbeks (1), Afghanistan
Vietnamese, USA
Wadiara Kohli, Pakistan
Wajita, Tanzania
Wanchoo, India
Wimbum, Cameroon
Yala, Nigeria
Yao (1), Thailand
Yei, Botswana
Zaranda Hill Peoples, Nigeria

INDIFFERENT
Afawa, Nigeria

REGISTRY OF THE UNREACHED

Kamuku, Nigeria
Kanarese, India
Karamojong, Uganda
Kepas, Papua New Guinea
Kimyal, Indonesia
Kissi, Sierra Leone
Kissi, Liberia
Komo, Ethiopia
Konkomba, Togo
Koreans, Japan
Korku, India
Krahn, Ivory Coast
Kudisai Vagh Makkal, India
Kui, Thailand
Kuknas, India
Kurds (1), Turkey
Lango, Ethiopia
Lao (1), Laos
Lokoro, Sudan
Maithili, Nepal
Manobo, Ilianen, Philippines
Masengo, Ethiopia
Meitei (1), India
Mimika, Indonesia
Mishmi, India
Mixteco, San Juan Mixtepic, Mexico
Mokole, Benin
Molbog, Philippines
Murngin (Wulamba), Australia
Nahua, North Pueblo, Mexico
Nepali, Nepal
Newari, Nepal
Ngen, Ivory Coast
Ningerum, Papua New Guinea
Nkoya, Zambia
Nuer, Ethiopia
Nuer (1), Sudan
Nyantruku, Benin
Pygmy (Mbuti) (1), Zaire

Rai, Danuwar, Nepal
Rava, India
Ryukyuan, Japan
Samo-Kubo, Papua New Guinea
Sanuma, Brazil
Sherpa, Nepal
Sindhis, India
Somagai, Indonesia
Tamang, Nepal
Tamil Brahmins, India
Tamils (Indian), Malaysia
Teenbu, Ivory Coast
Thailand Farmers (Ctl), Thailand
Tofi, Benin
Tonga, Rhodesia
Topotha, Sudan
University Students (1), France
University Students (1), German Federal Rep.
Urban Workers, Taiwan
Vai, Liberia
Warjawa, Nigeria
Wazinza, Tanzania
Yalunka, Sierra Leone
Yanomamo, Brazil (1)
Yanyula, Australia
Yucuna, Colombia

RELUCTANT
Afar (1), Ethiopia
Ajuran (1), Kenya
Alaba, Ethiopia
Alago, Nigeria
Barasano, Southern, Colombia
Busa, Nigeria
Butawa, Nigeria
Chitralis (1), Pakistan
Chola Naickans, India
Chuj of San Mateo Ixtatan, Guatemala

Degodia, Kenya
Druzes (1), Israel
Farmers, Japan
Fra-Fra, Ghana
Fulani (1), Cameroon
Ga-Dang, Philippines
Galla, Harar, Ethiopia
Gourency, Upper Volta
Government officials, Thailand
Guarayu, Bolivia
Gujarati, United Kingdom
Gurreh, Kenya
Hopi, USA
Ica, Colombia
Igbira, Nigeria
Indians (1), Fiji
Indust. Workers Yongdungpo,
   Korea, Republic of
Ixil, Guatemala
Jama Mapun, Philippines
Japanese (1), Brazil
Jews of Montreal, Canada
Jews, Sephardic, Canada
Kayagar, Indonesia
Kerewe, Tanzania
Kotokoli, Benin
Lamba, Togo
Lawa, Thailand
Maharashtrians, India
Malays (1), Singapore
Mapuche, Chile
Miya, Nigeria
Moken (1), Burma
Monpa, India
Mru, Bangladesh
Mualthuam, India
Nambikuara, Brazil
Ogadenya, Kenya
Palaung (1), Burma
Pwo Karen, Thailand

Rabinal-Achi, Guatemala
Rajbansi, Nepal
Sama Bangingi, Philippines
Sama Pangutaran, Philippines
Sama-Badjaw (1), Philippines
Sangil, Philippines
Senufo, Ivory Coast
Sinhalese, Sri Lanka
Swatis (1), Pakistan
Tagbanwa, Kalamian,
   Philippines
Tamil (Ceylonese), Sri Lanka
Tengger, Indonesia
Tin, Thailand
Tonga, Gwembe Valley (1),
   Zambia
Turkana, Kenya
Turkish Immigrant Workers (1),
   German Federal Rep.
Watchi, Togo
Winji-Winji, Benin
Woleat, Turks and Caicos
   Islands
Yakan, Philippines
Zapoteco, S. de Juarez, Mexico
Zowla, Ghana
Zuni, USA

VERY RELUCTANT
Achehnese, Indonesia
Algerian (Arabs), Algeria
Arawa, Nigeria
Balinese, Indonesia
Bugis, Indonesia
Caste Hindus (Andra Prd), India
Chamula (1), Mexico
Dendi, Benin
Fula, Guinea
Fulah, Upper Volta
Gugu-Yalanji, Australia

REGISTRY OF THE UNREACHED

Gwendora, Nigeria
Jemez Pueblo, USA
Kabyle (1), Algeria
Kotta, India
Libyans, Libya
Macu, Colombia
Madurese (1), Indonesia
Maguindano, Philippines
Malayo, Colombia
Mandingo (1), Liberia
Maranao (1), Philippines
Maures, Senegal
Middle-East Businessmen,
　Brazil
Minangkabau, Indonesia
Mirung, Bangladesh
Moor & Malays (1), Sri Lanka
mumuye, Nigeria
Muslim Malays, Malaysia
Muslims (West Nile Dist.),
　Uganda
Muslims (1), U.A.E.
Muslims, Yugoslavia
Muslims, Jordan
Muslims, Thailand
Ouaddai, Chad
Paiute, Northern, USA
Redjang, Indonesia
Soka Gakkai Believers, Japan
Somali, Ethiopia
Somali (1), Somalia
Spiritists (1), Brazil
Tausug, Philippines
Tem, Togo
Tuareg (1), Niger
Ulithi-Mall, Turks and Caicos
　Islands
Wolof, Senegal
Yaguis, Mexico
Yemenis (1), Yemen, Arab
　Republic

Zinacantecos (1), Mexico

UNKNOWN
Adamawa, Cameroon
Aka, India
Alak, Laos
Alas, Indonesia
Algerian Arabs, France
Ambonese, Netherlands
Ankwe, Nigeria
Anuak, Ethiopia
Anuak, Sudan
Arusha, Tanzania
Bagri, Pakistan
Bajania (1), Pakistan
Balanta, Senegal
Balante, Guinea-Bissau
Balmiki, Pakistan
Bambara, Mali
Bandi, Liberia
Banyun, Guinea-Bissau
Barabaig (1), Tanzania
Barasano, Northern, Colombia
Basakomo, Nigeria
Basari, Togo
Basari, Senegal
Biafada, Guinea-Bissau
Bimanese, Indonesia
Birifor, Ghana
Bobo, Mali
Boya, Sudan
Brao (1), Laos
Bua, Chad
Budugum, Cameroon
Builsa, Ghana
Bunu, Nigeria
Burungi, Tanzania
Bushmen (Heikum), Namibia
Bushmen, Botswana
Ch'ol Tila, Mexico
Chakossi, Togo

Kwere, Tanzania
Labans, India
Laka, Cameroon
Lampung, Indonesia
Lebong, Indonesia
Ligbi, Ivory Coast
Ligbi, Ghana
Limba, Sierra Leone
Lobi, Ivory Coast
Lohar, Pakistan
Loko, Sierra Leone
Loma, Guinea
Loma, Liberia
Lomwe, Mozambique
Loven, Laos
Lugbara, Uganda
Lungu, Nigeria
Maiongong, Brazil
Maji, Ethiopia
Makonde, Tanzania
Makua, Mozambique
Mambila, Cameroon
Mamprusi, Ghana
Mancang, Senegal
Manding, Senegal
Mangs, India
Manjack, Senegal
Mano, Liberia
Manobos, Pulangi, Philippines
Masa, Chad
Matakam, Cameroon
Matumbi, Tanzania
Mauri, Niger
Mbukushu, Angola
Meban, Sudan
Mende, Sierra Leone
Migrants of Cuiaba, Brazil
Minianka, Mali
Mo, Ghana
Moba, Ghana

Moba, Togo
Murle, Sudan
Muslim Community of Bawku, Ghana
Namshi, Cameroon
Nawuri, Ghana
Nchimburu, Ghana
Ndunpa Duupa, Cameroon
Neyo, Ivory Coast
Negeg, Laos
Ngere, Ivory Coast
Nigerians of Kano, Nigeria
Ntrubs, Ghana
Nyaheun, Laos
Nyamwezi, Tanzania
Nyzatom, Sudan
Od, Pakistan
Oi, Laos
Phu Thai, Laos
Podokwo, Cameroon
Pular, Senegal
Pygmy (Binga), Burundi
Pygmy (Binga), Central African Empire
Rabha, India
Rai, Nepal
Reshiat, Ethiopia
Rural Ranch Workers, Brazil
Safwa, Tanzania
Samburu, Kenya
Sapo, Liberia
Sarakole, Senegal
Sasak, Indonesia
Serawai, Indonesia
Serere (1), Senegal
Seychellois, Seychelles
Shanga, Nigeria
So, Laos
Sochi, Pakistan
Sonjo, Tanzania

INDEX
by
Principal
Professed
Religion

ANCESTOR WORSHIP
Akha* (1), Thailand
K'anjobal of San Miguel*,
  Guatemala

ANIMISM
Adamawa, Cameroon
Adi**, India
Adja*, Benin
Afawa, Nigeria
Afo*, Nigeria
Aka, India
Alago, Nigeria
Alak, Laos
Ambonese, Netherlands
Ankwe, Nigeria
Anuak, Ethiopia
Anuak, Sudan
Apatani*, India
Arusha, Tanzania
Asmat (1), Indonesia
Ata of Davao, Philippines
Atta, Philippines
Aymara*, Bolivia
Babur Thali*, Nigeria
Bakuba*, Zaire
Balante, Guinea-Bissau

Banaro**, Papua New Guinea
Bandi, Liberia
Banyun, Guinea-Bissau
Baoule**, Ivory Coast
Barabaig (1), Tanzania
Barasano, Northern, Colombia
Barasano, Southern, Colombia
Bariba, Benin
Basakomo, Nigeria
Basari, Togo
Basotho, Mountain** (1), Lesotho
Bassa, Liberia
Bassa*, Nigeria
Bhils* (1), India
Biafada, Guinea-Bissau
Bijogo*, Guinea-Bissau
Bilan*, Philippines
Birifor, Ghana
Bobo, Mali
Boko*, Benin
Bontoc, Central, Philippines
Bororo, Brazil
Boya, Sudan
Brao (1), Laos
Bua, Chad
Budugum, Cameroon
Builsa, Ghana
Bukidnon*, Philippines

303

REGISTRY OF THE UNREACHED

Bunu, Nigeria
Burungi, Tanzania
Busanse*, Ghana
Bushmen (Heikum), Namibia
Bushmen (Hiechware), Rhodesia
Bushmen (Kung) (1), Namibia
Bushmen in Botswana
Ch'ol Tila, Mexico
Chakossi*, Ghana
Chakossi, Togo
Chawai, Nigeria
Chiriguano*, Argentina
Chokwe Lunda, Angola
Chola Naickans, India
Chrau*, Viet Nam
Chuabo, Mozambique
Chuj of San Mateo Ixtatan,
    Guatemala
Citak**, Indonesia
Coreguaje*, Colombia
Cubeo, Colombia
Cuna (1), Colombia
Dagari, Ghana
Daka, Nigeria
Dani, Baliem (1), Indonesia
Dghwede, Nigeria
Didinga, Sudan
Dinka, Sudan
Diola, Senegal
Dogon (1), Mali
Dompago, Benin
Doohwaayo*, Cameroon
Dorobo, Kenya
Dorobo, Tanzania
Duka*, Nigeria
Dumagat, Philippines
Duru, Cameroon
Eggon, Nigeria
El Molo, Kenya
Fakai*, Nigeria

Fali*, Nigeria
Fra-Fra, Ghana
Ga-Dang, Philippines
Gade, Nigeria
Gagre*, Pakistan
Gagu, Ivory Coast
Galler, Laos
Gbande, Guinea
Gbari, Nigeria
Ghimeera*, Ethiopia
Gio, Liberia
Giryama, Kenya
Gisei, Cameroon
Gisiga, Cameroon
Glavda*, Nigeria
Godie**, Ivory Coast
Gonds, India
Gourency, Upper Volta
Gouro*, Ivory Coast
Grebo*, Liberia
Grunshi, Ghana
Guajiro, Colombia
Guarani** (1), Bolivia
Guayabevo, Colombia
Gude, Cameroon
Gugu-Yalanji, Australia
Gurensi, Ghana
Gwendora, Nigeria
Hewa*, Papua New Guinea
Hewa* (1), Papua New Guinea
Higi**, Nigeria
Hopi, United States
Huila*, Angola
Hukwe, Angola
Ibaji, Nigeria
Ica, Colombia
Ifugao, Antipolo, Philippines
Ifugao, Philippines
Ifugao (Kalangoya)*, Philippines
Ingassana, Sudan

Iraqw, Tanzania
Iwaidja, Austria
Izi*, Nigeria
Jaba, Nigeria
Jarawa*, Nigeria
Jeng, Laos
Jerawa, Nigeria
Jibu, Nigeria
Jiye, Uganda
Jiye, Sudan
Jukun, Nigeria
Kabre, Togo
Kadara, Nigeria
Kafirs* (1), Pakistan
Kagoro, Mali
Kaipeng-Koloi*, India
Kalagan*, Philippines
Kalanga, Botswana
Kalinga, Southern, Philippines
Kamantan, Nigeria
Kambari, Nigeria
Kamuku, Nigeria
Kankanay, Central, Philippines
Karamojong, Uganda
Karen (1), Thailand
Kasena*, Ghana
Kasseng, Laos
Kayagar, Indonesia
Kayapo, Brazil
Kepas, Papua New Guinea
Kerewe, Tanzania
Kichepo, Sudan
Kimyal, Indonesia
Kissi, Sierra Leone
Kissi, Guinea
Kissi, Liberia
Koalib (1), Sudan
Koma, Ghana
Komo, Ethiopia
Kond**, India

Konkomba, Togo
Konkomba, Ghana
Kono*, Sierra Leone
Konso, Ethiopia
Korku, India
Koro, Nigeria
Koroma, Sudan
Kotopo, Cameroon
Kotta, India
Kowaao*, Liberia
Kpelle, Liberia
Krahn**, Liberia
Krahn, Ivory Coast
Krongo, Sudan
Kuatinema, Brazil
Kubu, Indonesia
Kulango, Ivory Coast
Kurfei, Niger
Kusaasi*, Ghana
Kwere, Tanzania
Laka, Cameroon
Lamba, Togo
Lango, Ethiopia
Ligbi, Ivory Coast
Limba, Sierra Leone
Lobi, Ivory Coast
Loho Loho*, Indonesia
Loko, Sierra Leone
Loma, Guinea
Loma, Liberia
Lomwe, Mozambique
Luhya**, Kenya
Lungu, Nigeria
Macu, Colombia
Macuxi*, Brazil
Maguzawa** (1), Nigeria
Maiongong, Brazil
Maji, Ethiopia
Makua, Mozambique
Malayo, Colombia

REGISTRY OF THE UNREACHED

Mambila, Cameroon
Mamprusi, Ghana
Mangyan*, Philippines
Manikion*, Indonesia
Manjaco*, Guinea-Bissau
Mano, Liberia
Manobo, Cotabato*, Philippines
Manobo, Ilianen, Philippines
Manobo, Salug*, Philippines
Manobo, Tigwa*, Philippines
Manobo, Western Bukidnon,*,
    Philippines
Manobos, Pulangi, Philippines
Masa, Chad
Masai* (1), Kenya
Masengo, Ethiopia
Matakam, Cameroon
Mauri, Niger
Mbukushu, Angola
Meban, Sudan
Mejah*, India
Mende, Sierra Leone
Meo*, Thailand
Minianka, Mali
Mirung, Bangladesh
Mishmi, India
Miya, Nigeria
Mo, Ghana
Moba, Ghana
Moba, Togo
Mocha**, Ethiopia
Moken (1), Burma
Mokole, Benin
Mru, Bangladesh
Mualthuam, India
Mumuye, Nigeria
Murle, Sudan
Murngin (Wulamba), Australia
Nafaara* (1), Ghana
Nambikuara, Brazil

Nambya*, Rhodesia
Namshi, Cameroon
Nawuri, Ghana
Nchimburu, Ghana
Ndebele* (1), Rhodesia
Ndoro*, Nigeria
Ngamo*, Nigeria
Ngen, Ivory Coast
Ngeg, Laos
Ngere, Ivory Coast
Ningerum, Papua New Guinea
Nkoya, Zambia
Nocte**, India
Ntrubs, Ghana
Nuer, Ethiopia
Nuer (1), Sudan
Nyaheun, Laos
Nyamwezi, Tanzania
Nyantruku, Benin
Nyzatom, Sudan
Oeang Asli*, Malaysia
Oi, Laos
Pila*, Benin
Podokwo, Cameroon
Pwo Karen, Thailand
Pygmy (Binga), Burundi
Pygmy (Binga), Central African
    Empire
Pygmy (Mbuti) (1), Zaire
Quechua, Huanco*, Peru
Red Bobo*, Upper Volta
Reshiat, Ethiopia
Safwa, Tanzania
Samburu, Kenya
Samo-Kubo, Papua New Guinea
Santhali*, Nepal
Sanuma, Brazil
Sapo, Liberia
Save*, Benin
Senufo, Ivory Coast

Serere (1), Senegal
Shanga, Nigeria
Shirishana*, Brazil
Sisaala*, Ghana
So, Laos
Somagai, Indonesia
Somba*, Benin
Sonjo, Tanzania
Soruba, Benin
Spiritists (1), Brazil
Subanen (Tuboy)*, Philippines
Subanen, Sindangan*,
  Philippines
Suk, Kenya
Suri*, Ethiopia
Ta-Oi, Laos
Tagbanwa, Aborlan*,
  Philippines
Tagin**, India
Tampulma, Ghana
Tangsa*, India
Tatuyo*, Colombia
Tboli*, Philippines
Teenbu, Ivory Coast
Temne*, Sierra Leone
Tigon, Cameroon
Tin, Thailand
Tofi, Benein
Tonga, Rhodesia
Tonga, Gwembe Valley (1),
  Zambia
Topotha, Sudan
Tripuri*, India
Turkana, Kenya
Turkana Fishing Community* (1),
  Kenya
Turu, Tanzania
Uduk, Sudan
Vagala, Ghana
Vere**, Nigeria

Wajita*, Tanzania
Wala, Ghana
Wanchoo*, India
Warjawa, Nigeria
Watchi, Togo
Wazinza, Tanzania
Wimbum*, Cameroon
Wobe, Ivory Coast
Yala*, Nigeria
Yanomamo in Brazil (1)
Yao* (1), Thailand
Yei*, Botswana
Yinga, Cameroon
Zaranda Hill Peoples*, Nigeria
Zoliang, India
Zowla, Ghana
Zuni, USA

BUDDHISM
Banai*, Bangladesh
Cambodians, Thailand
Chinese, Thailand
Government officials, Thailand
Japanese (1), Brazil
Kui, Thailand
Lao (1), Laos
Lawa, Thailand
Lepers, N.E. Thailand*
Loven, Laos
Monpa, India
Palaung (1), Burma
Phu Thai, Laos
Sherpa, Nepal
Sinhalese, Sri Lanka
Soka Gakkai Believers, Japan
Thailand Farmers (Ctl), Thailand
Vietnamese, Laos
Vietnamese, USA*

CHRISTIANITY
Businessmen, Brazil*

REGISTRY OF THE UNREACHED

Calena*, Colombia
Chinese, Bangladesh**
Coloureds (1), South Africa
Elite Parisian** (1), France
Lapps*, (1), Norway
Middle-East Businessmen,
    Brazil
Migrants of Cuiaba, Brazil
Pakabeti of Equator**, Zaire
Portuguese, France*
Rural Ranch Workers, Brazil
Seychellois, Seychelles
Students in Cuiaba, Brazil
Suriguenos*, Philippines
University Students (1), France
University Students (1), German
    Federal Rep.
Zapoteco, S. de Juarez, Mexico

CHRISTO-PAGANISM
Ampeeli*, Papua New Guinea
Apayao*, Philippines
Azteca** (1), Mexico
Balangao*, Philippines
Bipim**, Indonesia
Black Caribs (1), Belize*
Black Caribs, Guatemala*
Black Caribs, Honduras*
Bontoc, Southern*, Philippines
Cebu, Middle-Class**,
    Philippines
pch'ol Sabanilla**, Mexico
Chamorro, Turks and Caicos
    Islands
Chamula (1), Mexico
Chayahuita*, Peru
Galla of Bucho, Ethiopia
Guanano (1), Colombia
Guarayu, Bolivia
Huave*, Mexico

Ixil, Guatemala
Jemez Pueblo, USA
Jivaro (Achuara)*, Venezuela
Ka'mis, Papua New Guinea
Kaffa, Ethiopia
Kalinga, Northern*, Philippines
Kunimaipa*, Papua New Guinea
Lokoro, Sudan
Mam Indian*, Guatemala
Mamanwa (Mamanua)*,
    Philippines
Mansaka*, Philippines
Mapuche, Chile
Mazahua*, Mexico
Mimika, Indonesia
Mixes*, Mexico
Mixteco, San Juan Mixtepic,
    Mexico
Mopan Maya*, Guatemala
Mopan Maya*, Belize
Nahua, North Pueblo, Mexico
Paez**, Colombia
Quechua*, Peru
Quechua*, Bolivia
Quiche*, (1), Guatemala
Rabinal-Achi, Guatemala
Shankilla (Kazza)**, Ethiopia
Suena*, Papua New Guinea
Tagbanwa, Kalamian,
    Philippines
Teribe*, Panama
Tsachila*, Ecuador
Ulithi-Mall, Turks and Caicos
    Islands
Woleat, Turks and Caicos
    Islands
Yaquis, Mexico
Yucuna, Colombia
Zinacantecos (1), Mexico

FOLK RELIGION
Apartment Residents—Seoul*,
    Korea, Republic of
Druzes (1), Israel
Gypsies (1), Spain
Indust. Workers Yongdungpo,
    Korea, Republic of

HINDUISM
Bagri, Pakistan
Bajania (1), Pakistan
Balinese, Indonesia
Balmiki, Pakistan
Bhil*, Pakistan
Bhojpuri, Nepal
Caste Hindus (Adra Prd), India
Dhodias*, India
Dubla*, India
Gujarati, United Kingdom
Hajong, Bangladesh
Indians (1), Fiji
Indians, Rhodesia
Indians, East* (1), Trinidad and
    Tobago
Kanarese, India
Koch*, Bangladesh
Kolam*, India
Kudisai Vagh Makkal, India
Kuknas, India
Kutchi Kohli*, Pakistan
Labans, India
Lohar, Pakistan
Magar*, Nepal
Maharashtrians, India
Maithili, Nepal
Mangs, India
Meghwar* (1), Pakistan
Meitei (1), India
Nepali, Nepal
Newari, Nepal

Od, Pakistan
Parkari Kohlis*, Pakistan
Rabha, India
Rai, Nepal
Rai, Danuwar, Nepal
Rajbansi, Nepal
Rava, India
Sindhis, India
Sochi, Pakistan
Tamang, Nepal
Tamil (Ceylonese), Sri Lanka
Tamil Brahmins, India
Tamil Plantation Workers**,
    Malaysia
Tamils (Indian), Malaysia
Tamils (Indian)* (1), Sri Lanka
Tengger, Indonesia
Tharadari Kohli*, Pakistan
Tharu, Nepal
Totis, India
Vagari, Pakistan
Wadiara Kohli*, Pakistan

ISLAM
Achehnese, Indonesia
Afar (1), Ethiopia
Ahl-i-Haqq (1), Iran*
Ajuran (1), Kenya
Alaba, Ethiopia
Alas, Indonesia
Alawites (1), Syria
Algerian (Arabs), Algeria
Algerian Arabs, France
Arawa, Nigeria
Ayao*, Malawi
Bambara, Mali
Bimanese, Indonesia
Boran, Ethiopia
Bugis, Indonesia
Busa, Nigeria

REGISTRY OF THE UNREACHED

Butawa, Nigeria
Cham, Vietnam
Cham (Western), Kampuchea,
   Democratic
Chitralis (1), Pakistan
Cirebon, Indonesia
Comorians (1), Comoros
Dagomba*, Ghana
Degodia, Kenya
Dendi, Benin
Dewein, Liberia
Diola, Guinea-Bissau
Fula, Guinea
Fulah, Upper Volta
Fulani (1), Cameroon
Fulani, Benin
Fulbe, Ghana
Gabra, Kenya
Galla (Bale), Ethiopia
Galla, Harar, Ethiopia
Gayo, Indonesia
Gbazantche, Benin
Gonja, Ghana
Gurage, Ethiopia
Gurreh, Kenya
Hunzakut* (1), Pakistan
Igbira, Nigeria
Jama Mapun, Philippines
Javanese (rural)* (1), Indonesia
Javanese of Central Java*,
   Indonesia
Javanese of Pejompongan*,
   Indonesia
Kabyle (1), Algeria
Kashmiri Muslims* (1), India
Kita, Mali
Kolbila, Cameroon
Koranko*, Sierra Leone
Kotokoli, Benin
Kurds (1), Turkey

Lampung, Indonesia
Lebong, Indonesia
Libyans, Libya
Ligbi, Ghana
Madurese (1), Indonesia
Maguindano, Philippines
Makonde, Tanzania
Malays (1), Singapore
Mandingo (1), Liberia
Maranao (1), Philippines
Matumbi, Tanzania
Maures, Senegal
Minangkabau, Indonesia
Molbog, Philippines
Moor & Malays (1), Sri Lanka
Muslim Community of Bawku,
   Ghana
Muslim Immigrants*, United
   Kingdom
Muslim Malays, Malaysia
Muslims (West Nile Dist.),
   Uganda
Muslims (1), United Arab
   Emirates
Muslims, Yugoslavia
Muslims, Jordan
Muslims, Thailand
Ndunpa Duupa, Cameroon
Nigerians of Kano, Nigeria
Nupe*, Nigeria
Ogandenya, Kenya
Ouaddai, Chad
Redjang, Indonesia
Saguye*, Kenya
Sama Bangingi, Philippines
Sama Pangutaran, Philippines
Sama-Badjaw (1), Philippines
Sangil, Philippines
Sarakole, Senegal
Sasak, Indonesia

Serawai, Indonesia
Sindhis, Pakistan*
Somali, Ethiopia
Somali (1), Somalia
Sundanese*, Indonesia
Swatis (1), Pakistan
Taucouleur, Senegal
Tausug, Philippines
Tem, Togo
Tuareg (1), Niger
Turkish Immigrant Workers (1),
    German Federal Rep.
Uzbeks* (1), Afghanistan
Vai, Liberia
Voko, Cameroon
Winji-Winji, Benin
Wolof, Senegal
Yakan, Philippines
Yalunka, Sierra Leone
Yao, Mozambique
Yemenis (1), Yemen, Arab
    Republic
Zaramo, Tanzania

JUDAISM
Falasha* (1), Ethiopia
Jewish Imgrnts.—American,
    Israel
Jewish Imgrnts.—Argentine,
    Israel
Jewish Imgrnts.—Australian,
    Israel
Jewish Imgrnts.—Brazilian,
    Israel
Jewish Imgrnts.—Mexican,
    Israel
Jewish Imgrnts.—Uruguayan,
    Israel
Jewish Immigrants, Other, Israel
Jews of Montreal, Canada

Jews, Sephardic, Canada

OTHER
Lotuka*, Sudan
Yanyula, Australia

PEYOTE RELIGION
Pauite, Northern, USA

SECULARISM
Chinese in Korea, Republic of
Chinese in West Germany,
    German Federal Rep.
Chinese Mainlanders, Taiwan
College Students, Japan
Japanese Students, USA*
Korean Prisoners*, Korea,
    Republic of
Koreans, Japan
Racetrack Residents* (1), USA

TRADITIONAL CHINESE
Chinese (Hoklo), Taiwan
Chinese Factory Workers, Hong
    Kong
Chinese Hakka (1), Taiwan*
Chinese, Australia*
Chinese, Austria
Chinese, Brazil*
Chinese, Burma
Chinese, Hong Kong*
Chinese, Indonesia*
Chinese, Japan
Chinese, Laos
Chinese, Malaysia
Chinese, New Zealand
Chinese in Sabah*, Malaysia
Chinese in Sarawak*, Malaysia
Chinese, South Africa
Chinese(1), United Kingdom*

REGISTRY OF THE UNREACHED

Chinese, USA*
Chinese in Vancouver B.C.*,
  Canada
Chinese, W. Malaysia
Chinese Refugees, Macau
Chinese Refugees, France* (1)
Chinese Restaurant Wrkrs.,
  France
Chinese Villagers, Hong Kong
Urban Workers, Taiwan

TRADITIONAL JAPANESE
Farmers, Japan
Industry Laborers, Japan
Inland Sea Island Peoples,
  Japan
Japanese in Korea, Republic of
Ryukyuan, Japan

UNKNOWN
Basari, Senegal
Bus Drivers, South Korea*
Chinese in Amsterdam,
  Netherlands
Chinese, Costa Rica
Chinese, Netherlands
Chinese in Osaka, Japan
Chinese Merchants, Ghana
Factory Workers, Young, Hong
  Kong
Gurung, Nepal
Khana, Nigeria
Koreans in Germany**, German
  Federal Rep.
Lugbara, Uganda
Neyo, Ivory Coast
Sumba, Indonesia

INDEX
by
Language

Achehnese	Achehnese, Indonesia
Adi	Adi, India**
Afanci	Afawa, Nigeria
Afar	Afar, Ethiopia (1)
Afo	Afo, Nigeria*
Agau	Falasha, Ethiopia* (1)
Aka	Aka, India
Akha	Akha, Thailand* (1)
Alaban	Alaba, Ethiopia
Alago	Alago, Nigeria
Alak	Alak, Laos
Alas	Alas, Indonesia
Albanian	Muslims, Yugoslavia
Aledjo	Nyantruku, Benin
Ambonese	Ambonese, Netherlands
Ampale	Ampeeli, Papua New Guinea*
Ankwai	Ankwe, Nigeria
Anuak	Anuak, Ethiopia
	Anuak, Sudan
Apartani	Apatani, India*
Arabic	Alawites, Syria (1)
	Algerian (Arabs), Algeria
	Algerian Arabs, France
	Druzes, Israel (1)
	Libyans, Libya
	Maures, Senegal
	Middle-East Businessmen, Brazil
	Muslims, United Arab Emirates (1)
	Muslims, Jordan

314

Arabic (Eastern)	Yemenis, Yemen, Arab Republic (1)
Arusha	Arusha, Tanzania
Asmat	Asmat, Indonesia (1)
Asurini	Kuatinema, Brazil
Atta	Atta, Philippines
Aymara	Aymara, Bolivia*
Bagri	Bagri, Pakistan
Bahasa Jawa	Javanese of Pejompongan, Indonesia*
Bahasa Malaysia	Muslim Malays, Malaysia
Balangao	Balangao, Philippines*
Balanta	Balanta, Senegal
	Balante, Guinea-Bissau
Balinese	Balinese, Indonesia
Bambara	Bambara, Mali
Banaro	Banaro, Papua New Guinea**
Bandi	Bandi, Liberia
	Gbande, Guinea
Banyun	Banyun, Guinea-Bissau
Barasano, Northern	Barasano, Northern, Colombia
Bariba	Bariba, Benin
Basari	Basari, Togo
Bassa	Bassa, Liberia
	Bassa, Nigeria*
Baule	Baoule, Ivory Coast**
Bengali	Banai, Bangladesh*
	Chinese, Bangladesh**
	Hajong, Bangladesh*
	Koch, Bangladesh*
Bhojpuri	Bhojpuri, Nepal
	Tharu, Nepal
Biafada	Biafada, Guinea-Bissau
Bidyogo	Bijogo, Guinea-Bissau*
Bilaan	Bilan, Philippines*
Bima	Bimanese, Indonesia
Bimoba	Moba, Ghana
	Moba, Togo
Bipim	Bipim, Indonesia**
Birifor	Birifor, Ghana
Bisa (Busanga)	Busanse, Ghana*
Bobowule	Bobo, Mali

315

REGISTRY OF THE UNREACHED

Boko (Busa)	Boko, Benin*
Bontoc, Central	Bontoc, Central, Philippines
Boran	Boran, Ethiopia
Bororo	Bororo, Brazil
Boya	Boya, Sudan
Brao	Brao, Laos (1)
Bua	Bua, Chad
Buamu (Bobo Wule)	Red Bobo, Upper Volta*
Bugis	Bugis, Indonesia
Buka-khwe	Bushmen, Botswana
Buli	Builsa, Ghana
Bunu	Bunu, Nigeria
Bura (Babur)	Babur Thali, Nigeria*
Burmese	Chinese Refugees, Macau
Burungi	Burungi, Tanzania
Burushaski	Hunzakut, Pakistan* (1)
Busa (Bokobarn Akiba)	Busa, Nigeria
Buta	Butawa, Nigeria
Cagayan	Jama Mapun, Philippines
Canarese	Chola Naickans, India
Cantonese	Chinese Factory Workers, Hong Kong
	Chinese in Amsterdam, Netherlands
	Chinese, Australia*
	Chinese, Costa Rica
	Chinese, Hong Kong*
	Chinese, New Zealand
	Chinese, South Africa
	Chinese in Vancouver B.C., Canada*
	Chinese, W. Malaysia
	Chinese Villagers, Hong Kong
	Factory Workers, Young, Hong Kong
Cebuano	Cebu, Middle-Class, Philippines**
Ch'ol	Ch'ol Sabanilla, Mexico*
Chakossi	Chakossi, Ghana*
	Chakossi, Togo
Cham	Cham, Vietnam
	Cham (Western), Kampuchea
Chamorro	Chamorro, Turks and Caicos Is.
Chawai	Chawai, Nigeria
Chayawita	Chayahuita, Peru*

REGISTRY OF THE UNREACHED

Eggon	Eggon, Nigeria
English	Coloureds, South Africa (1)
	Jews of Montreal, Canada
	Racetrack Residents, USA* (1)
English with Hindi	Indians, East, Trinidad and Tobago* (1)
Ewe	Zowla, Ghana
Faka	Fakai, Nigeria*
Fali	Fali, Nigeria*
Fouta Toro	Pular, Senegal
Fra-Fra	Fra-Fra, Ghana
French	Elite Parisian, France** (1)
	Jews, Sephardic, Canada
	University Students, France (1)
Fula	Fula, Guinea
Fulani	Adamawa, Cameroon
	Fulah, Upper Volta
	Fulani, Cameroon (1)
	Fulani, Benin
	Fulbe, Ghana
Ga-Dang	Ga-Dang, Philippines
Gade	Gade, Nigeria
Gagou	Gagu, Ivory Coast
Galla	Gabra, Kenya
	Galla (Bale), Ethiopia
	Saguye, Kenya*
Galler	Galler, Laos
Gallinya	Galla, Harar, Ethiopia
Gallinya (Oromo)	Galla of Bucho, Ethiopia
Gasari	Basari, Senegal
Gayo	Gayo, Indonesia
Gbari	Gbari, Nigeria
Gbazantche,	Gbazantche, Benin
Ge	Adja, Benin*
	Watchi, Togo
German	University Students, German Fed. Rep. (1)
Gimira	Ghimeera, Ethiopia*
Giryama	Giryama, Kenya
Gisiga	Gisiga, Cameroon
Glavda	Glavda, Nigeria*
Godie	Godie, Ivory Coast***

318

REGISTRY OF THE UNREACHED

Hebrew	Jewish Imgrnts.—American, Israel
	Jewish Imgrnts.—Argentine, Israel
	Jewish Imgrnts.—Australian, Israel
	Jewish Imgrnts.—Brazilian, Israel
	Jewish Imgrnts.—Mexican, Israel
	Jewish Imgrnts.—Uruguayan, Israel
	Jewish Immigrants, Other, Israel
Heikum	Bushmen (Heikum), Namibia
Hewa	Hewa, Papua New Guinea*
	Hewa, Papua New Guinea* (1)
Higi	Higi, Nigeria**
Hindustani	Balmiki, Pakistan
	Indians, Fiji (1)
Hopi	Hopi, USA
Huave	Huave, Mexico*
Huila	Huila, Angola*
Hukwe	Hukwe, Angola
Ibaji	Ibaji, Nigeria
Ica	Ica, Colombia
Ifugao	Ifugao, Philippines
Igbirra	Igbira, Nigeria
Ilianen Manobo	Manobo, Ilianen, Phillipines
Indonesian	Chinese, Indonesia*
Iragw	Iragw, Tanzania
Isaalin	Sisaala, Ghana*
Isneg	Apayao, Philippines*
Iwaidja	Iwaidja, Austria
Izi	Izi, Nigeria*
Jaba	Jaba, Nigeria
Janena	Barasano, Southern, Colombia
Japanese	Chinese in Osaka, Japan
	College Students, Japan
	Farmers, Japan
	Industry Laborers—Japan
	Inland Sea Island Peoples, Japan
	Japanese, Brazil (1)
	Japanese in Korea, Republic of
	Japanese Students, USA*
	Soka Gakkai Believers, Japan
Jaranchi	Jarawa, Nigeria*

Kissi, Southern	Kissi, Sierra Leone
Kizinza	Wazinza, Tanzania
Koalib (Nuba)	Koalib, Sudan (1)
Kolaka	Loho Loho, Indonesia*
Kolami	Kolam, India*
Kolbila	Kolbila, Cameroon
Kom Komba	Konkomba, Togo
Koma	Koma, Ghana
Komering	Lampung, Indonesia
Komo	Komo, Ethiopia
Konkomba	Konkomba, Ghana
Kono	Kono, Sierra Leone*
Konso	Konso, Ethiopia
Korean	Apartment Residents—Seoul, Korea*
	Bus Drivers, South Korea*
	Indust. Workers, Youngdungpo, Korea
	Korean Prisoners, Korea, Republic of*
	Koreans, German Federal Rep.**
	Koreans, Japan
Korku	Korku, India
Koro	Koro, Nigeria
Koroma	Koroma, Sudan
Kota	Kotta, India
Kotokoli	Kotokoli, Benin
	Tem, Togo
Kotopo	Kotopo, Cameroon
Kowaao	Kowaao, Liberia*
Kpelle	Kpelle, Liberia
Krahn	Krahn, Liberia**
Krahn	Krahn, Ivory Coast
Krongo	Krongo, Sudan
Kui	Kond, India**
	Kui, Thailand
Kukni	Kuknas, India
Kulango	Kulango, Ivory Coast
Kunimaipa	Kunimaipa, Papua New Guinea*
Kuranko (Maninka)	Koranko, Sierra Leone*
Kurdish (Kirmancho)	Kurds, Turkey (1)
Kurdish dialects	Ahl-i-Haqq, Iran* (1)
Kusaal	Kusaasi, Ghana*

Kusso   Mbukushu, Angola
Kwe-Etshari   Bushmen (Hiechware), Rhodesia
Kwere   Kwere, Tanzania
Lanaani   Labans, India
Laka   Laka, Cameroon
Lamba   Lamba, Togo
Lango   Lango, Ethiopia
Lao   Lao, Laos (1)
Lappish   Lapps, Norway* (1)
Latuka   Lotuka, Sudan*
Lawa   Lawa, Thailand
Ligbi   Ligbi, Ivory Coast
                         Ligbi, Ghana
Limba   Limba, Sierra Leone
Limbum   Wimbum, Cameroon*
Lobi   Lobi, Ivory Coast
local dialects   Kubu, Indonesia
                         Pygmy (Binga), Burundi
                         Pygmy (Binga), Central African Empire
local languages   Pygmy (Mbuti), Zaire (1)
                         Zaranda Hill Peoples, Nigeria*
Logoro (Bambara)   Kagoro, Mali
Loko   Loko, Sierra Leone
Lokoro   Lokoro, Sudan
Loma   Loma, Guinea
                         Loma, Liberia
Lorhon   Teenbu, Ivory Coast
Loven   Loven, Laos
Lugbara   Lugbara, Uganda
                         Muslims (West Nile Dist.), Uganda
Lungu   Lungu, Nigeria
Maba   Ouaddai, Chad
Maban-Jumjum   Meban, Sudan
Macu   Macu, Colombia
Macuxi   Macuxi, Brazil*
Madurese   Madurese, Indonesia (1)
Magar   Magar, Nepal*
Maguindano   Maguindano, Philippines
Maiongong   Maiongong, Brazil
Maithili   Maithili, Nepal

REGISTRY OF THE UNREACHED

Majangiir	Masengo, Ethiopia
Maji	Maji, Ethiopia
Makua	Makua, Mozambique
Malay	Malays of Singapore (1)
	Muslims of Thailand
Malayo	Malayo, Colombia
Malinke, Senegalese	Manding, Senegal
Mam	Mam Indian, Guatemala*
Mambila	Mambila, Cameroon
Mandarin	Chinese, Austria
	Chinese, Burma
	Chinese in Holland, Netherlands
	Chinese, Japan
	Chinese, Laos
	Chinese in Sarawak, Malaysia*
	Chinese in United Kingdom* (1)
	Chinese, USA*
	Chinese, West Germany
	Chinese Mainlanders, Taiwan
Mandingo	Mandingo, Liberia (1)
Mandyako	Manjaco, Guinea-Bissau*
Mandyale	Manjack, Senegal
Mangyan	Mangyan, Philippines*
Manipuri	Meitei, India (1)
Mankanya	Mancang, Senegal
Mano	Mano, Liberia
Manobo	Ata of Davao, Philippines
Manobo, Binokid	Manobo, Western Bukidnon, Philippines*
	Bukidnon, Philippines
Manobo, Pulangi	Manobos, Pulangi, Philippines
Manobo, Tigwa	Manobo, Salug, Philippines*
	Manobo, Tigwa, Philippines*
Mansaka	Mansaka, Philippines*
Mapuche	Mapuche, Chile
Maranao	Maranao, Philippines (1)
Marathi	Maharashtrians, India
	Mangs, India
Marwari	Bhil, Pakistan*
	Meghwar, Pakistan* (1)

Masa	Budugum, Cameroon
	Gisei, Cameroon
	Masa, Chad
Masai	Masai, Kenya* (1)
Masai, Samburu	Samburu, Kenya
Matakam	Matakam, Cameroon
Matumbi	Matumbi, Tanzania
Mazahua	Mazahua, Mexico*
Mejah	Mejah, India*
Mende	Mende, Sierra Leone
Meo	Meo, Thailand*
Mimika	Mimika, Indonesia
Minamanwa	Mamanwa (Mamanua), Philippines*
Minangkabau	Minangkabau, Indonesia
Mirung	Mirung, Bangladesh
Mishmi	Mishmi, India
Mixe	Mixes, Mexico*
Mixteco	Mixteco, San Juan Mixtepic, Mexico
Miya	Miya, Nigeria
Mo (Degha)	Mo, Ghana
Mocha	Mocha, Ethiopia**
Moken	Moken, Burma (1)
Mokole	Mokole, Benin
Molbog	Molbog, Philippines
Monpa	Monpa, India
Mopan May	Mopan Maya, Guatemala*
	Mopan Maya, Belize*
Moreno	Black Caribs, Belize* (1)
	Black Caribs, Guatemala*
	Black Caribs, Honduras*
Mualthuam	Mualthuam, India
Mumuye	Mumuye, Nigeria
Murle	Murle, Sudan
Murung	Mru, Bangladesh
Nafaara	Nafaara, Ghana* (1)
Naga, Zoliang	Zoliang, India
Nahua	Nahua, North Pueblo, Mexico
Nahuatl, Hidlalgo	Azteca, Mexico** (1)
Nambikuara	Nambikuara, Brazil

REGISTRY OF THE UNREACHED

Nambya	Nambya, Rhodesia*
Namshi	Namshi, Cameroon
Nandi	Dorobo, Kenya
Native Senoi	Oeang Asli, Malaysia*
Nawuri	Nawuri, Ghana
Nchumburu	Nchimburu, Ghana
Ndoro	Ndoro, Nigeria*
Ndunpa Duupa	Ndunpa Duupa, Cameroon
Nepali	Nepali, Nepal
Nevo	Neyo, Ivory Coast
Newari	Newari, Nepal
Ngamo	Ngamo, Nigeria*
Ngen	Ngen, Ivory Coast
Ngeg	Ngeg, Laos
Ningerum	Ningerum, Papua New Guinea
Nocte	Nocte, India**
Northeast Thai	Lepers, N.E. Thailand*
Northern Cambodian	Cambodians, Thailand
Ntrubo	Ntrubs, Ghana
Nuer	Nuer, Ethiopia
	Nuer, Sudan (1)
Nupe	Nupe, Nigeria*
Nyaheun	Nyaheun, Laos
Nyamwezi	Nyamwezi, Tanzania
Nyaturu	Turu, Tanzania
Odki	Od, Pakistan
Oi	Oi, Laos
Oluluyia	Luhya, Kenya**
Paez	Paez, Colombia**
Paiute, Northern	Paiute, Northern, USA
Pakabeti	Pakabeti of Equator, Zaire**
Palaung	Palaung, Burma (1)
Phu Thai	Phu Thai, Laos
Pila-Pila	Pila, Benin*
Podokwo	Podokwo, Cameroon
Portuguese	Businessmen, Brazil*
	Migrants of Cuiaba, Brazil
	Portuguese, France*
	Rural Ranch Workers, Brazil
	Spiritists, Brazil (1)
	Students in Cuiaba, Brazil

326

REGISTRY OF THE UNREACHED

Somagai	Somagai, Indonesia
Somali	Degodia, Kenya
	Gurreh, Kenya
	Ogadenya, Kenya
	Somali, Ethiopia
	Somali, Somalia (1)
Somali (Ajuran)	Ajuran, Kenya (1)
Somba (Detammari)	Somba, Benin*
Soninke	Sarakole, Senegal
Sonjo	Sonjo, Tanzania
Soruba	Soruba, Benin
Sough	Manikion, Indonesia*
Southern Bontoc	Bontoc, Southern, Philippines*
Southern Sesotho	Basotho, Mountain, Lesotho** (1)
Spanish	Calena, Colombia*
Subanen, Tuboy	Subanen (Tuboy), Philippines*
Subanun	Subanen, Sindangan, Philippines*
Suena	Suena, Papua New Guinea*
Sumba	Sumba, Indonesia
Sundanese	Sundanese, Indonesia*
Suppire	Minianka, Mali
Suri	Suri, Ethiopia*
Surigueno	Suriguenos, Philippines*
Swati	Swatis, Pakistan (1)
Ta-Oi	Ta-Oi, Laos
Tabi	Ingassana, Sudan
Tagbanwa	Tagbanwa, Aborlan, Philippines*
Tagbanwa, Kalamian	Tagbanwa, Kalamian, Philippines
Tagin	Tagin, India**
Taiwanese	Urban Workers, Taiwan
Taiwanese (Minnan)	Chinese (Hoklo), Taiwan
Tamachek	Tuareg, Niger (1)
Tamang	Tamang, Nepal
Tamil	Kudisai Vagh Makkal, India
	Moor & Malays, Sri Lanka (1)
	Tamil (Ceylonese), Sri Lanka
	Tamil Brahmins, India
	Tamil Plantation Workers, Malaysia**
	Tamils (Indian), Malaysia
	Tamils (Indian, Sri Lanka* (1)

Tampulensi	Tampulma, Ghana
Tandanke	Tandanke, Senegal
Tangsa	Tangsa, India*
Tatoga	Barabaig, Tanzania (1)
Tatuyo	Tatuyo, Colombia*
Tausug	Tausug, Philippines
Tboli	Tboli, Philippines*
Telugu	Caste Hindus (Andra Prd), India
Temne	Temne, Sierra Leone*
Tenggerese	Tengger, Indonesia
Teribe	Teribe, Panama*
Thai	Government officials, Thailand
	Thailand Farmers (Ctl), Thailand
Tien-Chiu	Chinese Refugees, Drance* (1)
Tigon	Tigon, Cameroon
Tila Chol	Ch'ol Tila, Mexico
Tin	Tin, Thailand
Tofi	Tofi, Benin
Toposa	Topotha, Sudan
Toposa, Donyiro	Nyzatom, Sudan
Towa (Jemez)	Jemez Pueblo, USA
Tripuri	Tripuri, India*
Tshiluba	Bakuba, Zaire*
Turkana	Turkana, Kenya
	Turkana Fishing Community, Kenya* (1)
Turkish	Turkish Immigrant Workers, German Federal Rep. (1)
Tzotzil (Chamula)	Chamula, Mexico (1)
Tzotzil, Chenalho	Zinacantecos, Mexico (1)
Uduk	Uduk, Sudan
Ulithi	Ulithi-Mall, Turks and Caicos Islands
Uzbeki, Turkic	Uzbeks, Afghanistan* (1)
Vagala	Vagala, Ghana
Vai	Vai, Liberia
Vere	Vere, Nigeria**
Vietnamese	Vietnamese, Laos
	Vietnamese, USA*
Waffa Dialect	Ka'mis, Papua New Guinea
Wali	Wala, Ghana
Wanchoo	Wanchoo, India*

329

REGISTRY OF THE UNREACHED

Warji	Warjawa, Nigeria
Winji-Winji	Winji-Winji, Benin
Wobe	Wobe, Ivory Coast
Woko	Voko, Cameroon
Woleat	Woleat, Turks and Caicos Islands
Wolof	Wolof, Senegal
Won Chow	Chinese Restaurant Wrkrs., France
Xu	Bushmen (Kung), Namibia (1)
Yakan	Yakan, Philippines
Yala	Yala, Nigeria*
Yalunka	Yalunka, Sierra Leone
Yanoman (Waica)	Yanomamo, Brazil (1)
Yanyula (Yanjula)	Yanyula, Australia
Yao	Yao, Mozambique
Yao (Mien Wa)	Yao, Thailand* (1)
Yaqui	Yaquis, Mexico
Yei	Yei, Botswana*
Yinga	Yinga, Cameroon
Yucuna	Yucuna, Colombia
Zapoteco, S. de Juarez	Zapoteco, S. de Juarez, Mexico
Zaramo	Zaramo, Tanzania
Zighvana (Dghwede)	Dghwede, Nigeria
Zuni	Zuni, USA

INDEX
by
Country

332

333

REGISTRY OF THE UNREACHED

Burma	Chinese, Burma	600,000
	Moken (1)	5,000
	Palaung (1)	150,000
Burundi	Pygmy (Binga)	30,000
Cameroon	Adamawa	380,000
	Budugum	10,000
	Doohwaayo*	15,000
	Duru	20,000
	Fulani (1)	250,000
	Gisei	10,000
	Gisiga	30,000
	Gude	100,000
	Kolbila	1,000
	Kotopo	10,000
	Laka	10,000
	Mambila	40,000
	Matakam	140,000
	Namshi	30,000
	Ndunpa Duupa	1,000
	Podokwo	25,000
	Tigon	25,000
	Voko	1,000
	Wimbum*	50,000
	Yinga	300
Canada	Chinese, Vancouver B.C.*	80,000
	Jews, Montreal	120,000
	Jews, Sephardic	26,000
Central African Empire	Pygmy (Binga)	2,000
Chad	Bua	20,000
	Masa	80,000
	Ouaddai	320,000
Chile	Mapuche	300,000
Colombia	Barasano, Northern	450
	Barasano, Southern	400
	Calena*	1,200,000
	Coreguaje*	500
	Cubeo	1,900
	Cuna (1)	600
	Guajiro	60,000
	Guanano (1)	1,000

	Guayabevo	600
	Ica	3,000
	Macu	1,000
	Malayo	1,000
	Paez**	40,000
	Tatuyo*	300
	Yucuna	500
Comoros	Comorians (1)	300,000
Costa Rica	Chinese, Costa Rica	5,000
Ecuador	Tsachila*	1,100
Ethiopia	Afar (1)	300,000
	Alaba	50,000
	Anuak	52,000
	Boran	37,500
	Falasha* (1)	30,000
	Galla (Bale)	750,000
	Galla, Bucho	1,500
	Galla, Harar	1,305,400
	Ghimeera*	50,000
	Gurage	750,000
	Kaffa	170,000
	Komo	20,000
	Konso	30,000
	Lango	8,000
	Maji	15,000
	Masengo	7,000
	Mocha**	45,000
	Nuer	70,000
	Reshiat	10,000
	Shankilla (Kazza)**	20,000
	Somali	1,000,000
	Suri*	30,000
Fiji	Indians, Fiji (1)	265,000
France	Algerian Arabs, France	804,000
	Chinese Refugees, France* (1)	100,000
	Chinese Restaurant Wrkrs.	50,000
	Elite Parisian** (1)	500,000
	Portuguese, France*	150,000
	University Students (1)	800,000
German Federal Rep.	Chinese, West Germany	5,200

REGISTRY OF THE UNREACHED

	Koreans, Germany**	10,000
	Turkish Immigrant Workers (1)	1,000,000
	University Students (1)	850,000
Ghana	Birifor	40,000
	Builsa	97,000
	Busanse*	50,000
	Chakossi*	22,000
	Chinese Merchants	40
	Dagari	200,000
	Dagomba*	350,000
Ghana	Fra-Fra	230,000
	Fulbe	5,500
	Gonja	108,000
	Grunshi	200,000
	Gurensi	250,000
	Kasena*	70,000
	Koma	1,000
	Konkomba	175,000
	Kusaasi*	150,000
	Ligbi	6,000
	Mamprusi	80,000
	Mo	13,000
	Moba	80,000
	Muslim Community, Bawku	20,000
	Nafaara* (1)	0,000
	Nawuri	10,000
	Nchimburu	7,000
	Ntrubs	5,000
	Sisaala*	60,000
	Tampulma	8,000
	Vagala	3,000
	Wala	60,000
	Zowla	800,000
Guatemala	Black Caribs, Guatemala*	1,500
	Chuj, San Mateo Ixtatan	17,000
	Ixil	45,000
	K'anjobal, San Miguel*	18,000
	Mam Indian*	470,000
	Mopan Mava*	2,000
	Quiche* (1)	500,000
	Rabinal-Achi	21,000

	Nocte**	19,400
	Rabha	10,000
	Rava	45,000
	Sindhis, India	3,000,000
	Tagin**	25,000
	Tamil Brahmins	98,112,000
	Tangsa*	10,700
	Totis	nc
	Tripuri*	400,000
	Wanchoo*	nc
	Zoliang	50,000
Indonesia	Achehnese	2,200,000
	Alas	30,000
	Asmat (1)	30,000
	Balinese	2,000,000
	Bimanese	300,000
	Bipim**	450
	Bugis	2,500,000
	Chinese, Indonesia*	3,600,000
	Cirebon	2,500,000
	Citak**	6,500
	Dani, Baliem (1)	50,000
	Gayo	200,000
	Javanese (rural)* (1)	60,000,000
	Javanese, Central Java*	20,000,000
	Javanese, Pejompongan*	5,000
	Kayagar	9,000
	Kimyal	7,000
	Kubu	6,000
	Lampung	1,500,000
	Lebong	nc
	Loho Loho*	10,000
	Madurese (1)	7,000,000
	Manikion*	8,000
	Mimika	10,000
	Minangkabau	2,000,000
	Redjang	300,000
	Sasak	100,000
	Serawai	60,000
	Somagai	nc

	El Molo	1,000
	Gabra	12,000
	Giryama	335,900
	Gurreh	54,165
	Luhya**	1,800,000
	Masai* (1)	100,000
	Ogadenya	99,129
	Saguye*	30,000
	Samburu	60,500
	Suk	133,200
	Turkana	224,000
	Turkana Fishing Community* (1)	20,000
Korea, Republic of	Apartment Residents-Seoul*	87,000
	Bus Drivers, South Korea*	26,000
	Chinese, Korea	35,000
	Indust. Workers Yongdungpo	140,000
	Japanese, Korea	5,000
	Korean Prisoners*	45,000
Laos	Alak	8,000
	Brao (1)	18,000
	Chinese, Laos	25,000
	Galler	50,000
	Jeng	500
	Kasseng	15,000
	Lao (1)	1,908,600
	Loven	25,000
	Ngeg	50,000
	Nyaheun	15,000
	Oi	10,000
	Phu Thai	100,000
	So	15,000
	Ta-Oi	15,000
	Vietnamese	20,000
Lesotho	Basotho, Mountain** (1)	70,000
Liberia	Bandi	32,000
	Bassa	200,000
	Dewein	5,000
	Gio	92,000
	grebo*	65,000
	Kissi	35,000

	Yao	220,000
Namibia	Bushmen (Heikum)	16,000
	Bushmen (Kung) (1)	10,000
Nepal	Bhojpuri	806,480
	Gurung	172,000
	Magar*	300,000
	Maithili	1,000,000
	Nepali	6,060,758
	Newari	500,000
	Rai	232,000
	Rai, Danuwar	12,000
	Rajbansi	15,000
	Santhali*	nc
	Sherpa	20,000
	Tamang	nc
	Tharu	495,000
Netherlands	Ambonese	30,000
	Chinese, Amsterdam	15,000
	Chinese, Holland	35,000
New Zealand	Chinese, New Zealand	9,500
Niger	Kurfei	50,000
	Mauri	100,000
	Tuareg (1)	200,000
Nigeria	Afawa	10,000
	Afo*	25,000
	Alago	35,000
	Ankwe	10,000
	Arawa	200,000
	Babur Thali*	75,000
	Basakomo	60,000
	Bassa*	100,000
	Bunu	150,000
	Busa	50,000
	Butawa	20,000
	Chawai	30,000
	Daka	10,000
	Dghwede	13,000
	Duka*	10,000
	Eggon	80,000
	Fakai*	15,000

REGISTRY OF THE UNREACHED

	Hunzakut* (1)	10,000
	Kafirs* (1)	3 000
	Kutchi Kohli*	50,000
	Lohar	nc
	Meghwar* (1)	100,000
	Od	40,000
	Parkari Kohlis*	100,000
	Sindhis, Pakistan*	4,000,000
	Sochi	nc
	Swatis (1)	600,000
	Tharadari Kohli*	40,000
	Vagari	30,000
	Wadiara Kohli*	40,000
Panama	Teribe*	1,000
Papua New Guinea	Ampeeli*	1,000
	Banaro**	2,500
	Hewa*	250
	Hewa* (1)	1,500
	Ka'mis	50
	Kepas	5,000
	Kunimaipa*	9,000
	Ningerum	3,000
	Samo-Kubo	1,200
	Suena*	2,000
Peru	Chayahuita*	6,000
	Quechua*	3,000,000
	Quechua, Huanco*	275,000
Philippines	Apayao*	12,000
	Ata of Davao	10,000
	Atta	1,000
	Balangao*	4,500
	Bilan*	75,000
	Bontoc, Central	20,000
	Bontoc, Southern*	12,000
	Bukidnon*	100,000
	Cebu, Middle-Class**	500,000
	Dumagat	1,000
	Ga-Dang	5,500
	Ifugao, Antipolo	5,000
	Ifugao	95,000

345

	Manding	208,400
	Manjack	44,200
	Maures	57,000
	Pular	281,900
	Sarakole	67,600
	Serere (1)	700,000
	Tandanke	1,000
	Taucouleur	464,700
	Wolof	1,500,000
Seychelles	Seychellois	51,000
Sierra Leone	Kissi	43,000
	Kono*	133,000
	Koranko*	103,000
	Limba	233,000
	Loko	80,000
	Mende	600,000
	Temne*	750,000
	Yalunka	25,000
Singapore	Malays, Singapore (1)	300,000
Somalia	Somali (1)	2,500,000
South Africa	Chinese, South Africa	10,000
	Coloureds, South Africa (1)	2,000,000
Spain	Gypsies, Spain (1)	200,000
Sri Lanka	Moor & Malays (1)	895,322
	Sinhalese	9,146,679
	Tamil (Ceylonese)	1,415,567
	Tamils (Indian)* (1)	1,195,368
Sudan	Anuak	30,000
	Boya	15,000
	Didinga	30,000
	Dinka	1,940,000
	Ingassana	35,000
	Jiye	7,000
	Kichepo	16,000
	Koalib (1)	320,000
	Koroma	30,000
	Krongo	121,000
	Lokoro	22,000
	Lotuka*	150,000
	Meban	130,000

Togo	Basari	100,000
	Chakossi	29,000
	Kabre	273,000
	Konkomba	25,000
	Lamba	29,000
	Moba	70,000
	Tem	100,000
	Watchi	400,000
Trinidad and Tobago	Indians, East* (1)	400,000
Turkey	Kurds (1)	4,000,000
Turks and Caicos Islands	Chamorro	15,000
	Ulithi-Mall	2,000
	Woleat	1,000
Uganda	Jiye	34,000
	Karamojong	24,000
	Lugbara	260,000
	Muslims (West Nile Dist.)	45,000
United Arab Emirates	Muslims, U.A.E. (1)	202,000
United Kingdom	Chinese, United Kingdom* (1)	105,000
	Gujarati	300,000
	Muslim Immigrants, U.K.*	500,000
USA	Chinese, USA*	550,000
Hopi		6,000
Japanese Students, USA*		nc
	Jemez Pueblo	1,800
	Paiute, Northern	5,000
	Racetrack Residents* (1)	50,000
	Vietnamese in the USA*	130,000
	Zuni	6,000
Upper Volta	Fulah	300,000
	Gourency	300,000
	Red Bobo*	60,000
Venezuela	Jivaro (Achuara)*	20,000
Viet Nam	Cham	45,000
	Chrau*	15,000
Yemen, Arab Republic	Yemenis (1)	5,600,000
Yugoslavia	Muslims in Yugoslavia	2,500,000
Zaire	Bakuba*	75,000
	Pakabeti of Equator**	3,000
	Pygmy (Mbuti) (1)	40,000

WHAT WORLD LEADERS SAY

BILLY GRAHAM Today in many parts of the globe there is an unprecedented interest in the Gospel. Yet nearly two-thirds of the world's people have yet to understand salvation in Christ. UNREACHED PEOPLES 1979 will help to pinpoint the need, stimulate intelligent prayer, and motivate informed obedience. Missions leaders, missionary-minded pastors, and lay persons with a heart for the world should be familiar with this important book.

DONALD McGAVRAN Three billion men and women have yet to believe on Christ and be saved. These unreached live in thousands of social groups: tribes, castes, classes, and neighborhoods. These are the peoples our Lord commands us to disciple in Matthew 28:19-20. We must see *each people* clearly if we are to disciple effectively. UNREACHED PEOPLES 1979 is essential reading for the contemporary Christian. Buy it and act on it.

THE EDITORS

EDWARD R. DAYTON is the founder of the Missions Advanced Research and Communication Center, a ministry of World Vision International. He currently heads the Evangelism and Research Division of World Vision. He has written extensively on mission strategy and management.

C. PETER WAGNER is chairman of the Strategy Working Group of the Lausanne Committee for World Evangelization. He is also associate professor of church growth at Fuller Theological Seminary School of World Mission and vice president of Fuller Evangelistic Association.

The UNREACHED PEOPLES series is a joint project of the Strategy Working Group of the Lausanne Committee for World Evangelization and the MARC ministry of World Vision International.

22921   A2557   ISBN 0-89191-484-4